Stage Turns

STAGE
TURNS

Canadian
Disability
Theatre

KIRSTY JOHNSTON

McGILL-QUEEN'S UNIVERSITY PRESS

Montreal & Kingston • London • Ithaca

ISBN 978-0-7735-3994-5 (cloth)
ISBN 978-0-7735-3995-2 (paper)

Legal deposit third quarter 2012
Bibliothèque nationale du Québec

Printed in Canada on acid-free paper that is 100% ancient forest free
(100% post-consumer recycled), processed chlorine free

This book has been published with the help of a grant from the Canadian
Federation for the Humanities and Social Sciences, through the Aid to
Scholarly Publications Program, using funds provided by the Social Sciences
and Humanities Research Council of Canada.

McGill-Queen's University Press acknowledges the support of the Canada
Council for the Arts for our publishing program. We also acknowledge the
financial support of the Government of Canada through the Canada Book
Fund for our publishing activities.

Library and Archives Canada Cataloguing in Publication
Johnston, Kirsty, 1971–
Stage turns : Canadian disability theatre / Kirsty Johnston.

Includes bibliographical references and index.
ISBN 978-0-7735-3994-5 (bound). ISBN 978-0-7735-3995-2 (pbk.)

1. Actors with disabilities–Canada. 2. People with disabilities
and the arts--Canada. 3. Theater–Canada–History. 4. Theaters–
Canada--History. 5. Canadian drama (English)–History and
criticism. I. Title.

PN1590.H36J64 2012   792.087'0971   C2012-903106-2

This book was designed and typeset by studio oneonone in
Minion 10.2/13.5

Contents

Acknowledgments

For their willingness to talk, send relevant links, correct, explain, argue, and joke with me throughout this process, I am indebted to Canada's many disability artists, presenters, and activists. Among these are a few people with whom I had informal conversations that I do not take up directly in the manuscript but for which I have been grateful nonetheless: MaryLynn Baum, Ruth Bieber, Leah Bradford-Smart, Nicole Dunbar, Wanda Fitzgerald, Catherine Frazee, Rachel Gorman, Rose Jacobson, Victoria Maxwell, Siobhan McCarthy, Geoff McMurchy, David Roche, Paul Santos, Patricia Seeley, Judith Snow, and Sam Varteniuk. The first day I met Lisa Brown, Terry Watada, Tom Free, and others at what was then called the Workman Theatre Project, I asked if I could write about them and was met with a firm "we'll see." I am therefore grateful that they let me hang out, volunteer, and eventually work at their theatre; moments from those days will stay with me always and the people I have met there continue to overwhelm me with their generosity, talent, and industry.

I am grateful for the support of a Social Sciences and Humanities Research Grant as well as a UBC Arts Undergraduate Research Award and a Humanities and Social Sciences small grant as these allowed me to hire excellent research assistants over the past few years. For their thoughtful assistance, I would therefore like to thank Dr Richard Ingram, graduate students Michelle

Kneale, Parie Leung, Lisa L'Heureux, AmyLynn Strilchuk, and undergraduate assistants Madeleine Copp, Kerry Duff, April Green, John Lum, and Sandra Chamberlain-Snider. A special thanks to Amanda Konkin and Marshall McMahen for their dedicated and careful work in the Vancouver theatre archives and their willingness to become experts in the vagaries of bibliographic style.

Some of this book draws from doctoral research at the University of Toronto. As I have begun my own work with graduate students, I have come to appreciate all the more the very fine mentoring I received there from my supervisor Richard Plant, committee members Deborah Levine and Domenico Pietropaolo, and professors Ann Saddlemyer, Michael Sidnell, Charlie Keil, and Caryl Flinn. Natalie Rewa and Julie Salverson at Queen's University as well as Susan Bennett at the University of Calgary have also long been supportive both through example and by helping me connect with important artists and works in the field. I have also gained a great deal from the excellent editorial advice shared by Ric Knowles and Glen Nichols.

Staff and faculty at the UBC Department of Theatre and Film have built access ramps on short notice, fixed computers, and shared teaching and research advice. My thanks to them, in particular Theatre Studies colleagues Errol Durbach, Siyuan Liu, Ernest Mathijs, and Jerry Wasserman. I am also grateful to Judy Segal in the UBC English Department for many helpful conversations about bodies, health, and rhetoric. Through the Unruly Salon, Leslie Roman organized an important and highly generative on-campus dialogue about disability arts. Also at UBC, Graeme Wynn, Sally Hermansen, and Brian McIlroy have been helpful supports and friends. They, Reid Gilbert, and my NFBI colleagues (Meryn Cadell, Lisa Coulthard, and Stephen Guy-Bray) regularly provided welcome distraction and perspective.

Beyond UBC, I have been grateful to Erin Hurley who read drafts of my work and helped me to imagine this book's possibility and form. Natalie Alvarez kindly included me in the Brock University conference described in chapter three and I would like to thank her and her colleagues for that opportunity. I would also like to thank more broadly colleagues in the Canadian Association for Theatre Research and the Society for Disability Studies whose scholarly feedback and advice has long been a support. Large thanks also go to Ann M. Fox, Bree Hadley, Petra Kuppers, Laura Levin, Denis Salter, Carrie Sandahl, Kim Solga, and Joanne Tompkins for sharing helpful ideas both on and off panels at a range of disability, theatre, and performance studies conferences. In relation to chapter 8, I am grateful for the feedback of conveners Jisha Menon and Patrick Anderson as well as other participants in the Destination "Health": Diagnosis, Prognosis, and the Residue of Clinical Presence working group of the American Society for Theatre Research. I would also like to thank Patricia Ybarra, Harvey Young, and Ramon Rivera-Servera for convening the Junior Faculty Publication Workshop jointly sponsored by the American Society for Theatre Research and the Association for Theatre in Higher Education.

At McGill-Queen's University Press, I have been extremely fortunate to work with editor Jonathan Crago whose expert guidance and encouragements have been invaluable. I have been equally supported by Kaarla Sundstrom's wise and careful editing. The anonymous reviewers offered rich and thoughtful responses which helped to improve the book, and for these I have been very grateful. Two chapters previously appeared as journal articles. I am pleased to thank Taylor and Francis (www.tandfonline.com) for permission to republish in revised form "New Strategies for Representing Mental Illness on Canadian Stages," *International Journal of Inclusive Education* (2009) 13.7: 755–66 as Chapter 3. I also thank the editors of *Modern Drama* for permission to republish a revised version of "Staging Schizophrenia: The Workman Theatre Project and Terry Watada's Vincent," *Modern Drama* (2004) 47.1: 114–32 as Chapter 7. In the course of preparing this book, I published a range of articles on disability theatre in Canada. Thanks to the editors of *Theatre Research in Canada* and *Canadian Theatre Review* for permission to draw on these articles in the final book.

In various ways, my family has made sure I haven't missed disability theatre productions due to blizzards, heat waves, or poor time management. For their ferrying of me, hardworking examples, longstanding patience with my interest in performance minutiae, and love, I offer big thanks to: David, Sharron, and Kate Johnston, Helen MacRae, Dianne Roulson, David and Jean Johnston, Margaret MacRae, Len and Polly Evenden, Kim Alexander, Emily Clore, Betty MacRae, David Miyauchi, the Frame-Adshead family, and Ann and Gary Leaf. My daughter Maggie is a constant source of wonder and welcome interruption. This book is for her and Matthew, whose capacity to exceed my hopes is astounding.

Illustrations

Preface

Disability is not, therefore, one subject of art among others. It is not merely a
theme. It is not only a personal or autobiographical response embedded in an
artwork. It is not solely a political act. It is all of these things, but it is more. It
is more because disability is properly speaking an aesthetic value, which is to
say, it participates in a system of knowledge that provides materials for and
increases critical consciousness about the way that some bodies make other
bodies feel.

Tobin Siebers 2010[1]

This book charts a theatre movement in Canada, its origins and development, its challenges, aesthetics, and innovations. Disability theatre is
neither easy to define nor homogenous in its expression, but in what follows I examine different attempts to make sense of the term and to press the
boundaries of disability on stage. I have taken snapshots of important companies, productions, and moments in the emergence of disability theatre in
Canada but make no claims to comprehensive coverage or a group portrait,
if one were even possible. Like the disability arts festivals I will discuss, this
book is a gathering – both hopeful and incomplete – of disparate companies
and artists. While this selective approach is in part due to the limits in
resources I could bring to this study, it is also indicative of the rich opportunities for further research. When I first started this project, I felt that while
there were articles written about individual artists and shows, often by the
artists themselves, and the main surveys of the Canadian field included compelling first-person accounts of why this work matters, there had been little
historical contextualization of the field or critical, comparative analysis of
the performances themselves. By attending to these important foundations
for discussion, I hope to contribute something to the artists whose works
have provoked, delighted, moved, and challenged me over the years.

In *Theatre & Feeling*, Erin Hurley demonstrates how feeling is what makes theatre matter.[2] As for those artists and audiences she describes, theatre has long been a passion for me. In 1995, I attended a conference at the University of Toronto that posed the simple question, "Why Theatre?" For me the answer began to turn increasingly around disability theatre, which I first discovered through the Workman Theatre Project and then through a whole field of emerging practice across Canada and internationally. It has been through disability theatre that I have experienced some of the most affectively powerful innovations in form, reinventions of tradition, and direct challenges to my understanding of humanity both in local contexts and around the world. In view of this, I have also been frustrated by how much of this work has been created in inhospitable and sometimes hostile contexts. Given how often disabled characters and productions involving disability themes arise in theatre, it is unacceptable that inaccessibility remains a problem in professional theatres and training programs. I am far from the first or only person to take issue with how often disability is and has been mined for pathos and comedy and enacted to demonstrate virtuosity in theatres that do not support people with lived disability experiences to take the stage or sometimes even a place in the audience. Writing from a Scottish context, Robert Rae insists that, "Theatre must acknowledge its active role in the construction of the disabling world. Whenever a playwright uses the metaphor of 'crippled' body for 'crippled' soul, a director uses an image of disability to signify terror, or an able-bodied actor employs a gesture from the vocabulary of impairment to evoke pity, the corrosive mixture of fear and pity that pervades the public conception of disability is unthinkingly reinforced."[3] The vibrant international community of disability theatre scholars upon whose studies I seek to build here have driven me to question my own feelings for theatre and seek out those moments in Canadian disability theatre where, in the words of Simi Linton, theatre has been rethought, rewritten, and recast.[4]

Acknowledging that disability theatre has a complex Canadian history is important. An exhibit of thirteen objects entitled "Out from Under: Disability, History & Things to Remember" was installed at Toronto's Royal Ontario Museum in 2008 and in the UBC Robson Square site in Vancouver during the 2010 Paralympic Winter Games. Curators Catherine Frazee, Kathryn Church, and Melanie Panitch from the School of Disability Studies at Ryerson University emphasized their determination "to situate disabled actors and their allies as the protagonists of their own history."[5] To claim a history, to bring it "out from under," they argue, is an activist enterprise; "There was – and is – much at stake in this enterprise. The claim to history is a declaration of self, place and solidarity at the same time as it is an articulation of new ground for debate. It is the brazen insurgency of outliers taking centre, refusing periphery. It is an announcement that we know, along with an affirmation that our knowledge matters. To make a claim of history is to count as author and social actor, to reach the tipping point from which entitlements to dignity, respect and the protection of human rights will be unstoppable."[6]

Theatre is one important place to look for disability history. The histories and performance analyses which follow act as invitations for more inquiry as the stakes are indeed high. In 2011, the Council of Canadians with Disabilities advised that "14.3% of Canadians report having a disability. Canadians with disabilities are more than twice as likely to live in poverty than other Canadians. They face exclusion from quality education, from employment and from participation in their communities."[7] Because my own answers to the question "Why theatre?" depend on its special capacities to fire up, delight, gird, and enjoin individuals and communities, I attempt to bring some of these Canadian disability theatre histories "out from under."

Stage Turns

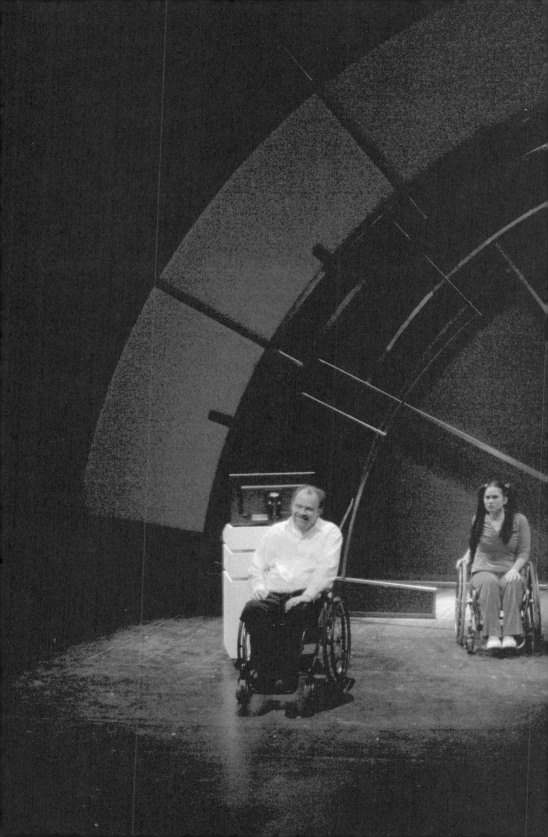

CHAPTER ONE

Introduction

Being able to get in and out of a building is not enough. You need meaningful access. That means being able to use the coffee shop and the bathroom, just like everyone else. You can get into theatres now, but can you also get on stage? That has to be the goal.

Rick Hansen, 2004[1]

Since the mid-1980s, a growing number of Canadian disability theatre artists have been doing exactly what famed athlete and disability activist Rick Hansen suggests: performing their work on Canadian and international stages. Not content simply to find or lobby for accessible audience seating, they have created and performed in their own theatres. The range of themes, genres, performance styles, dramaturgies, and production methods associated with this theatre is remarkably diverse. In Vancouver, a quadriplegic actor toured Canada in a production for which he modified swinging ballast technology to allow him to fly above stage for ninety minutes. A company of artists with mental illness experiences in Toronto have intervened in the ubiquitous dramatic theme of madness to claim more resonance with lived experience, creating over thirty plays in the past twenty years. In Calgary, a company comprising artists with a range of disabilities created a production confronting so-called mercy killings of people with disabilities. A twenty-five-year-old disability theatre company in Vancouver recently explored the place of disability in classical tragedy in the context of celebrated playwright Arthur Miller's decisions concerning his disabled son, Daniel. Two Vancouver solo performers have toured widely: one a deaf physical theatre and mime expert who has toured internationally as a clown with Cirque du Soleil and performed for countless deaf or hearing-impaired children in British Columbia;

while the other an artist whose autobiographical performance concerning bipolar disorder has won several theatre awards internationally. As these examples suggest, Canadian artists with disabilities have found many and provocative ways to "get on stage."

Disability has long been a theme, trope, and figure on world stages and performances by artists with disabilities are not new. Consider Sophocles' blind Oedipus and Shakespeare's "deformed, unfinish'd" Richard III; Isabella's *commedia dell'arte* mad scene and the mad scenes in Noh Drama; Beckett's cornucopia of disabled figures and Tennessee William's fragile limping Laura Wingfield. They all attest to disability's ubiquity and endurance in world theatre. Indeed, as we will explore in conjunction with specific performance analyses, a growing disability studies literature demonstrates how engaging with "disability as a critical category produces fresh and provocative readings" of these performance traditions.[2]

What is striking about the Canadian examples above is their self-conscious contribution to a growing international disability arts and culture movement. All of the artists cited have participated in Canadian disability arts festivals and many have also performed their works in similar venues internationally. What has drawn these artists and their international counterparts together? Why, of the myriad categories of identity and artistic practice, have some Canadian theatre artists chosen to position their work as "disability art?" What is theatre's place in the field? How have theatre practitioners animated, contested, and celebrated the term?

In her influential monograph, *Disability and Contemporary Performance*, Petra Kuppers explains her decision not to include definitions of core terms in her introduction by arguing that to do so would undermine her chief purpose of undoing certainties, questioning categories, and highlighting unknowability and difference.[3] Like Kuppers, I am wary of defining disability theatre as a fixed practice or aesthetic, especially as many artists whose works I explore are interested precisely in troubling received concepts of disability, ability, theatre, and art. Canadian activist and performer Judith Snow rejects the word disability outright as a term which impedes a greater politics of inclusion.[4] However, the terms "disability art," "disability theatre," "disability culture(s),"and "disability movement" have been used in Canadian artists' advocacy documents, festival programs, grant applications, publicity, and handbooks. The terms also hold currency among international artists, scholars, and activists. For these reasons, and for those who are new to the debates occasioned by the terms, I think it will be useful to begin by suggesting at least some of the key ways they have come to produce meaning in the field.

As a branch of disability art, disability theatre is most often described as a specific kind of artistic practice connected to the disability arts and culture movement. As such, it involves artists with disabilities who pursue an activist perspective, dismantling stereotypes, challenging stigma, and re-imagining disability as a valued human condition. For these reasons, *disability artists*, theatre and otherwise, are often distinguished from the larger category of *artists with disabilities*. In his survey of disability and art practices in the UK, Paul Anthony Darke argues for this distinction and suggests that Disability Art "is based upon legitimizing the experience of disabled people as equal within art and all other cultural practices ... Disability Art is a challenge to, an undermining of (as a minimum), traditional aesthetic and social values."[5] This drive to legitimize experiences of disability and connect to a broader emancipatory project links what might otherwise seem like an economically, nationally, racially, ethnically, aesthetically, and experientially disparate set of international artists and works.

While some have found value in the above distinctions, it is clear that identity politics play an important role both in claiming a place or being cast as a disability artist. For Darke, it is critical that disability artists challenge aesthetic and social values and he cautions those disability artists who achieve mainstream success against "drowning in the river Lethe" and undermining the activist aims that gave rise to disability art in the first place. By contrast, others find value in broadening the definition and argue that there is an inherent political challenge posed by being an artist with a disability. Oscar-winning documentarist and Vancouver's Society for Disability Arts and Culture co-founder Bonnie Klein argues that simply "to give permission to the artist within your disabled body is an outrageous act of defiance."[6] Further complications for the term disability art arise in its relation to or distinction from Deaf culture, art, and identities. While some Deaf and hearing impaired artists have connected with disability art and culture movements, others have argued that Deaf culture's unique and independent history, language, and cultural forms are necessarily distinct, especially among those who do not view deafness as an impairment. Thus, while for Darke and others who are invested in disability art's socially transformative roots, the definition is clear and critical, for others the waters are muddier. *Arts Smarts*, the Society for Disability Arts and Culture's (S4DAC) handbook for Canadian artists with disabilities, outlines a range of ways in which artists with disabilities might identify themselves and the role disability has in their art-making: "An artist with a disability may identify strongly as a person with a disability or as a member of the disability community, or they may not. Most

of us have more than one thing that makes up our identity – disability, sexual orientation, race, religion, gender, and so on … Artists who feel a strong
connection between their disability and their art tend to see themselves as
part of the disability movement."[7] Discussions of identity, the handbook also
explains, arise often among artists with disabilities and this is certainly true
of the artists with whom I engage in this book. What seems most important
to me in light of the ongoing debates circulating around the terms disability
and Deaf art is to be clear about how particular artists, companies, and organizations understand the term and their relationship to it.

By attending to these specific articulations of identity, coalition, and dis-
sent, I hope to demonstrate that disability theatre in Canada may best be understood as an intercultural project, one in which artists from a range of
disability cultures contribute to a polyvalent disability culture. In this reading, disability culture is not a monolith that essentializes one world-view or
disability experience. Rather, its chief presumption is a sense of shared and
open-ended identity rooted in disability experience that "rejects the notion
of impairment difference as a symbol of shame, and stresses instead solidarity and a positive identification."[8] The implied preference for pride over
shame, solidarity over isolation, and positive identification over negative il-
lustrates disability culture's connection to other human rights and minority
movements of the twentieth century.

The Disability Rights Movement: Advocacy, Policy, and Principles

A comprehensive history of the disability movement is not the focus of this
book and many rich sources are available which chart its development in the
US, UK, Canada, and beyond. Clearly, however, the arguments above demonstrate that disability theatre needs to be situated also within the broader history of disability rights advocacy. In part this is because many disability
theatre artists see their work – explicitly and implicitly – as contributing to
social change and disability rights. Further, it is difficult to understand the
emergence of disability theatre in Canada without understanding the social
struggles and context that helped shift definitions and understandings of disability in society and the law. Disability theatre is one important expression
of wider social changes.

The emergence of disability theatre in Canada in the 1980s coincided with
a rights revolution for persons with disabilities. Whereas many disability
activists point to the Americans with Disabilities Act (1990) as a major legal
turning point for disability rights in the US and internationally, in Canada

disability rights were strengthened in the early 1980s in the course of a broader re-evaluation of constitutional law. Under Liberal Prime Minister Pierre Trudeau, the Canadian government sought to patriate the Canadian constitution from the British Parliament and add to it a Charter of Rights and Freedoms. Early drafts of the Charter did not contain explicit reference to disability, but after sustained lobbying, particularly by the Coalition of Provincial Organizations of the Handicapped (CPOH), disability was added alongside other categories of systemic discrimination, including race, gender, and ethnicity. This significant addition set in train a series of legal changes and court cases as the federal and provincial governments sought to bring laws into compliance with the Charter and individuals and groups gained the ability to test discriminatory practices before the courts.[9] Although welfare measures pertaining to disability date back to the Old Age Pensions Act (1937) and to several initiatives surrounding vocational training in the 1950s, this broadened definition of citizenship had important effects at the inter-governmental level in terms of social spending, legal rights, and the articulation of disability access across the spectrum of governance.[10] The Human Rights Act (1985) extended the logic of the Charter and forbade discrimination in the delivery of goods, services, and accommodations. At the provincial level, further legislative reform followed, particularly in Ontario where several pieces of legislation culminating in the Accessibility for Ontarians with Disabilities Act (2005) laid out policies to remove discriminatory barriers in public and private sectors.[11] Much more needs to be done, of course, not least in the area of arts funding, but the Charter did mark an important break in the recognition of disability rights. As legal scholar Theresia Degener has noted, "To treat disability as a legally-recognized discrimination category implies an acknowledgement that disabled people are people with rights, not problems."[12]

Canadian disability politics – like disability theatre – developed also in an international context. In 1981 as the Charter debate unfolded, Canada participated in the International Year of Disabled Persons, a United Nations sponsored initiative of which Canada was a co-mover. Participation was more than symbolic as provincial governments took the opportunity to review disability policies and increased pressure was brought to bear on the federal government to include disability in the Charter.[13] In comparative terms, Canada's shift toward the constitutional recognition of disability rights can be viewed as an outlier event, produced in part by the coincidence of broader constitutional change in a period of rising disability activism. In the US and UK, legal change occurred more slowly. While changes to education and vocational training policy in the US in the mid-1970s were important landmarks, the Americans with Disabilities Act was not passed until 1990. In the UK, changes to civil law were not made until the 1995 Disability Discrimination Act. Despite this slower path toward legal recognition of disability rights in the US and UK, it is worth noting that both pieces of legislation also included provisions to support persons with disabilities in finding and keeping employment and in seeking education. These countries have also been leaders in other spheres of disability politics like funding, putting forward a range of special initiatives, and setting up arts councils for disability arts projects decades before any comparable effort was made in Canada.

As disability historians have argued, such shifts in formal policy and legislation, while important, only provide one particular vantage point on social change.[14] Beyond the parliamentary debates and UN initiatives lies a long and complex history of disability advocacy groups and disability rights organizations. In Canada, disability advocacy groups date to 1918 when A.E. Baker, a blind First World War veteran, helped to establish the Canadian National Institute of the Blind. Other such groups followed like the Canadian Association for the Deaf (1940), the Canadian Paraplegic Association (1945), and the Canadian Association for Community Living (1958) with a focus on persons with intellectual disabilities. These organizations proved important in delivering services to their members, but did not initially identify a cross-disability interest or advocate for the same. A shift toward such an expanded program occurred with the establishment in 1975 of the Coalition of Provincial Organizations of the Handicapped, later re-named the Council of Canadians with Disabilities. Although some other national organizational efforts had occurred previously, the CPOH distinguished itself as a national, consumer-led, cross-disability organization with a focus on issues of public policy.[15] Perhaps not surprisingly, it was the CPOH that proved effective in making the case for including disability in the language of the Charter.

The international emergence of disability advocacy, particularly in the UK and US in the 1970s, helped inspire Canadian disability advocates to organize national and cross-disability organizations. Modeling themselves to some extent on earlier civil rights campaigns for racial and sexual equality, disability rights advocates lobbied governments and sought to establish new experiments in political and social organization. For example, the Independent Living Movement (ILM), founded by Ed Roberts in Berkeley in 1972, established programs and services by and for people with disabilities to provide a dignified and independent life outside of institutional contexts. The ILM spread steadily across the US through the 1970s and by 1986, the concept came north with the formation of the Canadian Association of Independent Living Centres.[16] Initiatives like the ILM exemplified a new level of political organization, a self-conscious minority identity, and a positive redefinition of disability. These concerns were important in reshaping disability in politics and society and began to inspire a broader re-evaluation of disability in scholarship and the arts, leading to the new fields of *disability studies* and *disability arts* in the 1980s.

Disability Studies, Art(s), and Culture(s)

The concomitant rise of disability studies and disability arts was not accidental. The ideas and practices of both scholars and artists have been mutually informing and challenging. Since much of the logic that unites disability theatre artists has connections with scholarly re-framings of disability, it is important to understand the key paradigms and salient terms that have shaped the field.

Disability studies has become its own academic field of inquiry, but it is also more than that. It seeks at once to study the questions that animate disability politics and culture from a range of perspectives in the humanities and social sciences, and to push these questions across disciplinary boundaries. Prominent disability historian Catherine Kudlick argues that the emergence of disability studies as an interdisciplinary scholarly field in the mid-1980s also invited scholars and others "to think about disability not as an isolated, individual medical pathology but instead as a key defining social category on a par with race, class and gender."[17] In this paradigm, commonly referred to as the social model or social construction model, disability is often distinguished from impairment. This language underlines the argument that disability is not located in any individual's condition of difference (impairment) but emerges instead from disabling social systems that inhibit the full social inclusion and valuing of individuals with impairments. Disability studies scholarship in this vein often emphasizes how these social systems have varied over time, space, and according to a host of economic, religious, cultural, and other factors.[18] As such, the social model has been a generative source for re-thinking disability and has encouraged both elaboration and further debate.

Building on the social model's positive ideals, the minority model of disability suggests a shared identity among those who view disability "not as personal misfortune or individual defect but as the product of a disabling social and built environment. Tired of discrimination and claiming disability as a positive identity, people with disabilities insist on the pertinence of disability to the human condition, on the value of disability as a form of diversity and on the power of disability as a critical concept for thinking about human identity in general."[19] The minority model has been productive both in scholarly and political terms, but it has also given rise to critical debates. Disability scholars have been attentive to layers of potential distinction and difference among people, examining how class background, ethnicity, sexuality, and age "exacerbate or modify" experiences of disabilities, whether these are physical or cognitive, visible or invisible, life-long or acquired, medically and socially recognized or not, severe or less so.[20] This range of perspectives points not to mere differences of opinion about disability experience or semantics, but opens a much broader discussion about the identities and *cultures* of disability, their boundaries, meanings, and limits.

Disability arts scholars have investigated artists' capacities to articulate, enact, or otherwise express ideas and feelings drawn from a range of disability perspectives. Interest in the arts within disability scholarship and activism draws in part from a recognition that the "pursuit of equality and inclusion is a cultural task as much as a political one."[21] However, early disability scholarship was generally wary of the arts, seeing them at first "mainly as purveyors of negative images of people with disabilities" or too often tied to arts therapies that supported the medical model and its interest in cures.[22] Over the past fifteen years, however, as disability artists have gained prominence in the movement, scholars have become increasingly interested in their efforts to express disability identities and re-imagine the representation and meaning of disability. Moreover, as Canadian disability scholar, activist, and s4DAC co-founder Catherine Frazee explains, art's role in shaping disability cultures is vital: "In Canada, the United States and around the world, artists and performers with disabilities are contributing to one of the most radical and effective aspects of disability culture – challenging conventional notions of beauty, form and motion."[23] There are signs that this "culturing" of disability studies has reached a point of general acceptance. Three recent texts in disability studies, for example, devote space to the role of disability arts in culture formation.[24]

It is important to note, however, that the social model, minority model, and their extensions are not without detractors. For example, in their 2001 article "The social model of disability: An outdated ideology?," Tom Shakespeare and Nicholas Watson point to problems which arise from the social model's framing of impairment, identity, and the dualism of disability/ impairment. Their arguments favour instead a more nuanced ontology of embodiment.[25] As Mairian Corker and Shakespeare argue, "the global experience of disabled people is too complex to be rendered within one unitary model or set of ideas. Considering the range of impairments under the disability umbrella; considering the different ways in which they impact on individuals and groups over their lifetime; considering the intersection of disability with other axes of inequality; and considering the challenge which impairment issues to notions of embodiment, we believe that disability is the ultimate postmodern concept."[26] In the context of theatre and performance, these critiques of the social model and their embrace of greater intricacy and precision suggest the importance of attending carefully to the everyday realities of living with particular impairments at the same time as we consider how disability performers respond to and challenge socially based stigmas, stereotypes, and forms of oppression which shape their self and social perception.

Debates and tensions aside, disability studies scholars are relatively united in their fundamental opposition to traditional medical models. Disability studies theorist Tobin Siebers provides a particularly clear account of the primary differences between the medical and disability studies approach to disability:

> The medical model defines disability as an individual defect lodged in the person, a defect that must be cured or eliminated if the person is to achieve full capacity as a human being ... Unlike the medical approach, the emerging field of disability studies defines disability not as an individual defect but as the product of social injustice, one that requires not the cure or elimination of the defective person but significant changes in the social and built environment ... [I]t studies the social meanings, symbols, and stigmas attached to disability identity and asks how they relate to enforced systems of exclusion and oppression, attacking the widespread belief that having an able body and mind determines whether one is a quality human being.[27]

Like Shakespeare and Watson, Siebers challenges the field of disability studies to move beyond the basic conclusion that disability is socially constructed. Rather, he urges, we must be attentive to the materiality of bodies and read specific constructions for their "blueprints." We must examine how disability is constructed in a specific time and place[28] and by whom and with what kinds of "complex embodiment."[29] In the following chapters I will bring Siebers' questions to bear in the field of disability theatre studies to ask what kinds of "blueprints" have informed Canadian disability theatre policies, practices, and performances. This exploration of Canadian disability theatre builds on the premise that disability cultures must be understood in the light of their artistic contributions. The more particular focus on theatre as a specific kind of performance, however, draws on a lively, emerging, international,

and interdisciplinary scholarship which argues for the centrality of performance to any critical thinking about disability.

Performance, Disability, and Interdisciplinary Dialogue

Emerging in the 1990s, a robust interdisciplinary scholarship has formed to
bridge disability, theatre, and performance studies. This work begins from
the position that disability – like other identities related to biology and bina-
ries such as gender and race – is performed.[30] As such, the analytical tools
and methods of performance studies may be applied to disability as it is performed in everyday life and in more particular contexts like theatre, dance,
photography, or television. Studies in this vein have investigated performance traditions and activities that shape disability identities and experiences.
Understanding these traditions and contexts is critical because, as Petra Kuppers has demonstrated, disabled performers' bodies are overwhelmingly read
by audiences as "*naturally* about disability," whatever disability might mean
in a particular cultural context.[31] Disability and performance scholars have
also investigated how various disabled performers have confronted stereotypes of disability to innovate artistically. How, for example, have they unsettled such common representational shorthands as the "blind seer," the
inspirational "heroic overcomer," or the sweet, innocent, and morally deserv-
ing "charity case?" Interdisciplinary exchanges also run in the reverse direction and there has been growing interest in how the analytical methods and
tools of disability studies challenge performance studies to address ableist
biases in their approach. As Sandahl and Auslander argue in *Bodies in Commotion*, disability and performance studies, despite having different histories and epistemological bases, invite interdisciplinary engagement due to
the "theatricality of disability and the centrality of performance to the formation of disability cultures and identities."[32]

Why Theatre?

While the broader field is interested in a vast range of performances, from
everyday life to extraordinary spectacles, in this book I am more specifically
concerned with those offered in a theatrical frame. Theatre is a particularly
rich art form for study because of its capacity to generate focused, convivial,
and sometimes inspirational forums in which bodies gather to perform and
receive artistic expressions rooted in disability experience. In such settings,

opportunities for bodies to "talk back" abound and it becomes difficult to disavow any particular body's materiality in aesthetic responses or discussions. These features are some of the most generative for challenging traditional aesthetics and stereotypes.

Originating in Europe and the US in the 1980s, disability theatre has since become a major international field with innovative companies and artists. Outside Canada, for example, such companies include England's Graeae Theatre, Sweden's Moomsteatern, Australia's Back to Back Theatre, Germany's Theater Sycorax, the Other Voices Project at the Mark Taper Forum, and PHAMALY in the US. Individual solo performers have also established substantial reputations such as Lynn Manning (US), Philip Patston (NZ), Mat Fraser (UK), Julia Trahan, and Terry Galloway (US). Although disability theatres have established their own growing body of key works and developed vibrant communities of interest, they have also begun to influence mainstream theatres. This can be seen not only in their performances at venues like Canada's National Arts Centre and the Kennedy Center for the Performing Arts in Washington, DC, but also in the ways that practitioners and theorists articulate and demand inclusive aesthetic standards, challenge casting choices which favour able-bodied performers, and agitate for inclusive performance venues and production practices.

The larger field of international disability theatre is important to bear in mind when thinking about the Canadian scene. Where other countries have developed strong national programs to provide targeted support and encouragement for disability art, in Canada this has been less evident until recently. Canada nonetheless boasts important and pioneering artists, companies, and events that have helped shape the international field. Disability arts festivals in Vancouver, Calgary, and Toronto, for example, have become hubs for artistic exchange between Canadian and international artists. Calgary's MoMo Mixed Ability Dance Theatre has organized several artistic exchanges, bringing international innovators to Canada and sending Canadian artists to work with disability theatre groups abroad. Performers Lyle Victor Albert, Alex Bulmer, Max Fomitchev, David Roche, Alan Shain, and Victoria Maxwell have toured their works in Canada and internationally. Toronto's Workman Arts founded a large-scale moving international festival dedicated to re-imagining mental illness on stage. In the growing international literature focused on disability theatre, however, these Canadian contributions have not yet been adequately documented or analyzed.

In what follows, I bring the questions of disability performance scholarship to bear on disability theatre in Canada. What impulses drive disability theatre practices in Canada? How have disability artists articulated cultures and identities? Where have they set, pushed, or disregarded the boundaries for both? What dramaturgical, production, and collaborative methods have been employed or rejected in their practice? What aesthetic principles have informed artists' works? What kinds of audiences have they realized and to what effects? How has disability theatre challenged all Canadian theatre artists and audiences to question their casting, staging, publicity, and other production choices? How have critics and audiences responded to this work? What kinds of theatre practices and infrastructures have hindered or fostered disability theatre's development? What changes would Canadian disability theatre artists like to see in theatre more broadly? How have they connected with international counterparts to achieve these goals?

This comparative analysis of disability theatre in a national framework seeks to understand the origins and growth of disability theatre in Canada, the aesthetic choices and challenges of the movement, and the multiple scales at which disability theatre operates, from the local to the increasingly global. A comparative approach also allows for consideration of disability theatre's internal divisions. By examining Canadian disability theatre, it is possible also to say something about the field elsewhere and to recognize Canadian innovations. My conclusions suggest that disability theatre presents profound challenges to mainstream aesthetics that have not yet been fully recognized, and that disability theatre must be understood in its diversity to appreciate fully its creative tensions and opportunities.

This book is divided into two halves, with an emphasis on theatre histories in Part I and performances in Part II. The ordering is suggestive rather than absolute but offers a useful division between a concern in the first half of the book for the mechanics of how disability theatre has found its way onto Canadian stages (to borrow again from Rick Hansen) and a more detailed look at what has been performed in the second half. With a view to providing appropriate focus as well as range, I have paired theatre histories in Part I with performance analyses in Part II. This means that some companies come in for greater attention than others. This is not a statement about quality or importance on my part, but rather the result of the research process as well as an assessment of interesting and illuminating cases, both representative in some ways and distinctive in others.

The book opens with a reconnaissance. Chapter 2 surveys disability theatre in English Canada in its three principal centres (Toronto, Calgary, and Vancouver) and seeks to identify and analyze the range of disability theatre in each. Surveying the contemporary landscape leads to observations about company origins and mandates, practices and performances, and different approaches to the very idea of disability theatre. In addition to the city/company focus, I also identify the importance of solo-autobiographical performers in the contemporary disability theatre scene.

Chapter 3 provides a history of Workman Arts, a Toronto company that has focused primarily on serving artists with mental illness and addiction concerns and only more recently has begun to develop ties to the broader disability arts and culture movement. Looking at a company at the edge, as it were, allows for a reconsideration of just what is at stake in disability theatre more generally and what issues attend the theatrical representation of mental illness in particular. A focused investigation of this company's development also allows for an analysis of training programs, performances, and critical reception.

Chapter 4 offers a historical analysis of one of Canada's oldest disability theatre companies, Vancouver's Theatre Terrific. Situated in the rich archival evidence of this company which dates to the mid-1980s, it is possible to ask questions about origins, the role of artistic direction, the importance of mandates, and the role of funding. Theatre Terrific's history offers textured detail about one company's journey to disability theatre practice and its struggles and triumphs, while also providing insight into a range of structural issues that have faced disability theatres in Canada and elsewhere, including the balance between artistry and vocational training, and the struggle to maintain consistent funding.

The move from the local scale to the international in disability theatre animates Chapter 5. Just how have local groups tried to build coalition among themselves, and to what ends? Apart from identifying the increasingly international reach of Canadian disability theatre companies and performers, I seek to explain how such mobilization has occurred, particularly in the form of disability arts festivals and regional coalitions. The national scale, I argue, has until fairly recently been relatively less active compared to the field's grassroots and local scales. Disability theatre thus largely operates in Canada at the interface of the local, regional, and international. The use of the festival to activate the field, however, has introduced new challenges which I assess by way of conclusion.

The book's second part opens with a paired reading in Chapter 6 of two particularly contrasting and important productions in Canadian disability theatre history: Stage Left's *Mercy Killing or Murder: The Tracy Latimer Story*, and Realwheels' *Skydive*. While both productions operated within the assumption of a broader disability theatre framework, they did so from profoundly different starting points and with different artistic and political ambitions. By comparing and evaluating the content of these two shows, it is possible to sketch out some of the core debates of disability theatre and aesthetics in Canada. Engaging the work of Catherine Frazee and Tobin Siebers on disability aesthetics, I seek to raise critical questions about just what a disability theatre aesthetics might entail.

Chapter 7 considers two of Theatre Terrific's recent performances, *The Secret Son* and *The Glass Box*, to analyze the place of the clinic in disability theatre. The clinic is a recurring metaphor and site of conflict in disability arts, and Theatre Terrific's recent work suggests some of the ways in which its performance figures in the representation of disability. While *The Secret Son* takes up ideas of classical tragedy and disability, partially through the biography of Arthur Miller's family, *The Glass Box* explores disability and sexuality. Although they offer strikingly different narratives, both shows express a critical perspective on the medicalization of disability and the place of disability in theatre and society.

Chapter 8 turns on the question of how to perform disability on stage, by what visual signs and cues. In *Vincent*, one of Workman Arts' most performed works, the main character, controversially, never appears physically on stage. Although some audience members worried that this implied the absence of a voice for disability, I argue that the production employed negativity, a term theorized by Sanford Budick and Wolfgang Iser, to signify how the deliberate absence of something can imply its ambiguous presence. I also explain why such ambiguity might be important for mental illness representations in particular.

Chapter 9 offers a contemporary reading of three performances staged in Vancouver during the Olympic and Paralympic winter games in 2010: the Vancouver Playhouse production of the *Miracle Worker*; Manitoba Theatre's *Rick: The Rick Hansen Story*; and Realwheels and the University of Alberta's co-production, *Spine*. Although all of the plays deal with disability issues and themes, they handle them in distinct ways, some with seemingly little appreciation for the perspectives developed by disability theatre practitioners in Canada. Apart from analyzing the productions and considering the context of the Olympic and Paralympic games, I ask how these shows suggest both the influence and the lack of influence disability theatre has had on mainstream theatre, critics, and audiences.

By way of conclusion, I reflect on an early disability theatre script, David Freeman's *Creeps*, against which it becomes possible to measure the contemporary development of disability theatre in English Canada. How far has this arts practice travelled and what distances remain?

PART ONE

Histories

CHAPTER TWO

Surveying the Scene

Artists create and flout labels. Playing with, defining, and pushing organizing principles are their truck and trade. Most theatre artists choose from a range of labels (Canadian, mainstream, radical, feminist, queer, aboriginal, postmodern, avant-garde, experimental) when they solicit audiences, apply for grants, or account for their work in media interviews. Disability theatre artists are no different, but what do they mean when they pair the words disability and theatre? How do they put the terms into practice and performance?

This chapter surveys disability theatre companies and performers in the main Canadian urban centres where disability arts and culture have gained hold: Toronto, Calgary and Vancouver. Apart from introducing many of the companies and groups considered in later chapters, I will map the contours of disability theatre's meaning, debates, and resonances for theatre practitioners in these hubs. While important groups like Edmonton's SOS Players and Montreal's Pourquoi Pas Nous fall outside this frame, focusing on three cities allows for a survey of groups and artists who have developed their sense of the field through interactions with one another. The comparisons and contradistinctions that have arisen through this dialogue help explain how disability theatre has come to have shared and disputed meanings in Canada.[1] Solo performers have also been critical contributors in each of these three centres through their performances at disability arts festivals and related events; an overview of their approaches extends the comparison and helps to explain their particular importance in the field. This survey perspective suggests the emerging coherence of disability theatre as a particular type of practice, while also pointing to its tensions and diverse impulses and incarnations.

It is important to note that this is not the first survey of the field; three surveys, all within the last decade, have been produced by disability artists, scholars, and presenters, offering an instructive look at how others have charted the history and practice of disability arts and culture in Canada. One of the first introductions to the field of disability arts and culture both on a national and international scale was produced in 2004 by a team of leading disability scholars from Toronto's Ryerson-RBC Institute for Disability Studies Research and Education, including Jihan Abbas, Kathryn Church, Catherine Frazee, and Melanie Panitch. In that same year, Rose Jacobson, a project manager and artistic principal with Picasso PRO (a Toronto-based arts organization that aims to integrate disability and Deaf artists in the performing and media arts) and co-author Alex Bulmer, an actor and award-winning playwright with a vision impairment, sought to convey the depth of the field internationally and the growth of a Canadian disability arts and culture scene in a report for the Trillium Foundation.[2] Five years later, this time under contract for the Canada Council, Jacobson collaborated with Geoff McMurchy, a disability artist and co-founder of Vancouver's Society for Disability Arts and Culture (s4DAC – now known as Kickstart) and the Kickstart festivals, to write an overview of disability arts and culture across the country, with attention to artists, groups, coalitions, and festivals.[3]

The contrasts between these documents, written so close together in time, speak volumes about the rapid growth of the field in Canada in the first decade of the twenty-first century. The Ryerson 2004 report emphasized the importance of the institute's own arts activities in catalyzing disability arts in Toronto, and highlighted the national importance of the Kickstart festivals in Vancouver. Incorporating a host of particular examples across the visual and performing arts, the report addressed accessibility issues, disability politics, and urged increased funding for the field. Jacobson and Bulmer's report paid particular attention to disability arts and culture in Britain (where Bulmer had recently re-located) and Vancouver, where Jacobson highlighted the impact of the Kickstart festivals and noted the range of exciting companies, actors, and groups which had formed surrounding these events. Like the Ryerson report, Jacobson and Bulmer called for increased funding with the particular goal of launching a festival like Vancouver's Kickstart in Toronto.

The Canada Council report that Jacobson authored with McMurchy in 2009 set out more deliberately to explore the extent of disability arts and culture organizations and funding sources across Canada. Again Vancouver garnered considerable attention. This is not surprising as the city continued to be a major festival and performance centre for disability arts and culture, and one of its most prominent contributors (McMurchy) was co-author. In contrast to the 2004 report which highlighted pioneering groups and organizations that the authors judged to be particularly innovative, the 2009 report aimed for broader inclusion and representation. Some Vancouver groups, however, received only passing mention, most notably Theatre Terrific, the oldest disability theatre company in western Canada, which we will discuss in detail in Chapter 3. The report also explained the development of a range of coalitions that had grown up in the past five years, partly out of the Kickstart experience, to knit together new regional and national alliances. A national presenters network, for example, spearheaded by Michele Decottignies of Stage Left and the British Columbia Regional Integrated Arts Network (BRIAN), organized to build alliances within a diverse disability arts and culture scene in British Columbia. The 2009 report also touched down in Calgary, acknowledging the range and extent of Stage Left's contributions to regional and national activity, as well as in Toronto, where a variety of groups, including Workman Arts, drew attention. Some French language efforts in Quebec were noted, but no groups were mentioned in Saskatchewan or Manitoba, nor in Atlantic Canada. As McMurchy and Jacobson noted, alongside the explosion of disability arts and culture in some regions of the country, other areas remained "underserved."[4]

It is important to recognize the purpose of these exercises. The 2004 reports offered broad introductions and called for greater funding. The 2009 report, in advance of a wider Canada Council initiative to engage disability arts and culture, laid out the parameters of the field, introduced groups, and provided context. The aim was to clarify "how Canadian funding and cultural support networks can better serve the art regionally and nationally."[5] None were designed to offer a historical perspective or to be exhaustive. The very existence of these reports signaled that different funding bodies recognized that something was happening in disability arts and culture in Canada and wanted to get a sense of its scope. These exercises should be read partly for their content, but also as statements about an emerging self-consciousness of a field of artistic practice, operating first on a regional scale before expanding to a national arena. These practices are tied both broadly and in various specific ways to disability activism and politics.

My aim in offering another kind of survey is not simply to repeat this work. My focus is on disability theatre not disability arts and culture, and I approach the problem with no particular policy relevance in mind. While some recent work, such as Michele Decottignies and Andrew Houston's co-edited *Canadian Theatre Review* issue on "Theatre and the Question of Disability," offers a wide-ranging examination of different companies and performers, often from the perspective of the artists themselves, my survey also analyzes comparatively how such different artists envision their work.[6] In some cases, goals have been formalized into mandates; in others they have developed and evolved in the context of practice. Whatever the process, those companies and performers who self-identify as engaged in disability theatre seek to express a principled artistic approach. How they do so, however, has been highly varied.

Toronto

As Canada's largest city, with a lively arts and theatre community, it is little surprise that Toronto has become one of the primary centres in English Canada for disability arts and culture. Witness, for example, the many disability arts festivals which originated in or call Toronto home. Since 1999 the Ryerson-RBC Institute of Disability Studies Research and Education has organized an annual Art with Attitude event as well as a series of Culture Cauldrons – programming that has regularly featured Canadian and International disability theatre artists. The inaugural Madness and Arts World Festival produced by Workman Arts was mounted at Toronto's Harbourfront Centre in 2003 and the city's annual Abilities Arts Festival: A Celebration of Disability Arts and Culture began in 2005. These and other disability arts related series and events have created lively and regular spaces for dialogue about disability arts and culture in the city. Within this broader activity, disability theatre plays an important role. A striking feature of Toronto's disability theatre scene, however, is that most of the city's enduring companies have been more focused on one disability community in particular, rather than cross-disability experience. These companies coalesce instead through festival culture or facilitative organizations like Picasso PRO.

   The oldest disability theatre company in Toronto bears witness to the origins of disability organization and activism in Canada. Founded in the early 1940s by the Ladies' Auxiliary of the Canadian National Institute for the Blind (CNIB), the Glenvale Players began as a theatrical group for blind and vision-impaired actors. Through the post-war decades, the company developed a regular program of performances and entered a host of regional drama competitions. By the early 1960s, the company performed an annual show of popular mainstream plays at the CNIB auditorium on Bayview Avenue.[7] By the 1980s, the company's activity grew in scope and importance. Under the direction of Gregory Heyn, the players performed and toured his original plays, including *A House Called Pride* and *Juno is Missing*, in Metro Toronto schools. In 1985 and 1986, they also produced his *Braille Manuscript* about Louis Braille, which was nominated at the Association of Community Theatres of Central Ontario Festival for Best Production of a Canadian play.[8] At this stage, because the Glenvale Players were engaging in theatre that not only involved actors with disabilities but also explored disability themes in performance, they could be seen as operating at the inception of disability theatre in Canada.

The company began to engage disability theatre more deliberately after the turn of the century. At a time of growing membership and increased activity, the company began to explore the links between blind performance and disability theatre. In a 2005 précis of the company's activities, Artistic Director Wanda C. Fitzgerald insisted that "Glenvale is not a 'blind theatre group' but a company stepping from the wings to present an outstanding theatre experience for everyone and to enable some very talented artists to develop and share their gifts."[9] Apart from developing the talent of blind and vision-impaired artists in all facets of production, the company sought to educate directors and production companies in the entertainment industry about inclusive audition and casting procedures as a means both to support blind and vision-impaired artists seeking work in the industry and to mitigate against the negative portrayals of blind and vision-impaired people that company members have felt dominate mainstream media.[10] Fitzgerald and other company artists have also connected with disability arts initiatives in the city, including those of Picasso PRO. Through these growing associations and their explicit attention to unsettling longstanding negative representational patterns related to vision impairment, over the past decade the company has become a more self-conscious contributor to the emerging disability theatre scene in Canada.

Although its history in Canada is more brief, Alex Bulmer's SNIFF (Sensory Narrative in Full Form) Inc. theatre company also aims to foster work by and for vision-impaired or blind artists and audiences by creating work with "a more diverse use of sensory perception."[11] Responding to what she describes as a contemporary bias for "bumping up spectacle" instead of, say, the aural, tactile, or olfactory features of theatre, Bulmer's company aims to devise work which begins by thinking about sound, movement through space, and/or smell.[12] In 2000, in association with Nightwood Theatre and at the Tarragon Theatre Extra Space, SNIFF Inc produced Bulmer's one-woman, Chalmers Award nominated play, *Smudge*. The play follows the central female character of Freddie who, like Bulmer, has been diagnosed with a degenerative eye disease, retinitis pigmentosa. Having known that she wanted to be an actor since she was three and having trained and performed regularly in Toronto, Bulmer explains the importance of the play in her own artistic development: "Writing the play made me realize – and fear – how much I love theatre, which I've been drawn to my whole life. I thought my connection with the arts was over when my sight disappeared, but I've survived. It's been vital to write about it, to reproduce it as a useful experience."[13] Despite the company's success with *Smudge*, however, Bulmer subsequently relocated to London, frustrated by the lack of opportunities and support for her professional artistic development in Canada.[14] The company has nonetheless played a critical role in raising disability theatre issues through its buttressing of the Picasso Project and success with the high-profile *Smudge*. While maintaining her London base and developing connections from there between Canadian and London-based disability artists, Bulmer returned to Toronto briefly in 2009 to develop and perform in the provocative and acclaimed *Book of Judith*, a production which involved inclusion activist Judith Snow, Fitzgerald, and several other Picasso PRO-affiliated artists. To protest pervasive problems of inaccessibility in Toronto's professional theatre, the production erected a revival-style tent on the lawns of the Centre for Addiction and Mental Health at the Queen Street site where they performed using a purpose-built stage with a long graded ramp for wheelchair access and flexible seating for patrons. For Bulmer, the opportunity to develop this innovative professional work and demonstrate how the boundaries of Canadian professional theatre might be pushed toward inclusion was worth the travel effort involved.

Two more longstanding theatre companies in Toronto serve a range of artists who have, at some point in their lives, been diagnosed with mental illness. Like the Glenvale Players and SNIFF Inc. they have tended to focus on one branch of disability experience, but often from different perspectives. Workman Arts (formerly the Workman Theatre Project) and Friendly Spike Theatre Band both began in the late 1980s. In Chapter 4, I will chart the organizational and production history of Workman Arts as one of two case studies which suggest the complex ways that companies have found connections with disability theatre over time. It is important to note here, however, a few key similarities and distinctions in approach between Friendly Spike Theatre Band and Workman Arts. Some Toronto artists have been involved with both companies and both have produced works which aim to shift public perceptions of mental illness. The companies' histories suggest, however, that each holds different ideas about how this shift might best be accomplished, through what kinds of aesthetic choices, and with what kinds of connections to activist groups, medical institutions and theatre professionals.

Friendly Spike Theatre Band originated in the late 1980s with an activist spirit and agenda. Named after two dogs associated with the "band" or circle of three equal founding members, Ruth Ruth Stackhouse, Ken Innes and Miles Cohen, the company incorporated as a registered charity in 1989 and has gone on to produce a range of theatrical productions, many of them related to the lived experience of psychiatric survivors and people with disabilities. The original three members of the band all had theatrical backgrounds. Innes and Cohen met working at Second City and Stackhouse met Cohen through a theatre for street youth.[15] Stackhouse, a leader in the Mad Pride movement, who had studied at the American Academy of Dramatic Arts in New York, credits Cohen with her interest in the company's ideals: "We formed the company in 1989 because we shared a vision. Theatre should reflect Canadian culture and turn regular folks on. Regular folks don't usually make up your typical audience ... It was Miles who turned me onto the concept of integration – bringing together professionals and amateurs and anyone else who's interested – and wiping out the categories that differentiate theatre."[16] These ideals translated into a practice emphasizing the collective development of plays through workshops.

Over the last twenty years Friendly Spike Theatre Band has developed many original productions in this way, the themes of which are often connected to the experiences of people who self-identify as psychiatric survivors. One example of their collectively devised work is *The Edmond Yu Project* (first created in 2000 and remounted in 2007), which follows a theatre group composed of psychiatric survivors that frees itself from a director who accepts government money to direct them and tries to press them into a production of Euripides' *Electra*. Instead, the group asserts its desire to produce work that is more connected with their own experiences and sense of truth-telling. The metatheatrical and multi-media play ultimately explores society's treatment of people diagnosed with mental illness and the tragic case of Edmond Yu, a Toronto man diagnosed with schizophrenia who was killed by police in 1997.[17] Another key example of the company's drive to feature the local lived experiences of psychiatric service was its 2000 production, *Angels of 999*. Written by historian Geoffrey Reaume, the play drew from his doctoral thesis that examined the history of patient experience at the Toronto Hospital of the Insane (and was subsequently published as *Remembrance of Patients Past*) to tell the stories of patients who lived at the institution.[18] More recently, Stackhouse developed a second play drawing from the stories of three women cited in Reaume's book: May F., Audrey B., and Mathilda K. Entitled *Tied Together*, it toured to Vancouver as part of Simon Fraser University's 2008 Madness, Citizenship and Social Justice Conference. The Friendly Spike Theatre Band has been a leader in the Toronto Mad Pride scene, organizing a grassroots event that began in 1993 and has grown to become a city-designated week-long annual celebration with connections to similar events internationally. In addition to organizing Mad Pride, the company has continued to offer theatre workshops, develop members' plays, and regularly produce theatre both for and by interested "regular folks" in the community.[19]

Workman Arts, by contrast, began as a theatre company operating out of the Queen Street Mental Health Centre on the site of the former Toronto Hospital for the Insane. Some of the company's members have also been active in the psychiatric survivor movement while others are unaffiliated with the movement and describe their relationship to psychiatry or mental illness differently. Like Friendly Spike, Workman Arts has also sought to integrate professional and amateur artists and has aimed in its productions to have an even balance of company members and trained professional theatre artists. While Friendly Spike Theatre Band has had focused and fixed allegiances to the specific goals of psychiatric survivor and Mad Pride movements, Workman Arts has connected with a range of Canadian and international disability activist groups as well as professional theatres. A further distinction is that Friendly Spike Theatre Band has been interested in integrated processes that dissolve distinctions between professional and amateur, whereas Workman Arts has been focused on providing professionally oriented theatre training and performance opportunities to members who may not be able to develop their talents through standard professional training programs.

While the Glenvale Players, SNIFF Inc., Friendly Spike Theatre Band, and Workman Arts have pursued programs largely independently of one another, Picasso PRO has been an important facilitating body for connection and collaboration in the city (see Figures 2.1 and 2.2). Although the work has been accomplished under various project names, each led by Rose Jacobson, overall Picasso PRO has been shaped by the core mission of facilitating "genuine opportunity and integration for artists with disabilities and Deaf artists in the performing and media arts. It springs from the passionate conviction that artists with disabilities and Deaf artists belong on Ontario and Canada's stages and screens, among our audiences, professional staffs, teachers and cultural leaders."[20] Although theatre has not been the only focus, disability theatre artists have been strong participants in the

2.1
Picasso PRO's Talking Movement
Workshop led by Miriam Rother,
September 2010.

2.2
Picasso PRO's Jammin' with
Josette, an Actors Lab for Deaf
and allied artists led by Josette
Bushell-Mingo, May 2010.

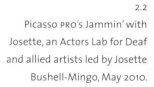

project, especially as Jacobson began the work as a satellite of the Toronto
Theatre Alliance (TTA) Cross Cultural Caucus entitled *Dis This!* (1993–2003).
She renamed it the Picasso Project when it became a collaboration between
the TTA and Alex Bulmer's SNIFF Inc theatre company (2001–2003), then re-
configured it as Picasso PRO when it proceeded both in partnership with the
Equity Showcase Theatre (2005–2007) and during its independent operations (2007– 2009). Renamed again as Picasso PRO/CT in 2009, it currently
functions as a collaborative effort with Creative Trust. From an original core
of 8 people, the endeavour now involves more than 70 active participants,
many of whom have ties to disability theatre. Bulmer has explained that it
was important that the enterprise "not become yet another production company that might simply be pushed to the side," but rather be a force for
change in the community at large.[21] Picasso PRO has supported individual
performances like *Dis This!* at Kickstart, the 2006 Toronto Summerworks
production of John Feld's *Oops!* (winner of the Toronto arts weekly, *NOW
Magazine*'s Audience Choice Award), and the 2007 production of Marivaux's
La Dispute (with an integrated ensemble of Deaf, disabled, and non-disabled
actors). It has also organized many theatre training initiatives (eg. Shake-
spearean scene study, vocal and movement workshops), sponsored local
opportunities to connect with disability theatre practitioners like Australia's
Back to Back Theatre and Sweden's Tyst Teater, and supported the professional development and extended practice of ASL interpretation and audio
description services in live performance, including theatre. As a chief aspect
of Picasso PRO's mandate has been to support the regional development of
disability arts and culture, the initiative has been primarily interested in
connecting with and supporting disability artists, providing training, career
development, and employment opportunities, and serving as an umbrella
for activism, advocacy, and organization of disability artists in the region.
Thus, while its broader mandate has not been to serve theatre alone, a range
of disability theatre artists in the city have gained from the opportunity to
connect across artistic disciplines and specific disability orientations.[22] This
has been important in Toronto for, unlike Calgary and Vancouver, most
disability theatre companies in the city have developed art and supported
artists connected to specific kinds of disability experience.

Calgary

Calgary is a significantly smaller urban centre than Toronto (with a population just over a million compared to 5.5 million in the Greater Toronto Area),

yet it boasts one of the most active and diverse urban disability arts scenes in the country. Among prairie cities it is the primary hub of disability theatre, and has shown national and international leadership, particularly through its annual disability arts festival, Balancing Acts. Since the 1990s, three primary companies have emerged and been sustained in the city: Stage Left Productions, the Association of the Inside Out Integrated Theatre (Inside Out), and MoMo Mixed Ability Dance Theatre (MoMo). Whereas disability theatre in Toronto has been marked by connections to particular disability communities, these three Calgary companies have pursued a cross-disability approach. Although each emphasizes a different perspective and connection to disability politics, crossover personnel between Inside Out and Momo and Stage Left's programming of both Inside Out and MoMo in their Balancing Acts festival suggests the companies' mutual awareness of each other's work.

Stage Left Productions, one of Calgary's most wide-ranging companies, defines itself as a performance company rather than strictly theatre, pointing to its commitment to multi and interdisciplinary approaches and alternative practices. In fact its efforts are not exclusively oriented toward disability issues; it also supports a range of art forms and social activism. Founded in 1999 by disabled artist and activist Michele Decottignies, Stage Left Productions later incorporated as a non-profit in 2003. Since its early days, the company has been inspired by and engaged in Augusto Boal-based Theatre of the Oppressed, and in 2005 they were recognized by Boal as an official Centre for Theatre of the Oppressed. The techniques and social justice interests of the company are evident in its ethos which states: "We are radical artists and activists. We are personally, not just professionally, located within marginalized community groups and deeply connected to the interrogative politics of intersectional identity, diversity, and social justice. We are equally accomplished in community engagement and professional arts practices, and we relentlessly strive to ensure that both strongly adhere to our vision. We shape the artwork to the people, rather than shape the people to the work – making our practice welcoming, accessible, culturally-respectful, and anti-assimilationist."[23]

The company also publicly asserts its place as "Canada's leading contributor to the global Disability Arts movement."[24] Decottignies has been careful to explain that the company's primary impulse was not to lead but to "redress barriers to the advancement of [their] dis arts practice."[25] Distinguishing its concerns from "the arts and disability," the company explains that:

Disability Arts forms an integral part of disability politics and contributes to the expression of disability culture. This artistic practice is based on the unique movements, sounds, thoughts, and perspectives of disabled artists – patterns that cannot be authentically replicated by non-disabled artists. It is informed by disabled people's experiences, values, and beliefs, and by a sense of identity as collective members of a distinct community group with a distinct culture and unique experiences as the recipients of social prejudice. Disability Arts is a unique production modality, that is primarily concerned with representations of individual disabled identity and collective disability culture, rather than with gaining access to traditional arts practices.[26]

Importantly, Stage Left's connection to the global movement has meant that Decottignies cites the company's primary disability arts goals as the generation and dissemination of a "national understanding, among all dis arts stakeholders (artists, service providers, academics, critics, funders, arts and community service organizations, the media, parents and families, etc.), of exactly what disability arts practice is and what factors are at play that are impeding its continued evolution."[27] Decottignies and Stage Left ascribe to the global disability arts movement's promotion of a distinctive artistic practice which resists "dominant norms that frame disability as undesirable," advances new ideas of equity, and reflects a disability aesthetic, "which means that we (Stage Left and my colleagues in radical dis arts) understand disability as a unique culture in society – the value of which can be commented on and shared with a largely ignorant and biased society in artistically engaging ways – just as 'queer' or 'feminist' art contributed a new understanding of humanity to society through artistic channels."[28] Decottignies' emphasis on radical disability arts distinguishes the company's approach to disability theatre more generally. As a modifier, the term radical emphasizes a political commitment to profound social change. As we shall see, other groups place less emphasis on this dimension. For Stage Left, however, this radical politics is a foundational component and marker of their connection to the global movement.

Although Stage Left's own performance work has largely been produced locally, their Balancing Acts festival has built critical connections between Canadian and international disability theatre artists. The festivals have featured, for example, acclaimed international disability theatre artist Mat Fraser as well as many of the leading Canadian disability theatre solo artists (e.g. Jan Derbyshire, Victoria Maxwell, Meg Torwl, Alan Shain). They have also showcased such groups as Inside Out and MoMo, which we will consider further below.

Beyond presenting activities, the company has developed a distinctive performance practice that builds from both an artistic and a community foundation. With regard to the former, the company explains that all of its work "is a combination of Popular Theatre genres (e.g. Theatre of the Oppressed, Agit-Prop, Guerrilla Theatre, Theatre of the Streets, Workers' Theatre), Political Theatre, Documentary Theatre, Performance Creation, Digital and New Media, Multidisciplinary Production, and Artist-Community Collaboration with anti-oppressive, arts-based change processes."[29] In terms of community, the company insists that its work centre around its collaborators in a manner that engages "other marginalized artists and community members directly in a radical process of further discovering, representing, and transforming individual, cultural, and social realities through art."[30] In Chapter 6, I investigate a critically important example of the company's work that draws from these two foundations, *Mercy Killing or Murder: The Tracy Latimer Story*.

In contrast to companies like Workman Arts and Friendly Spike Theatre Band, Stage Left Productions has not sought charitable status. Decottignies has explained this choice as consonant with the company's need to resist at all costs the charitable model, which they consider anathema to the disability movement's drive for disabled peoples' agency and call for social responsibility. "If we can't bite the hand that feeds us," she explains, "then we need to eat at a different table. Or cook a different meal for those others, like us, who find ourselves on the margins."[31] Instead, Stage Left seeks to operate largely through a partnership model in which most of its funding opportunities "have logically and naturally emerged from the strength of our relationships with many organizations and/or individuals ... We identify programming needs from long-standing and continued engagement with specific communities. We work with our partners to figure out how best to offer programming that may meet those needs. We apply for funding to support that programming."[32] The model has proven successful and in recent years some funders have approached Stage Left to shift from program-based to operational funding, a transition critical for long term planning and sustainability which, as we will explore more fully in the next two chapters, are perennial challenges for most disability theatre companies.

Even before Stage Left began to give some regularity to disability arts programming in Calgary with the Balancing Acts festivals, there were early signs of activity. Inside Out, for example, originated in the early 1990s in a University of Calgary Rehabilitation Studies program. A 1991 production entitled *Belonging* invited audiences to watch people with and without disabilities perform stories related to the challenges and humour that shape the lives of people living with disabilities. Founding artistic director Ruth Bieber, who is blind and holds an MA in Education with a specialty in disability and theatre, began the group's incorporation process in 1994. Two years later, Inside Out

separated from the university and formed an independent, non-profit corporation dedicated to providing training and performance opportunities for
people with disabilities.

Bieber has cited critical parallels with feminist practices in the company's
development and activities.[33] During her studies in the 1980s, she had been
struck by a seeming disconnect between feminist and disability rights discourses. Inside Out's work, by contrast, has been informed by ideas from
both fields of study. Bieber suggests that, like feminists who support women's
aspirations in a patriarchal society that traditionally denies them access to
power, the company aims to promote and serve the theatrical abilities of
people who, because of physical, developmental, and sensory disabilities, or
mental health disorders, would normally be denied performance opportunities. Thus, as with Stage Left, Inside Out's approach to disability theatre
involves a broader spectrum of activist practices which resist the "myth that
creativity belongs to a talented few who are able to earn a living through their
craft" and promotes instead the creative and artistic rights of all people.[34]
Drawing parallels with feminist consciousness raising from the 1960s that
went beyond individual women to address a broader social base, Bieber
explains that Inside Out has also "had to embrace the greater context of raising the consciousness of its audience ... Just like the early feminists who tried
to turn themselves into little men and discovered that this was not the answer,
Inside Out, through its occasional efforts to accommodate mainstream
traditional theatre, discovered that ultimately this compromised its own
authenticity. We could not try to be something we were not. We ARE disability theatre."[35]

The company's practice of disability theatre involves, as their name asserts,
an integrated approach in which people with and without disabilities develop
and perform work together, coming up with roles specifically designed for
individual artists and using a rehearsed improvisation approach to include
participants who have difficulty reading. The company adopts a collective,
inclusive approach, in which each participant is respected and valued, with
members contributing their particular blend of responsibility, trust, and willingness. "We simply build on strengths and abilities," notes Bieber, "rather
than focusing on a deficit and exclusive approach."[36] The company's tagline
also indicates a core artistic strategy: "Our message is serious, our delivery
humourous!" Finding comedy wherever possible in the challenging stories
shared by participating artists, the company aims to woo audiences "through
the use of humour and soul connection."[37] This strategy has helped it to
find a wide range of audiences both at home and abroad. Inside Out has
performed at Canadian and international disability arts festivals (such as

Balancing Acts, Kickstart, Australia's High Beam Festival) and more main-stream local events like One Yellow Rabbit's annual High Performance Rodeo and several Canadian Fringe Festivals.

In their 2004 touring show, *Help Unwanted*, for example, performers enacted comic scenarios drawn from real-life experiences coping with "help" from misguided but well-meaning members of the public. Describing laughter as a "good tool," Inside Out's Nicky Peeters explained the show's development process: "There is a real story behind every vignette. These can be very little tiny things. Someone might say 'Y'know what really bothered me this week? I went on a bus and someone was looking at me.' OK, how can we say to the audience that's what's happening to us? We act it out. We laugh about it. We make fun of it."[38] For Helen LeBaron, an actor who worked with the group for many of its early years, finding the comedy helps her push past the frustrations of the incidents themselves: "I have this anger, and it helps me to get over things. The stories that we do make me laugh and be happy again … [P]eople get the hint that we don't need as much help as they think we do."[39] Bieber has noted that the company places a great deal of emphasis on the journey to production: "Within our process a sense of social cohesion is established, simultaneously empowering the individuals by encouraging self-expression, by emphasizing the process over the product. This is not to say that performance in and of itself is without value, it simply limits its potential if it is the only value. This does not mean that the professional quality of the performance is compromised."[40] Thus, a critical part of the process is finding the humour which will allow the company to connect with audiences in generative ways. Comedy, Bieber argues, helps to navigate the fear of disability that pervades society in ways that will make audiences think but not "leave them feeling guilt-ridden, oppressed and bewildered" so that they would not attend company shows again.[41] The company thus seeks a broad public in its efforts to shift social attitudes and create a more inclusive society. In comparison to Stage Left's emphasis on more radical approaches, Bieber has suggested that this shift, like "all true change," is slow and incremental.[42]

In further contrast to Stage Left, Inside Out has held charitable status since 1997. Like Decottignies, however, Bieber has been thoughtful about the polit-ical difficulties involved in supporting disability theatre financially. She has expressed frustration at outsiders' perceptions that disability theatre artists receive "'easy dollars' by virtue of the fact that they have access to govern-ment funding for the disabled."[43] Refuting this idea, she argues that disabil-ity theatre is often "between a rock and a hard place" when rehabilitation funding bodies and arts funders both pressure the group to look to the other for funding.[44] Bieber acknowledges that mainstream theatres take on risk

when they program disability theatre but she also points out that the actual
absence of "easy dollars" means that disability theatre companies face the
challenge of educating audiences and critics about disability culture as well
as engaging in the work itself. Drawing parallels again with feminism, Bieber
demonstrates how the rhetoric of "easy dollars" for disability theatre draws
from a logically flawed discourse of dependency akin to that which belittles
women's labour.[45]

In 2003, a third company, MoMo Mixed Ability Dance Theatre, emerged
on the Calgary scene (see Fig. 2.3). One of the company's founders, award-
winning playwright Pamela Boyd, began the work after forty years of
professional theatre practice, three years with InsideOut and many years as a
frontline disability support worker. As part of InsideOut, Boyd had been able
to attend the Australian High Beam Festival with Bieber. There she saw a performance by Australia's Restless Dance Theatre, a company of young
performers with and without disabilities that dazzled Boyd: "Restless is a 25-
year-old company that performs 10-day, sold-out runs, sometimes twice a
year, in a 400-seat theatre. Its audience demographic is completely mainstream. I knew I had to make this happen in Calgary."[46] In 2003, Boyd teamed
up with choreographer and dance teacher Laurie Montemurro and yoga and
movement instructor George McFaul to offer open-contact improvisation
workshops. The success of these convinced them of a strong community
need, and they founded the company. Although McFaul and Montemurro
later left to pursue other projects, Boyd has remained committed to the company's original roots in movement and dance.

Like "MoMo," the eponymous heroine of Michael Ende's children's book
who can see beyond the restrictions of her current society, each term in the
company's name has been carefully chosen to suggest its mandate.[47] While
some companies with similar mandates have adopted the term "integrated
theatre," Boyd explains that MoMo favours "mixed ability" because they feel
it is less confusing language and represents more precisely the company's
goals and process. As their website explains, MoMo aims to bring together
"professional artists and prospective artists, with and without disability or
ability, to explore movement, voice, instrument, theatre, dance, visual art and
improvisational disciplines. Artists of all abilities and skills, professional or
not, are supported and challenged in the practice, creation and performance
of distinctive works of dance theatre that reflect our unique community and
its individuals."[48]

Practically, Boyd is careful to explain that MoMo's creative process is not
simply about one group teaching or adapting to another; nor is it about erasing or ignoring the differences among people that can make collaboration

2.3
MoMo Mixed Ability Dance Theatre,
Momentum, 2010.

challenging.[49] Instead, the company pays careful attention to the perceived strengths and weaknesses specific to the group. As the group pursues a particular artistic goal, Boyd suggests, a fundamental part of their process is problem solving, "itself a very creative activity."[50] Company artist Thomas Poulsen suggests that the early part of the process is often about getting to know one another – each person's disabilities and abilities. All participants in the process, he explains, "need to have flexibility and the ability and willingness to work with people as they are. The process is not going to be about taking a person with a disability and making them fit into a preconceived theatre or dance box."[51]

Finding financial support for the increasing scope of MoMo's workshops and productions has been important. In its early days the company was driven by the inspiration and volunteerism of Boyd and her co-founders. MoMo later gained from the generous support of a benefactor, glasswaters foundation, as well as project and operating arts funding from both the municipal and provincial levels. They have also partnered with the Kinsmen and the City of Calgary to present the annual Freak Out! activist disability event at City Hall.

MoMo's particular form of mixed abilities dance and theatre, Boyd argues, "asks audiences to see and hear in new ways, to suspend their preconceptions about beauty and art."[52] In support of this end, Boyd insists that each of their performances adhere to a high production standard; she always hires professional stage managers, designers, and operators. In addition to distinguishing MoMo's work from "a school skit," Boyd believes these professional production standards honour the work and help the audience look and listen in new ways. Audiences have responded positively to their work, and Boyd argues that the company has "been completely accepted by Calgary's independent dance and theatre community and we're happily busy."[53] External critical reception of the work is more difficult to gauge. Like many Canadian disability artists and innovative dance theatre artists who have become frustrated with the lack of attention from mainstream critical presses, MoMo has been more previewed than reviewed.

Connections among the three major disability theatre companies in Calgary are manifest in the case of Boyd and Bieber's work history and Stage Left's featuring of work from all three companies in its annual Balancing Acts Festival. Each has also explicitly noted and forged ties to the global disability arts and culture movement. What is perhaps most striking in the Calgary context are the different niches that each company has carved out within the local scene. Formally, MoMo's focus on dance theatre is different than Inside Out's focus on consciousness-raising devised comedy. Structurally, Stage Left's partnership model differs from MoMo and Inside Out's charitable status model. Calgary is served by several different disability theatre models, each of which has a growing track record and an evolving, internationally-connected sense of its place and purpose.

Vancouver

Like Toronto and Calgary, Vancouver is a prominent theatre and festival city. In the past thirty years, it has also demonstrated leadership in disability activism and civic policies supporting accessibility.[54] The Kickstart festival in 2001 highlighted the importance of Vancouver as a national hub of disability arts and culture. This critical event, however, followed and drew from years of local activity, not least in disability theatre.

Two disability theatre companies stand out in the Vancouver scene: Theatre Terrific and Realwheels. While Realwheels is a relatively young company that emerged self-consciously in relation to disability arts and culture, Theatre Terrific's local and international ties to disability theatre have grown in tandem with the disability movement itself. While I will consider Theatre Terrific in more depth in Chapter 3, it is important to note here that, like Workman Arts and Glenvale Players, its earliest operations emerged from local initiatives to provide theatre training and performance opportunities for people with disabilities, impulses that can be connected to disability culture but, as we have seen, are not their only animating principles. In the course of its development, however, the company became an early proponent of disability arts and culture in the city, modifying its practices in this direction over time, supporting the foundation of the Society for Disability Arts and Culture in 1998, and performing at the first Kickstart festival in 2001. The company also has complex ties with Realwheels founder James Sanders, who took classes and explored creative opportunities with the company in the 1990s. Further, former Theatre Terrific co-Artistic Director Trevor Found formed an ad hoc collective with Sanders in 2000 and sat on Realwheels Society's founding board of directors.[55] In 2006, the two companies also shared funding for a collaborative Classical Project, an initiative that ultimately fractured at least partially due to different visions for disability theatre. Sanders has suggested that the collapse of the shared project was valuable because it helped each company to sharpen its mandate and demonstrated that the city could support different kinds of disability theatre practice.[56] To gain a sense of what these kinds are, we will first explore Realwheels' own comparatively short history, its mandate, and remarkably swift commercial and professional success.

Realwheels, founded and incorporated as a not-for-profit organization and registered federal charity by Sanders in 2003, is best known for its touring production of *Skydive*, a technologically innovative show that brought together the artistic team that would also reconnect in the company's second major production, *Spine*. This team included Sanders, much-lauded local professional actor Bob Frazer, and award-winning playwright Kevin Kerr. Of the three, only Sanders, who became paraplegic following a spinal cord injury in 1990, claims to have a disability. Sanders was in his third semester of a professional theatre training program at Vancouver's Douglas

College when he sustained the injury. Returning to classes after a year of rehabilitation, he felt more hampered by attitudinal than physical barriers, a situation which pushed him to think about how he might challenge these through theatre itself.[57]

One of the chief attitudes that Sanders sought to challenge after graduation was the idea that he should always play characters with disabilities or create work related to disability. With this aim in mind, in 2000 he and Trevor Found created the Realwheels Ad Hoc Collective to produce two plays explicitly not about disability: *Getting In* and *The Store* by famed Canadian arts leader Mavor Moore. The aim was both to cast Sanders in roles which did not reference disability and, as each play's narrative turned on a struggle over status, show him playing the high status position to "challenge assumptions with a very plausible situation that does occur in the real world but not with any great frequency."[58] In 2001, Found's company Theatre Bagger joined with s4DAC and the collective to present the works. Moore himself attended the production and responded positively: "What absolutely knocked me out was your collective fidelity to the text and texture of the plays. I don't think there was a nuance missed, and the tough challenges in the staging (which include subtle ways of snapping out of the static situations) were all met with ingenuity and skill."[59]

Encouraged and challenged by feedback of the production, Sanders moved forward with the idea of creating work in which disability was "simply present without any cited issue, allowing for a natural and honest representation of disability through universal issues."[60] He collaborated with his friend from Douglas College, Bob Frazer, and they commissioned playwright Kevin Kerr to help them develop what would eventually become *Skydive*. The play would premiere at Vancouver's PuSh festival in 2007, garner several professional theatre nominations and awards, and go on to play for over 30,000 people as it toured to Calgary, Montreal, Ottawa, and Kamloops. In subsequent chapters I explore *Skydive* and *Spine* in more detail. Here, it is critical to note how the company's interest in locating disability within universal themes has been a guiding impulse since its earliest days.

The swift success of *Skydive* and grants for the company's subsequent projects meant that its budgets grew quickly in tandem with its professional reporting and business responsibilities. To help with this rapid growth, they applied for and received a Canada Council Flying Squad grant which they used to consult with professionals to hone their mandate and vision. In response to this work, the company identified its core values as excellence, innovation, authenticity, and inclusiveness while defining itself through the following mission statement: "Realwheels is a professional theatre company that creates and produces world-class art that deepens the audience's under-standing of the disability experience. We tell stories in which disability itself is not the focus of conflict, but rather disability forms the landscape upon which universal issues are debated onstage."[61] The stated commitment to pro-fessional status separates Realwheels from those companies like Friendly Spike Theatre Band, for example, who seek to elide traditional distinctions between professionals and amateurs in a new disability theatre. Further, as we shall see in Chapter 6 where I compare Realwheels' *Skydive* with Stage Left's *Mercy Killing or Murder: The Tracy Latimer Story*, Realwheels' artistic interest in universal themes and invocation of disability as landscape rather than focus works in opposition to those who seek more radical interpella-tions between disability and the public sphere. Realwheels is also distinctive in that, unlike all of the other groups explored above, it does not run theatre training programs. It also avoids connection with any particular disability activist or community group, preferring instead to focus on the specific con-cerns of productions and core professional development. In this regard the company has been adept at capitalizing on its home city's lively professional theatre and disability arts and culture scenes. For example, many of the tech-nological and performance innovations of *Skydive* drew from Sanders' participation in the Kickstart festivals. The production also gained main-stream theatre exposure through its premier at Vancouver's annual PuSh International Performing Arts Festival, an event that aims to expand "the horizons of Vancouver artists and audiences with work that is visionary, genre-bending, multi-disciplined, startling and original."[62] Realwheels has pitched its work as boundary-pushing for professional theatre practice and has found a place in a city whose performing arts and disability arts scenes both seek global connections.

Realwheels has also pushed boundaries through its artistic collaborations and explorations with Vancouver-based Deaf artist, Max Fomitchev, a Russian-born and professionally trained mime artist best known locally and internationally as Max-i-mime. After receiving his MFA from Schukin University of the Arts, Fomitchev toured internationally with the Zakutok Players. When in 1991 the troupe visited Washington, DC's Gallaudet Uni-versity (an institution dedicated to the undergraduate education of people who are Deaf or hard of hearing), Fomitchev determined to leave Russia: "I will never forget meeting all these empowered 'normal' deaf students, so full of confidence for their futures. I could not believe there were deaf people studying to be doctors and lawyers and engineers, whatever they wanted, as if they were free ... And I saw they were free. And I wanted to be free."[63] In 1992 Fomitchev performed in Vancouver with Zakutok and decided to stay, establishing a career in Canada as a professional mime artist in film, television, and theatre. Although more recently he has been on tour as a lead clown in Cirque du Soleil's touring production of *Alegria*, he has performed his solo works in the context of disability arts and culture events (Toronto's Abilities Festival in 2005 and the Kickstart-sponsored Unruly Salon in 2007) as well as Deaf-World events (Deaf Way II in 2002 and the Deaf Olympics in 2005). His decision to engage with both is interesting given that some Deaf-World advocates argue for firm distinctions between disability and Deaf cultures. Indeed, Fomitchev's willingness to collaborate artistically with Sanders in 2008 is suggestive of his resistance to borders of many kinds; he has performed for adults and children in festivals targeting a wide range of communities, disability, Deaf, and otherwise. His work with Sanders used text from Shakespeare's *Richard III* to explore "the simultaneous representation of a single character on stage through two performers: a quadriplegic actor (whose body language is limited by their physicality, but who can expertly vocalize the text) and a Deaf mime artist (who is expertly capable of combining sign and mime into a powerful physical performance)."[64] Both Sanders and Fomitchev have found means to connect across difference and serve audiences with and without disabilities.

Another Vancouver enterprise that has promoted crossover between professional, mainstream, and disability theatre is Siobhan McCarthy's absolut theatre company which was founded in 1997 and registered as a not-for-profit society in 2003. With an Honours BA in Theatre and a degree in arts administration from the University of British Columbia, McCarthy is currently engaged in broader performance work as a producer, director, instructor, and actor for film, television, and theatre. She is also a well-known contributor to disability theatre through festivals, workshops, and productions. In 2003, for example, she shared her perspectives on a panel at the inaugural Madness and Arts World Festival in Toronto. In 2005 she headlined at Stage Left's Balancing Acts where the programmers described her as one of Canada's foremost "cross-over" artists "using her dynamic blend of physical theatre to explore disability and to dazzle audiences with risky, challenging performance art work that stretches the boundaries of both disability and theatre."[65]

Like "radical," the modifier "cross-over" is suggestive of disability theatre's features and limits. It infers boundaries between mainstream and disability theatre practices, while nonetheless reflecting a desire to connect with different communities of artists and audiences. While McCarthy's current company, blyssful PRODUCTIONS, does not align itself with disability arts explicitly, it retains her commitment to socially and politically aware, issue-based storytelling. Through absolut theatre company, she had sought "to foster relationships between distinct communities – disability and main-stream – and within artistic disciplines – visual art and performing arts."[66] Like MoMo in Calgary, the company was committed to high standards of artistic integrity and professionalism in their productions because they did not want their work to "be dismissed or not taken seriously because of soci-ety's misconceptions of 'disability.'"[67] Like Bieber at Calgary's Inside Out, McCarthy also stressed the importance of humour in its work: "It is our experience that humorous elements allow for the difficult issues of mental illness to be more approachable, leaving the audience and participants more open to their experiences."[68] Although neither absolut theatre company nor blyssful PRODUCTIONS engage with disability theatre exclusively, in both cases the pressing social and political concerns of people with disabilities have been important motivators for their artistic development processes.

McCarthy and Sanders are both examples of artists who trained in Cana-dian mainstream university theatre programs and then proceeded to form professionally-oriented companies with "cross-over" aims and appeal. Given their training, it is perhaps not surprising that both aim to create theatre that succeeds at least in part according to mainstream professional theatre stan-dards. Further, while McCarthy has done some solo performance work, both have also produced work involving ensembles of artists with and without dis-abilities. By contrast, a significant number of other Canadian theatre artists have followed a different path to generate a rich and active sub-field: solo dis-ability theatre performance.

Solo Disability Theatre

Solo performers have been key contributors to Canadian disability theatre. These performers' works, to varying degrees, have explicitly addressed the particular performer's relationship to disability, usually in ways that have challenged related stigma and stereotypes. Performances of this kind have been regular features of Canadian disability arts festival programs in the major urban centres. Lyle Victor Albert's *Scraping the Surface*, Victoria Maxwell's *Crazy for Life*, Alan Shain's *Still Waiting for that Special Bus*, and David Roche's *The Church of 80% Sincerity*, for example, have toured to acclaim both in Canada and abroad.[69] Apart from the extended touring efforts of Realwheels and Workman Arts, solo disability theatre performers have easily been the most mobile group of disability theatre artists in the country. As opposed to ensemble or company-generated shows, solo per-formers have created work to serve their artistic and professional goals, often performing the same productions over many years in a range of Canadian and international venues. In these ways, they have helped to connect ideas, practices, and people involved in the form both in Canada and abroad. Some works have been wholly self-generated while others have been developed in partnership with disability theatre companies or disability arts presenters. Theatre Terrific produced Albert's *Scraping the Surface*, for example, while Alan Shain's 2009 *Time to Put My Socks On*, a sequel to his 1999 *Still Waiting for that Special Bus*, was developed through Stage Left's Balancing Acts Commissioning Project, an initiative that also supported multi-media artist Meg Torwl's *That's so Gay!* in the same year.[70] Some artists, Victoria Maxwell and Alan Shain for example, have focused on solo performance while others are also regularly involved in ensemble performances. Jan Derbyshire, for example, who has performed her one-woman comedy about mental illness entitled *Funny in the Head* at Kickstart and an array of other venues, is also active in Vancouver as a director, dramaturg, and performer in mainstream and disability theatre. The range of ways that solo performance has figured in Canadian disability theatre artists' careers attests to its importance for the field.

Disability performance scholar Carrie Sandahl has previously demonstrated the critical role that solo performances have played in engaging audiences in disability identity politics and collective re-imagining of stigmatized understandings of disability experience. Analyzing the work of American solo performance artist Lynn Manning, for example, Sandahl has demonstrated "the power of live performance, and the solo performer in particular, to galvanize community activism."[71] Sandahl finds value in the specific autobiographical nature of the experiences shared by such performers and argues that they play "the vital role of interpreting individual experience, gained through epistemic privilege, for the collective. In so doing, [they bring] people together, adding to the collective's framework for understanding systems of oppression, as well as providing access to phenomenological frameworks that only actual bodies of difference, with their unique corporealities, have access to."[72]

Canadian solo performers have likewise mobilized their "unique corporealities" in the service of disability theatre. In his analysis of Albert's performance of *Scraping the Surface*, for example, Andrew Houston demonstrates the critical importance of Albert's performance of the play's central action and metaphor: shaving. In Albert's autobiographical coming of age narrative as a young man with cerebral palsy in rural Alberta, manually shaving his face becomes a metaphor for achieving adulthood and, Houston argues, a means by which Albert asks audiences to consider "the life-altering

benefits of scraping the surface of our own first impressions of him, of cerebral palsy and of the long-term effects this 'shave' may have upon how we
define identity in theatre."[73] Houston emphasizes how the production
achieves profound effects precisely because, after underlining the potentially
lethal significance of the act ("With a razor and a can of cream, I push the
envelope of my existence"), he actually shaves himself on stage, an act that
takes only a few minutes in performance but that, as Albert explains in the
play, in his first real-life attempt took thirty-seven. As in Sandahl's analysis of
Weights, Houston links the play's affective power to Albert's capacity to invest
audiences in his unique corporeality; the shaving is meaningful because it is
accomplished by Albert's particular body on stage in a narrative he framed to
emphasize both its literal and metaphorical significance.

Striking a balance about the place of one's disability in theatre is an enduring concern for disability theatre artists, particularly those involved in solo
autobiographical performance. As disability performance scholar Petra Kuppers has noted, "Disabled performers are often aware of the knowledges that
have been erected around them: tragic, poor, helpless, heroic, struggling, etc.
In the laboratory of the performance situation, these knowledges can be re-
examined, and questioned again and again."[74] Several Canadian theatre artists
have emphasized the power of connecting to their own lived experience to
accomplish this kind of re-examining or questioning.[75] For example, both of
Alan Shain's solo shows have autobiographical elements: "I work from my
own experience as a person with a disability. I focus on the challenges, the
attitudes I come across, and I use comedy to share with people what some of
the issues are, how it affects my life. I also use theatre to show people that I
live in the same world. I see the artist's role in the disability movement as
making a connection with the general public – that we're human, too. What
artists can do is show who they are on stage rather than necessarily talking
about disability rights."[76] While he cites the powerful role that artists can play
in shifting public attitudes about disability, Shain is careful to note that he
also wants to explore more than just disability in his work: "I have many concerns that might not have anything to do with disability like, 'Is the world
going to blow up?' I think it's important for me as an artist to talk about
issues like that or to talk about things like dating and trying to find that special someone to share with. I have the same hopes and dreams as anyone
else."[77] Having attended several consecutive performances of *Socks* in 2009,
it was striking to me that the audiences invariably offered a loud collective
and appreciative "awww!" when Shain's character Marc opened a present of
his favoured white tube socks from Linda, his girlfriend in the play. This scene
signaled her growing understanding of and love for him. Like the moment of

shaving in *Scraping the Surface*, the evident affective power of this moment built upon audience investment in Shain's particular physicality within a performance that demonstrated his specific physical relationship with what would otherwise be utterly banal objects.

In addition to its aesthetic and political potential, solo autobiographical performances have also served important practical ends for Canadian disability theatre artists. Victoria Maxwell, for example, has explicitly identified the form's practical value for her professional career: "Frankly, I wrote the one-person show because I knew I could sell it as a theatre piece and, with it, create work for myself as an actor. I wanted to re-enter the arts and believed this was the only financially wise way to do it."[78] Maxwell has been remarkably successful in marketing and internationally touring productions that draw from her real-life experiences living with mental illness: *Crazy for Life* and *Funny ... You Don't Look Crazy?!*[79] While Sandahl reminds us that solo performances rarely involve only one artist (most productions' direction, dramaturgy, and technical personnel belie the "solo"), the material costs of production can be lowered and potential profits raised by only having one performer to support. Further, the production may be more easily coordinated, rehearsed, and toured to suit the artist's needs. In a large country like Canada where travel to and from various performance sites can be costly and time-consuming, particularly when they involve planning for disability access, these practical features are significant both for disability artists and disability arts presenters.

One final structural feature of solo performances that must be noted is their capacity to side-step disability arts arguments within the frame of a single production. As James Sanders has noted, "There's in-fighting within the disability movement, and I think one camp is saying, 'Embrace disability, talk about it, tell the stories, get it out there' and the other camp is saying, 'ignore disability and just do your work.' I think both of them have strong arguments. For me, I want to be able to take from both. I want to be able to talk about it, but I don't want it to be the driving force."[80] Whether or not they would agree with Sanders' parsing of the debate, most disability theatre artists would agree that there can be irreconcilable approaches to disability theatre production that solo performers, having only to answer to their own aesthetic and practical interests prior to showing audiences, can avoid. Victoria Maxwell's willingness to perform regularly in conjunction with psychiatric medical conferences or events, for example, is not something that artists from Friendly Spike Theatre Band would easily embrace. Further, the current scene seems to hold space for a range of such performers. While Maxwell and Jan Derbyshire have each performed solo shows about mental illness experience at disability arts festivals, for example, their comic sensibilities are different and the disability theatre scene has demonstrated an interest in programming both artists' works rather than featuring one to the exclusion of the other. In short, the scene as a whole does not seem to reserve a particular disability niche for specific performers.

Conclusion

This three-city and solo performer survey suggests some of the ways in which Canadian artists have taken the stage under the banner of disability theatre. It is clear that the artists cited have adopted both complementary and competing stances with regard to the term. In most cases, however, they have explicitly recognized their connection to broader disability culture and activism and all are committed to creating theatre which invites critical reflection about the place and understanding of disability in society. Thirty years ago, a survey similar to this one would have turned up very different results. The term disability theatre would have been unknown and confusing. Only a few theatres discussed here would have been in operation. In the intervening period, disability culture and politics in Canada have been transformed and the disability arts and culture movement, through festivals and other networking forums, has forged links between artists. Disability theatre has proven to be an important facet of this movement, and its principal companies and artists have made enduring commitments to revise the performance of disability on stage.

It is important to emphasize that the links noted above are not always defined by goodwill and fellow feeling. It is remarkable how strategic coalition is shaping disability theatre communities in the face of stark differences between some groups. Indeed, at festivals, roundtables, after shows, in interviews, on websites, in archival materials, organizational meetings, formal correspondence, and informal discussion, I have witnessed and been party to a great deal of friction between artists who are passionate about their particular way of creating disability theatre and equally passionate that others' approaches inhibit the field's reach. In the second part of this book, I analyze performances and aesthetic tensions, but it is worth noting that many tensions are not simply aesthetic. While Alex Bulmer, on the *Book of Judith* blogspot, calls herself a "born-again blinky" and riffs comically on the hierarchy of disability in an effort to educate her non-disabled castmates, her jokes belie the seriousness of some rifts. That disability theatre artists return to festivals, roundtables, and each other's work, however, demonstrates how much is at stake for artists who see disability theatre as a critical means for reshaping the lives of people with disabilities and all Canadians. Further, in these growing days of recognition and interest from national funding bodies like the Canada Council for the Arts, not everyone has wanted to go on record with their specific views on these matters because livelihoods and the potential to build the field are at stake. Moreover, due to the poverty and disenfranchisement which shape the lives of people with disabilities more than any other group (Canada being perhaps better in some instances than many places but no exception in this regard), as well as to the often insurmountable inaccessibilities related to travel, the vast majority of the artists involved in the companies described herein have not yet seen the range of each other's work live. I believe that this has further augmented tensions in the field.

It may be striking for readers familiar with other disability or disability arts contexts to note the comparatively low level of contact and conflict between Deaf theatre and disability theatre practitioners and advocates in the Canadian urban contexts described above. Although some Deaf artists have collaborated with disability artists within individual festivals, companies, and initiatives, the Canadian disability theatre scene has not yet featured a critical mass of Deaf artists.[81] While elsewhere this might be a choice by Deaf theatres to distance themselves from disability culture, it is important to note that Canadian Deaf theatre initiatives have not yet met with the same levels of success and stability as such renowned companies as the US National Theatre of the Deaf (NTD), Russia's TOYS Theatre or Sweden's Tyst Teater. In her richly detailed 1998 University of Alberta MA thesis, "Deaf Theatre in Canada: Signposts to An Other Land," Rachel E. Tracie charts the rise and fall of the Canadian Theatre for the Deaf, comparing it directly to NTD, and makes several arguments about why "attempts at deaf theatre in Canada have been unsuccessful."[82] Not least among these is the absence of a professional theatre training program for Deaf artists and other gaps in infrastructure that parallel those noted in relation to disability theatre.[83] In 1997, international performer and comedian Angela Petrone Stratiy argued, "There's no Canadian Theatre of the Deaf right now, no money, no funding."[84] Since then, there have been some focused efforts to cultivate Canada's own Deaf theatre.[85] In many ways Tracie's conclusions suggest ways that strategic coalition with disability theatres might be productive, but the complex arguments for and against this have yet to be fully explored.

Some groups have connected to the term disability theatre more explicitly than others; some have used it with modifications. Most artists surveyed here have sought to distinguish their particular understanding of the term or the relationship of their theatre to disability arts and broader cultural spheres.

While some favour radical approaches to create social change, others value incrementalism. While some emphasize the power of humour to forge connections with audiences, others emphasize narratives that alarm or resonate with audiences because of their authentic expression. A number of companies are open to the broad involvement of people without disabilities, variously describing this approach as integrated or mixed, while others seek to limit or balance their involvement. Some target specific disability communities while others address a broader public. Many have sought charitable and not-for-profit status and some operate deliberately outside these frameworks. There have been different sources for funds and attitudes toward their appropriate use. Further, scales for production and attitudes toward production standards have also varied as have processes for developing theatre. Importantly, however, these many statements of difference also highlight broad commonalities and shared fields of debate. In short, the debates also indicate that there is something at stake for these artists in the idea of disability theatre. While here we have painted these debates in broad strokes, the next two chapters will explore in finer detail the operational choices made by two companies that are both over twenty years old, each with a complicated, distinctive relationship to disability theatre. Both have features that make them outliers and engines in the Canadian disability theatre context. In section two, we will return to these two companies as well as some others considered above to see just what kind of theatre this range of approaches has produced.

CHAPTER THREE

Workman Arts

> Madness has been and remains an elusive thing.
> Roy Porter, *A Social History of Madness: Stories of the Insane*

In spring 2008, over a hundred students, faculty, artists, researchers, and interested community members gathered in a large circle at Brock University in St Catharines, Ontario, to watch a short performance by Toronto's Workman Arts entitled *The Chant*.[1] Building a strong rhythm through clapping, stamping, gesture, choral speech, monologue, and dialogue, three performers, initially indistinguishable from the audience, emerged from the circle and invited those present to question what they knew about mental illness. What, they asked, would you do when confronted with a broad range of practical scenarios drawn from lived mental illness experiences?

Following the performance, a panel discussion allowed the performers to field many questions about their artistic processes and the issues raised by the piece. In addition to offering answers, however, performers also turned questions back to the audience because the problems they raised were complex and required dialogue and reflection. One performer spoke candidly about personal struggles with schizophrenia and noted how much of what is represented in the media confuses the experience, fuelling stigma and making it difficult for people to recognize or seek help for their illness. Another performer explained how mental illness experience had interrupted a successful professional performing arts career but that Workman Arts had afforded an opportunity to get back on stage, reinvigorating his performance

skills and passion. A number of students came up at the end of the performance to ask how they, friends, or family could become more involved in
Workman Arts. The day's events were routine for Workman Arts performers
in the sense that post-performance panels are a common feature of the company's work and versions of *The Chant* have toured to dozens of venues since
the piece debuted as part of the play *Worlds Away?* by John Gregory, which
the company first produced for a nine-city tour in 1992. The day's particular
cast followed in the footsteps of other company members who have mounted
the work, but each also enriched the broader performance and talkback
session with his or her particular talents and experiences. Given these routine
qualities, the brevity of the piece, and its low production costs, I wondered
as I sat in the audience, how did this performance garner such high levels of
audience engagement and discussion?

Theatre depicting mental illness is not rare. In fact, few dramatic figures,
tropes, and themes are as ubiquitous. We can think, for example, of the
Dionysian frenzy, Hamlet and Ophelia, *commedia dell'arte*, and Noh drama
mad scenes. Among the countless twentieth century mad figures are Luigi
Pirandello's Enrico IV, Tennessee Williams' Blanche Dubois, the asylum
inmates presented in Peter Weiss' *Marat/Sade*, and the list goes on and on.
Although Workman Arts productions also often include characters with
mental illness and their works have mental illness themes, the company's
mandate and artistic processes break from tradition in an important way:
they privilege the voices, perspectives, and artistry of people with mental illness experience. What was striking and unusual for audiences at *The Chant*
was the opportunity to see theatre in which people who have received mental health or addiction services held artistic control and innovated with
representational choices.

While short, invited, touring productions aimed at generating discussion
in local audiences form an important arm of the company's activity, they
have only been made possible by the project's past two decades of sustained
artistic training and production activities. The company's pioneering mandate and years of experience have also allowed them to reach beyond the local
and regional to create larger-scale productions and forums for exchange
about mental illness and artistic representation. In stark contrast to the low
production costs of *The Chant*, the company's 2003 Madness and Arts World
Festival ran for ten days at Toronto's prestigious Harbourfront Centre with a
three quarters of a million dollar budget and included an international multidisciplinary program. The festival was the first event of its kind and has
since inspired subsequent incarnations in Germany (2006) and another in
Holland (2010). Featuring over 100 artists from eight different countries, the

Toronto program offered a range of diverse performances as well as formal opportunities to share ideas about the role of the arts in shaping attitudes toward mental illness in a range of cultures.

Of all the companies considered in this book, Workman Arts is the one I have studied the longest. My association with it began during my doctoral studies when I approached staff and members to investigate their particular strategies for community theatre engagement. They generously shared their time and views and gave me full access to the company archives. In due course, I volunteered at the company and was hired to act as the research and education coordinator for their Madness and Arts World Festival. As I have moved on to study Canada's disability theatre at large, it has become clear to me that Workman Arts holds an unusual place in the field.

Whereas most of the companies considered in Chapters 2 and 4 emerged from within the disability arts and culture movement in Canada and helped lead the way, Workman Arts has until recently evolved outside its bounds. Rather than engage primarily with other disability artists, it has built connections with a range of artists in the Toronto theatre community and with international companies that also explore mental illness on stage. This approach has brought the company considerable local attention and success while simultaneously building its international profile and cementing its position as a key organizer of an international network of cognate companies. How and why the company has developed in this way relates to its particular institutional origins, its training and artistic mandate, and its members' goal to work at the intersection of the local community and the international field. While Workman Arts shares many ideals with other disability arts companies, its means of reaching them do not suggest a fundamentally national vision of disability arts and culture or a particular affinity with a movement defined around disability in general so much as a focus on mental illness experience in particular.[2]

Workman Arts' members are driven to challenge the kinds of stigmas surrounding mental illness, chiefly by innovating with works that upset artistic tropes identified by company members as contributing to stigma, especially the longstanding custom of marking people with mental illness with some kind of visible physical or aural signal of difference. For those disability artists and scholars who labour to unseat the negative connotations associated with physical difference, the company's aims present a challenge. Rather than add to such negative connotations, however, the company works to devalue the axiom that mental illness needs to be written on the body just as, in the other direction, disability artists have demanded re-evaluations of how physical difference is read. Thus, the specific aesthetic questions that the company raises, while deeply rooted in their local context, concerns, and community, have nonetheless made significant contributions to the international disability arts and culture movement.

Origins, Mandate, and Institutional Structures

Workman Arts is the first and most enduring Canadian performing arts company to support the professional training and practice of artists who have received mental health services.[3] While other innovative Canadian companies have worked in this area (Toronto's Friendly Spike Theatre Band and Edmonton's SOS players are notable examples), Workman Arts has the longest production history, largest membership, most comprehensive training program, and greatest formal connections with external artists and organizations at the local, national, and international levels. Any analysis of Workman Arts must take into account the particular institution in which it was founded: Toronto's Centre for Addiction and Mental Health (CAMH), formerly known as the Queen Street Mental Health Centre.[4] Fully affiliated with the University of Toronto, CAMH is a Pan American Health Organization and World Health Organization Collaborating Centre. The centre is located in a recently gentrified neighbourhood promoted as a design and arts district, but the site nevertheless has a long history as an asylum, stigmatized by its association with mental illness. The Centre's modern concrete architecture still retains the outer brick walls of the nineteenth century institution but these walls and the entire institutional space are currently being redeveloped to strengthen community connections. That Workman Arts has played a significant role in this redevelopment and will have a prime space in the renovated centre attests to the significance of its partnership with CAMH and the distance the company has traveled from its more humble origins.

The company emerged from a talent night series in the late 1980s at the Queen Street Mental Health Centre organized by then psychiatric nurse, Lisa Brown. The performers' considerable talent and commitment to the production process convinced Brown of the need to create more sustained professional training and showcasing opportunities both with and for them.[5] With the help of five performers and the cooperation of the Centre's administrators, Brown established a company over the 1988–89 winter season. The group arranged for local theatre professionals to offer training sessions and scheduled a Christmas performance to work toward. The company's name was drawn from the Joseph L. Workman Auditorium, the Centre's 300-seat theatre out of which the company has rehearsed, operated, and performed from its earliest days until its 2009 temporary relocation to St Anne's Parish Hall while a new theatre and creative arts space is being developed on the former site. Workman himself served as the site's first medical superintendent and held a reputation as an early advocate of patients' arts activities. In 1991, Brown left nursing to lead the company fulltime and incorporated it as a non-profit charitable organization, outside of the Centre's formal control. The primary drive to incorporate concerned the critical issue challenging so many of the companies studied in this book: fees for labour. As Artistic Director, Brown wanted to pay all the members at least minimum wage, something she would have been unable to do within the hospital's pre-existing vocational structures.[6] In retrospect, Brown believes that this move allowed the company to grow according to its own vision, attract a range of external funding, and enter into partnerships with the Centre only when it felt appropriate and was on equal footing.[7] Incorporation, to some extent, created a level of independence.

Workman Arts' mission statement has been adjusted in two significant ways since the company's founding. First, when the Centre expanded to become the Centre for Addiction and Mental Health, the company began to include people facing addiction issues as members. Second, while theatre training and production comprised the company's primary artistic focus prior to 2005, the subsequent range of artistic engagements expanded to include the visual and literary arts, film, and music, necessitating the name change from the Workman Theatre Project to simply Workman Arts. Since its earliest days, the company has distinguished its activities from any form of drama therapy, including psychodrama, medical, or clinical work. As the first call for members to join the emerging group outlined: "The WTP is not a clinical or therapy program for people who receive mental health services. Instead it is a forum for these individuals to explore new interests or develop their skills in theatre, either on the stage or behind the scenes."[8] Members are still defined as artists, whether amateur or professional, who, at some point in their lives have received mental health or addiction services.[9] This approach resists the specific labels of any particular diagnosis of mental illness and members are not required to disclose specific details of their medical history. While this definition can be cumbersome to explain, it is one that company members settled upon after much deliberation. Membership is understandably broad and includes people who are anti-psychiatry activists, individuals who self-identify as consumer survivors, and people who are more positive about their mental health care or addiction treatment experiences.[10] The membership thus has a range of attitudes, many of them highly critical toward the medical model of mental illness and addiction. The company's commitment to this range is fuelled by its need to serve a diverse group of artists who have received mental health and addiction services, to explore mental health and addiction issues from a range of perspectives, and to resist the idea that they are in any way the communications or propaganda arm of the institution on whose property they operate.

While Workman Arts productions have often criticized medical protocols, and the company is adamant that its services are artistic and social rather than medical or therapeutic, connections to CAMH have nonetheless been pivotal in the Workman Arts enterprise. Toronto is a city with a strong theatre community but many vibrant companies have struggled to survive in the absence of performance and operational spaces of their own. Workman Arts, by contrast, has had relatively consistent access to both through its partnership with CAMH. In addition, CAMH helped the company build its professional capacity by providing funds for core staff, including Lisa Brown. Brown's training and familiarity with CAMH undoubtedly helped convince the Centre to open its doors and share resources with the company. However, while Brown's employment history at the centre and the institutional location of the theatre certainly knit the company to CAMH operationally and in the public imagination, the relationship has also had boundaries. Workman Arts maintains its own budget and board of directors. This has allowed it to seek and receive funding from such diverse sources as private foundations, municipal, provincial, and national arts councils, as well as health and drug companies. Although accepting funding from pharmaceutical companies was a choice rigorously debated by members, the majority has ultimately elected to accept it provided that no limits are imposed on their artistic freedom of expression. Maintaining artistic control over its output is a primary concern for the company, whether funding sources are derived from CAMH or other external sources. CAMH, in turn, does not categorize Workman Arts as any kind of health service delivery nor does it take ownership or responsibility for the content of the company's efforts unless it has explicitly collaborated on a project.

Although the company began with five participants, it now counts over 400 members. As the demand for places has grown, the process for becoming a company member has become more formalized. In its earliest years, it was possible for members to enter into training sessions fairly casually and many joined as much for the lively social atmosphere as the arts training.[11] Now, however, interested individuals, all self-referred adults, meet with the membership coordinator, bringing along a résumé and indicating the specific areas in which they seek training. While the company has tightened its focus to aspiring, emerging, and established artists, the chief criteria for participation

in the company's training program remain having received either mental
health or addiction services and the willingness to commit to the training
process.[12] It is important to note, however, that the kind of commitment the
company seeks is mindful of the exigencies of living with mental health or
addiction issues. Members are not expelled for having to withdraw from
projects or commitments due to illness. This is in contrast to normative
conservatory programs or other arts training environments in which accommodations for mental illness or addiction issues or breaks from the
program can be more difficult to obtain.

A fundamental set of issues in the field of disability arts concerns access
to professionally-oriented arts training. Disability performance scholar Carrie Sandahl has demonstrated how a lack of access undermines the cultural
currency of disabled artists' voices and allows stigmatizing representational
patterns of disability to flourish unchallenged.[13] Workman Arts' training falls
broadly into two categories. First, members refine their skills by working on
particular productions. For example, the cast of the production *Third Eye
Looming* included many company members (see Fig. 3.1). In the early years,
most company productions aimed to involve company members and theatre
professionals equally. More recently, especially as members have used their
training and productions to gain professional status with the Canadian
Actor's Equity Association, the divisions between members and professionals have blurred. During productions, the company encourages one-on-one
mentoring relationships between those with more professional experience
than others, and members have used productions to gain valuable skills and
training in such areas as acting, design, and technical theatre. The second
kind of training is more formal. Workman Arts decided in the beginning to
focus on hiring respected arts professionals to teach in its programs. As the
programs have grown, the company has also aimed to make their content,
policies, and structures as accessible as possible by creating several streams
of training activity to address the diverse needs of its members.

The company's membership comprises a range of people from those with
significant formal arts training and prior professional arts accomplishments
to complete novices or amateurs. The 2007–08 season and training brochure
explains that members have the opportunity to take courses in four instruction
streams designated as beginner, intermediate, advanced, and "professionally-oriented."[14] In its registration materials, the company describes the
primary features of its training philosophy by noting that their programs
are "instructional, structured, have defined start and end dates and are
stream specific." While member evaluations of instructors occur in each
stream and individual course, evaluation of participants only occurs in the

advanced stream programs. With regard to access, no previous training or skill is required for any member to participate in the introductory courses although participation in advanced streams "may require the successful completion of prerequisite training programs, auditions, submissions and/ or applications." While members are encouraged to advance along the streams if this suits their longer-term goals, they are neither required nor expected to do so within a particular time frame. This strategy aims to be inclusive of people who seek to progress at the pace best suited for their mental health needs. The company also promises that the program instructors will each be respected professionals in their particular artistic fields. Examples of the professionals the company has engaged include award-winning director Sarah Stanley, professional improviser and television actor Kate Ashby, John Turner of the internationally successful clowning duo Mump and Smoot, acclaimed singer Salome Bey, Topological Theatre Artistic Director Ed Roy, and John Palmer, a celebrated playwright, dramaturg, and cofounder of the Playwrights Union of Canada, the Guild of Canadian Playwrights, and several important Canadian theatres. As Palmer also

3.1
Workman Arts, *Third Eye Looming*, 2010.

instructs playwriting at the National Theatre School (NTS) in Montreal, he was able to offer the following comparative insight: "WA members tend to be more mature, older and life-experienced than NTS students. The primary struggle for both, however, is with insecurity although it is evidenced in different ways. At NTS it may stem from their youth, at WA it may stem from their mental illness experiences ... Talent, in both cases, is either there or not but the craft of writing can be taught."[15] His comments reflect the broader aims of the program: building an inclusive artistic training and production environment which meets members on their own terms to refine their skills, build their confidence and support their artistic growth and achievement. Several company members have achieved full or apprenticeship status in the Canadian Actors' Equity Association, the professional association of performers, directors, choreographers, fight directors, and stage managers in English Canada working in live performance in theatre, opera, and dance.

Artistic Impulses and Innovations

What drives this company to re-imagine mental illness on stage? One answer is the need to address and overturn stigmatizing stereotypes offered by theatre and other representational arts. All of the company members I have interviewed cite their profound frustration with the representations of mental illness they encounter daily in the media. One member explained how his efforts with Workman Arts are directed at producing more educational material: "A lot of people don't know much about mental illness so when it happens to them or a family member they are in the dark. Plays can educate and help them to find good services, good treatments, good doctors. If people knew more, they could access treatment more efficiently and quickly. I would like to see a play where people could learn about pitfalls, what to avoid, what to access, how to advocate for better services and reduced stigma."[16] Like this member, journalists Scott Simmie and Julia Nunes argue in *The Last Taboo: A Survival Guide to Mental Health in Canada* that there is a strong connection between stigma and ignorance.[17] They reveal that many people with mental illness in Canada describe the stigma and discrimination as worse than the mental disorder itself. Workman Arts members similarly note many deleterious effects of stigma; social discrimination and isolation may compound or exacerbate suffering. Moreover, stigma may prevent people from seeking professional help. Left to cope with an illness on their own, people risk deterioration and being vulnerable to a host of ill effects, destructive behaviours, or suicide. For company members, such high stakes create a forceful need to combat stigma and this informs much of their creative work.

Over the past two decades the company has produced over thirty original plays. Company productions drawn from this collection have played locally and toured to over thirty different theatres in Ontario, Manitoba, and Germany. All of the plays have been generated either through various Workman Arts playwriting programs or via the company's innovative and distinctive dramaturgical process. The latter involves the creative work of company members and the theatre professionals with whom they collaborate. These plays generally begin with a company member's idea although the company has on occasion accepted commissions. Members then interview prospective professional playwrights and/or dramaturgs to find someone with whom they will feel comfortable working. Once a partnership is formed, the company and collaborating artists share ideas through workshops, readings, and drafts. While the company benefits from the professional involvement, the collaborating artists also gain from the process. Award-winning playwright Louise Arsenault was one of Workman Arts' earliest such collaborators. Her 1991 play, *Innerspeak*, told the story of Mark, a poet diagnosed with manic-depression, and his relationships with family, friends, and a community of others with similar diagnoses. Arsenault gives credit to Workman Arts members for sharing their own stories and views: "The script has an undeniable authenticity because of the involvement of people in the project. I frequently heard someone say 'Wait – that's not how it happened to me, that's not what mood swings are like.'"[18] The collaborative process also aims to create more than simple public service announcements about the issues. In the case of *Innerspeak*, for example, *Toronto Star* critic Vit Wagner praised the production for "not getting mired in its didactic purpose."[19] This early example set a blueprint for the distinctive dramaturgical process driving the company's subsequent mainstage and touring productions.

Although each Workman Arts production has explored different themes and issues, in analyzing their works over time I have identified a recurring attempt to destabilize longstanding patterns of mental illness representation. For example, Lisa Brown suggests the company has worked to unseat "the drooling mouth, shuffling gait and vacant or wild-eyed" representations that have been used so often in film, theatre, and television to mark the person who has a mental illness as visibly different.[20] Brown's description suggests how the company has developed its aims independently from the broader disability movement and may seem at odds with the work of those who seek to disrupt negative associations with physical difference. At core, however, her example aims not to reify such associations but rather to query an entrenched representational pattern that insists upon visual and physical clues to distinguish mental illness.

Grounded in their particular dramaturgical process, Workman Arts' productions have frequently challenged visual stereotypes.[21] Surveying company productions, I have been struck by how often these attempts have relied on formal innovation. In *Vincent*, a play about schizophrenia, to which we will return in Chapter 7, the audience is given limited visual access to the central character, a man diagnosed with schizophrenia. He is heard only in voiceovers that seem to emanate from the audience space, and the other characters speak to the audience as though, collectively, they are the character with schizophrenia. In *Tale of a Mask*, a play about competing cross-cultural understandings of mental illness, the central character wears a mask to signal her mental illness, but the play also uses a range of formal traditions (Noh staging, pantomime, realistic acting, and cinematic detective conventions) to demonstrate how the mask is a social construction read differently by different cultures. Leaving the precise experience of mental illness ambiguous, the play focuses on the role of cultural understanding in shaping that experience. In contrast to these earlier productions, *Joy. A Musical. About Depression.* presents a central character diagnosed with depression, a wealthy forty-year-old named Joy, who is not only visually present on stage, but also sings, dances, and speaks about her illness. A more familiar and naturalistic representation of depression might have found the character of Joy sobbing quietly with diminished affect in a kind of 1:1 ratio with an aspect of actual depression experience. In the *Joy* production, however, the ratio between the performance dynamics and the lowered energy associated with actual depression experience seems more like 10:1. Depression experience is not simply visually indicated through Joy's vocalizations and movements but also through things like the blue colour scheme of the décor and her costume as well as the singing and dancing performances of three of her embodied depression symptoms: anxiety, fatigue, and headache. Thus in *Joy*, multiple excesses collide, contrast, and play off each other in a kaleidoscopic exploration of Joy's experience of depression and drug treatment. The company's most recent production, *Third Eye Looming*, devised and directed by Ed Roy in collaboration with Workman artists, uses only the ensemble's movement and multimedia scenography to tell the story of one member's particular mental illness experience.

Although almost all have cited the company's unusual mandate and artistic practices somewhere in their reviews, critics have responded to the company's various works in a range of ways. Many disability artists have expressed frustration with local critics, most often because they feel ignored by the pri-

mary arts reviewers in their area and seek greater critical feedback and dialogue about their work. This has been less of a problem for Workman Arts.
This difference may be attributed to several factors beyond the company's
artistic reputation. First, the company's stable financial base and operating
space allow them to mobilize publicity funds and manage press packages efficiently. Second, the prominence of the professional artists collaborating with
Workman Arts also brings their works greater attention within the city's artistic communities. Having received reviews since its incorporation in 1991, the
company has gained more critical attention from the major dailies over time.
Like most theatre companies, critical appraisal of these various works has
varied according to the production. Brown and other company members
suggest that positive reviews of their first production, *Innerspeak*, are what
galvanized them to continue in their efforts. Both Terry Watada's *Vincent* and
Shirley Barrie's *Tripping through Time*, the two productions most often
requested for remounts by outside groups, also garnered strong reviews. The
company has also received negative and mixed reviews, most notably with
regard to their 2005 production of *Joy. A Musical. About Depression*. *National
Post* critic Robert Cushman felt that the company's strategy of using musical
form to bring a difficult topic to more mainstream attention was unsuccessful: "[Musicals] may make [forbidding subjects] more superficially approachable, but they are likely to make the most important issues harder to get at."[22]
Although *Toronto Star* critic Richard Ouzounian praised many artistic aspects
of the performance, his comments favoured the production's message more
than anything else: "This is a message show, urging us to deal with depression,
and it makes its points boldly. Although it has nothing to apologize for,
I would be misleading you if I said that its primary appeal was theatrical.
No, it's what it says, not how it says it, that makes it so important."[23] Ouzounian's remark points to the most common theme running through critical
responses to the company's work over the years: the balance between artistic,
educational, and activist aims. In view of this, Cushman's *National Post* review
of the company's most recent production, *Edward the Crazy Man*, is striking:
"Here, writing and acting leave us wanting more in a good way. Two of the
actors, it was revealed at a first night talk back, are mental-health patients
themselves, and one of them is actually a schizophrenic in remission. The
quality of their work here shows that a social good can also be an artistic
good."[24] While Cushman's labelling of the actor by his medical diagnosis
does not follow disability arts practice, his review seems ready to find both
artistic and social merit in the enterprise.

Beyond theatre productions, the company has organized a range of forums
in which members and the public have gathered to discuss issues pertaining

to mental illness or addiction. They have produced multi-disciplinary festivals, art exhibitions, and Rendezvous with Madness Film Festivals, the latter an annual event that screens features, shorts, and documentaries. Eye-catching advertisements for this festival with Freud wearing 3-D glasses are seen annually on buses, subways, and billboards throughout Toronto and give the company wide visibility. Post-screening panels have involved many well-known and award-winning directors, actors, and screenwriters as well as company members, mental health workers, and other people who are familiar with the film's particular issues. Such panels have also followed most of the company's theatre productions and they have been a means both for giving public voice to people affected by mental illness and addiction experiences and assessing the company's level of success in generating community engagement with the issues.

In 2000, the company began to reach beyond its region to engage with a broader international community. After over a decade of work, Brown and the members felt a strong need to seek and connect with artists working in similar ways worldwide. It is important to note, however, that they retained their specific focus on mental illness and addiction issues. While many Canadian disability arts companies have forged connections through local, national, and international disability arts networks, festivals, and exchange programs, Workman Arts stands alone as the founder of a roaming international festival series specifically focused on featuring artists who have received mental health services and on re-imagining how mental illness is represented on international stages. Brown pitched the idea of an international festival that would draw such groups together to CAMH administrators and they provided seed money for research. After finding many more groups than they had anticipated, the company went forward with its plans, this time with the support of the CAMH Foundation and an Honorary Fundraising Council which raised a further $650,000.00 to help cover the visiting artists' travel and accommodations as well as local staffing and production costs. Toronto's Harbourfront Centre, a venue with international experience and a reputation for producing large-scale performing arts events, also partnered with the company, sharing its expertise and providing full use of its various performance, studio, and exhibition venues. In 2003 from 21–30 March, the company hosted the inaugural Madness and Arts World Festival, playing to an estimated total audience of over 10,000 people. Although the company found relevant arts companies in a diverse range of places (Zaire, Cuba, New Zealand, and Iceland, for example), it ultimately selected artists on the basis of artistic merit with the additional goal of including a broad range of artistic disciplines and international representation. The festival research also produced a database of companies with similar mandates and a blueprint for subsequent festivals.

A heterogeneous collection of performances, actors, and languages marked the festival program as well as a shared sense of exploration and purpose. Japan's Ryuzanji and Company opened the festival performing *Educating Mad Persons*, a hyperkinetic interpretation of Shuji Terayama's puppet play about a family in which one member has been diagnosed as mad. The festival closed with the Los Angeles-based dance group Rosanna Gamson/World Wide, whose production *Lovesickness* explored Freudian concepts of hysteria and unsatisfied desire. Other performances included a production from Wisconsin's TAPIT/new works called *Soul Journey*, which used tap-dance, jazz music, and monologues to explore one woman's journey through depression. Canadian actor Victoria Maxwell performed her acclaimed one-woman show about manic-depression entitled *Crazy for Life*. Productions for young audiences included: *Cracked*, a play about teenage depression and suicide, written by Nicola Baldwin and produced by London, England's Y Touring Theatre Company; and *Iris the Dragon*, a Workman Arts production of Gayle Grass' play investigating early indicators and coping strategies for children with mental illness. Other company contributions to the festival included *The Climps*, which combined improvisation and clowning by company members; and a remount of Terry Watada's play *Vincent*. Germany's Theater Sycorax, perhaps the theatre most akin to Workman Arts in terms of mandate and process, offered their production of Buchner's classic story of mental illness, *Woyzech*. Their performance drew upon company members' contemporary experiences and professional expertise to give the drama a contemporary resonance.

The drive to build networks among various national arts initiatives was most evident in the festival's closing performance: an international collaborative performance called *In the Room*. Organized by Workman Arts' collaborative workshop director, Ed Roy, the performance involved two actors and a director from each of three companies: Australia's RAG Theatre Troupe, a group which involves theatre professionals and provides theatre training and opportunities to people with mental illnesses; Denmark's Billed-spor, a company focused on mask work and also dedicated to creating training and performance opportunities for people who have received mental health services; and Workman Arts itself with two members directed by Ed Roy. In the year leading up to the festival, each of these groups developed a fifteen-minute production based on the phrase "in the room." During the festival, the three groups collaborated for ten days with the aim of combining all three productions into a one-hour performance to be presented at the

festival's end. The individual group productions each offered strikingly original and idiosyncratic approaches, while the whole presentation blended
masks, properties, and performers together to create a new shared performance language. For many of the festival artists and audiences, this occasion
proved to be the most moving and inspirational, as it capped the festival's
explorations and pointed to future collaborations.

Before the first festival, none of the ten companies that would be involved
had collaborated; few had even heard of each other. Now they more routinely
interact. In 2006, one of the participating groups in the 2003 festival, Germany's Theater Sycorax, produced a second and larger scale Madness and
Arts World Festival in Münster. In 2010, the third festival took place in the
Netherlands, hosted by Het Dolhuys, a Dutch museum that participated in
the 2006 event. Workman Arts' productions have been key features of each
of the subsequent festival lineups (*Vincent* in 2006 and *Third Eye Looming* in
2010) and Brown has consulted with both Theater Sycorax and Het Dolhuys
in their planning. As the catalyst for cementing this international network,
Workman Arts has managed to provide an expanding forum for the artists
they support and to further their mission of promoting a greater understanding of mental illness.

While Workman Arts is careful to refer to individuals in ways which
respect and recognize their personal value and agency, other projects and
artistic conceptualizations also embrace the term "madness," whose associations with stigmatized interpretations of mental illness may at first seem to
undermine this purpose. The company has used this term in the titles of
some of its broader projects because it is an often used, diversely interpreted
term whose political, historical, social, and ideological meanings continue to
influence contemporary experiences of mental illness. Drawing on the term
themselves, company members invite audiences to their own artistic investigations and explorations of "madness," its relationship both to broader
cultural perceptions of mental illness and particular lived experience.

Connecting at the Edges

Like the "nothing about us without us" refrain that animates so much disability arts and cultural work, Workman Arts is fundamentally dedicated to
carving out both public space to attend to the voices, perspectives, and
artistry of people who either claim mental illness experience or have been
labelled mentally ill, and private space where the same people can develop
their own artistry.[25] The refrain has a particular resonance for company

members whose own perspectives have so often been neglected or discounted, in large part due to the issues of stigma described above. Foucault suggested that this type of silencing experienced by people labelled mentally ill in modern western culture is linked to the social and cultural construction of mental illness as abnormal behavior or will, which has attenuated their access to public space and led to the adversarial notion that they must be confronted with model behaviour.[26] Foucault also insisted upon the individual's conscious experiences of mental illness, which built the foundation for historians Dale Peterson and Roy Porter to examine the conscious expressions of people labelled as mentally ill. In the groundbreaking work, *A Mad People's History of Madness*, for example, Dale Peterson asks:

> Is there meaning in madness? Can we know it? What is madness? What was madness? What is the history of madness? What is the history of how people have seen madness? Is it a disease, or is it simply a private religion, a little harmless deviance of thought and action? Which is better, psychiatry or no psychiatry? Are we all, in our own obscure ways, mad, and is madness really so close to sanity? Experts and authorities have addressed these questions for centuries, with confused results. It is time to hear from those who, by experience, are more closely connected to the issues – mad people, mad patients, themselves. Perhaps they are less confused.[27]

Rather than discount, objectify, pathologize, or romanticize the artistry of those labelled mentally ill, Peterson seeks an exploration of conscious artistic production. Workman Arts' artistic expressions are similarly not offered to be read symptomatically for signs of mental illness or addiction but rather as valuable on their own artistic terms. Thus, although the company tackles a particular kind of stigma, its art-making processes and impulses contribute to the project which UK disability scholar Paul Darke has argued animates all disability art: "re-presenting a more accurate picture of society, life, disability and impairment and art itself."[28]

Workman Arts claims an unusual place in the local, national, and international disability arts communities. Of all the festival producers examined in this book, it is the only company not to use the word "disability" in its festival rubric. Further, the word is remarkably absent in their production history and mandate. Yet, the company's ties to disability theatre are evident in important ways. First, their mandate is rooted in the same activist impulses that inform so much disability theatre and performance in Canada. These include the need to claim cultural space and artistic training opportunities for

people with mental illness and disability experience. Although the focus is
on a specific kind of disability experience, over the past two decades the company has become an international leader in fostering the artistry of people
who have received mental health and addiction services. They have generated a body of work which fights stigma and re-imagines mental illness from
the perspective of lived experience. Further, many of the company artists,
some of whom have sensory, intellectual, or physical disabilities, have ties to
disability arts communities beyond Workman Arts. The company has hosted
Toronto's Picasso Pro and other local disability arts companies' rehearsals
and performances and these have often included artists who are also Workman Arts members. The company has also helped to facilitate the National
Disability Arts Presenters Network initiated by Stage Left's Michele Decottignies. Brown was invited to participate in these early network meetings and
Workman Arts hosted a regional meeting for disability artists to voice their
concerns and ideas for how the network might best serve disability arts in
Canada. These regional meetings generated a great deal of conflict between
disability artists and presenters with many expressing concern about leadership, exclusivity, and incompatible artistic and political agendas. For many
Workman Arts members, the vociferous nature of the arguments was new
and turned on a set of issues that seemed different from their more focused
interest in fighting stigma related to mental illness and addiction specifically.

Despite seeking links to disability theatre, therefore, the company is also
keen to maintain its unique identity and not blur its boundaries to become
a disability arts company more broadly defined. While many company
members have had a range of impairment experiences, the primary mandate
at Workman Arts is to support the artistic development and creative expression of people with mental illness and addiction experiences. The
company's willingness to contribute to – but not be wholly defined by –
disability arts and culture raises questions about institutional affiliations, the
politics of disability, and the meaning and goals of disability arts and culture.
While considered a major disability performing arts company by many,
Workman Arts nonetheless stands at the edge, within and without, locally
connected, but internationally engaged in a project whose terms sometimes
cut more narrowly than the broader disability arts and culture movement.
Its complex and unique evolution reminds us that disability arts and culture
is not a unified and homogeneous movement, but profoundly diverse and
internally fractious.

CHAPTER FOUR

Theatre Terrific

> In the 1980s the community of disabled artists needed a tornado
> to wake them up.
>
> Longtime Theatre Terrific artist, Candice Larscheid[1]

Over the last decade, Vancouver has emerged as one of the primary centres in Canada for disability arts and culture. Theatre Terrific Society, one of Canada's oldest and most enduring disability theatre companies, has been an important engine in this process. Founded in 1985 as a small-scale education-oriented theatre to support the artistic development of adults with "mental and physical handicaps," it has grown in scope and ambition.[2] Today it is a multi-award-winning avant-garde disability theatre company with international connections, commissioning and producing original plays while also offering educational programs and artistic development opportunities. In addition to its significant artistic and social successes, however, the company's twenty-five year history has also been marked by friction, debate, problems, and moments of near-collapse. The company's development, as well as its problems, can be read on one level as the results of idiosyncratic, local circumstances, shaped by a changing cast of artistic directors. The company's trajectory, and the nature of its challenges, however, shed light on broader structural problems in the emergence of disability theatre in Canada and abroad. Like early disability theatre programs in the United States, such as the National Theatre Workshop of the Handicapped in New York or Theatre Unlimited in San Francisco, Theatre Terrific has wrestled over time with several competing agendas, partly informed by available funding and partly by changing ideas about what a theatre involving disabled people ought to do.[3] Should it focus on professional training, artistic innovation, or community involvement and expression? Is its primary goal educating the public through mainstream theatre forms or contributing to an emerging disability arts and culture aesthetic? In Theatre Terrific's case, the answers to these questions have changed over time, and this chapter seeks to explain how and why.

Compared to the theatre companies discussed in Chapter 2 – many of whom have developed connections to the disability arts and culture movement more recently – Theatre Terrific emerged before this wave as a pioneering effort. In a large and diverse city, it sought to meet a range of needs and spread its efforts across a broad front of activity. This left it particularly susceptible to debates over purpose and focus, and raised questions from funding agencies about its mandate; was it vocational, educational, or artistic? Whereas more recent companies such as Stage Left or Realwheels have developed with specific motivations and aims and been led by a single artistic director operating within a relatively fixed mandate, Theatre Terrific has seen six artistic directors since 1985 and numerous changes to its mandate language and orientation. Mandate changes arguably have not unsettled the company's primary impulses, but have refined them in relation to the discourse and expanding practice of disability arts and culture movement in the city and beyond. The evolution of this company, its survival as well as its successes and struggles, provide an important opportunity to consider how disability theatre emerged in Canada, how its proponents held the enterprise together, and how its goals evolved. Not only is disability culture understood unevenly across the landscape of disability theatre (a point made in Chapter 2), but also, as the case of Theatre Terrific demonstrates, across time.

In the spring of 1995, Theatre Terrific artists and supporters met at the Heritage Hall in East Vancouver to mark ten years of activity. It was a celebration and a high point, as well as a transition. The company was functioning well with a range of educational programs, touring shows, and annual productions that drew increasing professional recognition. The previous June it had won the Vancouver Professional Theatre Alliance's annual Jessie Richardson Theatre Award for its "Distinctive Mandate," and a script commissioned and toured by Theatre Terrific, John Lazarus' *Good Looking Friends,* had been nominated for "Outstanding Original Script for Young Audiences." The Heritage Hall event, however, also served as a send-off for Sue Lister, Theatre Terrific's founding artistic director, who was returning to her native England. Lister had helped carve a niche for Theatre Terrific in the local theatre community and in terms of its educational programming. A new era, with a new artistic director, as well as new challenges, beckoned. This night of "FRIVOLITY and FUN" was not conceived as a fundraiser, though organizers could not help mentioning parenthetically that "we'll happily relieve you of any spare cash you've got."[4] It was a reminder that despite the company's persistence, its many performances and range of outreach activities, holding Theatre Terrific together, mounting an annual program, and paying its staff continued to be a challenge.

While many theatre companies struggle to sustain themselves artistically and financially, Theatre Terrific also faced the common disability theatre problem of trying to answer a surfeit of community needs. In a city with limited accessible professional theatre training and community arts opportunities for people with disabilities, which of these needs should trump the other? From its origins in the mid-1980s, Theatre Terrific developed a dual mandate, focusing on theatre training and educational outreach on the one hand, and artistic development and innovation on the other. Ideally, these mandates were to mesh seamlessly. Practically, they often pulled the company and its supporters in different directions. This was due in part to the different conceptions of the company's primary purpose, but it was also a tension exacerbated by the pattern of funding available. The vocational and outreach emphasis could attract government funding for work with students and in the schools, while some of the performances were able to attract Canada Council and other foundation funds for the arts. But which set of goals, outreach, or artistry, ought to hold priority? This basic question had informed Lister's tenure as artistic director and it would continue to shape discussion and debate in the next decade.

Theatre Terrific began from small foundations in 1984, when Connie Hargrave replaced a friend working for the Community Living Society, a service organization for people described then as mentally and physically handicapped persons.[5] Hargrave began to wonder if, "theatre could fill a void in the lives of people whose creativity is stifled by the role society forces on them."[6] More than this, she wondered if the local theatre scene could include disabled actors. In the mid-1980s, as Hargrave later recalled, no stage in Vancouver had wheelchair access.[7] Candace Larscheid, an actor who began with the company in the 1980s, remembers the period as a time when people with disabilities did not command public space or attention: "you got so trained to be sheltered and good at giving others what they wanted to hear … [W]e weren't allowed to have a voice and if you did speak up it was looked upon as inappropriate. That was the basis of disability in the 80s and it unfortunately carried into the field of art."[8] For several company artists, Theatre Terrific would be their first opportunity for artistic training and expression. Although a longstanding theatre enthusiast, Hargrave had no formal theatre training or experience. She had read plays, watched theatre for years and participated in self-development groups using theatrical techniques. She also had an MA in sociology and experience in community organization.[9] Building on an initial idea of providing creative drama classes for adults with mental handicaps, she began to canvas funding opportunities with different organizations and foundations. As an individual with a notion, not a company with a program, however, it was difficult to convince funding agencies to take a risk. Added to this, her proposal was relatively unusual. Was it properly within the realm of arts funding or training?

After several false starts, in 1985 Hargrave placed Theatre Terrific on firmer institutional footing. First, she registered Theatre Terrific as a non-profit society and established a board.[10] The first funding break came when Hargrave managed to secure a substantial, two-year grant from Employment Canada for a pilot vocational training program for persons with disabilities.[11] This allowed Hargrave to hire Sue Lister as an instructor and Paul Beckett as an assistant to launch educational courses for adults with disabilities focusing on movement, props, and musical instruments. Lister had an extensive theatre background, having previously managed a theatre-in-education company in London, as well as professional experience in social work with persons with mental illness and elderly physically disabled persons.[12] In 1982, she had immigrated to Edmonton and her work there included directing a successful Fringe Festival play that involved seven actors with disabilities.[13] At this early stage, the company had no performance space and operated out of a small office on West 12th Avenue, hosting classes in a range of locations across the city offered freely by institutions, hospitals, and churches. Larscheid remembers Lister's commitment to professional training that both supported and challenged artists: "You had to progress up the levels, from introductory work to more focused upper levels involving focused scriptwork and memorization."[14] By the fall of 1986, the first round of courses had gone well, funding from Employment Canada had been renewed for another year, and several participants had developed *Dancing on the Head of a Pin with a Mouse in My Pocket*, a musical revue written by Leonard Angel with nine scenes exploring disability themes. This would be the first of many shows the company would perform at the annual Fringe Festival in Vancouver, which in 1986, was only in its third year. Hargrave recalled that the show was "not exactly a runaway hit" but it did get local notice and a cable station broadcast the performance.[15] Whereas the educational programs had emphasized inclusion and reached a wide clientele across the Vancouver region, this production had involved competitive auditions and an integrated cast of people with and without disabilities.

With two years of activity behind them, and the first large grants to Theatre Terrific winding down, Hargrave and Lister took stock. They separately composed notes outlining the company's mandate, accomplishments, and future directions and discovered they had complementary views in their broad outline, but placed emphases on different things. In response to the question "What do we do?," Hargrave wrote, "Theatre Terrific provides training in the theatre arts for people with disabilities for personal and professional development."[16] Lister, coming at the same question, suggested that the company "has been formed to bring disabled people into theatre and to bring the ability of disabled actors into the mainstream of artistic life in the community."[17] The founder with the managerial responsibility emphasized vocational training, while Lister, the instructor and artistic director, also sought to underline the importance of performance, artistry, and outreach. When Hargrave explained the reasons for Theatre Terrific's existence, however, she revealed a much more wide-ranging set of ambitions. "Disabled people are a part of our community," she wrote, "and as such should be represented in film, on radio and on T.V. and on stage in Canada." Theatre Terrific existed "to be a catalyst for the disabled to be a creative and effective part of our community. To present the best that our community has to offer in terms of creative professionals, in drama, movement, voice, mime, etc. in courses specifically designed for people with disabilities. To develop dramatic materials with people who have disabilities for entertainment and education. To have the public and school children experience disabled people as active, interesting and creative people on stage and in educational workshops."[18]

Hargrave and Lister were, to some extent, hashing out something new in the Vancouver theatre scene in 1986, but they understood that their work built on past experience elsewhere. The company was emerging at the early phase of expansion in disability theatre internationally, at a time when a handful of theatres in Europe and the Anglo-American world pointed the way. Theatre Terrific's 1986 mandate documents also included summaries and descriptions of the activities of the National Theatre Workshop of the Handicapped (NTWH) based in New York City and the Graeae Theatre in London. Lister had observed Graeae before immigrating to Canada, and both directors had studied the policies and mandates of these international leaders.[19] They particularly noted the balance that these theatre companies struck between training, outreach, and performance. The NTWH had operated since

1977, with a vocational training focus, they noted, but had only begun to form a repertory group in 1986. Graeae, on the other hand, offered a different model and ambition, with mandate language that emphasized innovation, education, and outreach. Hargrave and Lister were also aware of the activities of the Famous People Players Theatre in Toronto and set a goal to train individuals to be in a position to find work with the company.[20]

With these different points of reference in mind, Theatre Terrific sought a unique fusion. Like the NTWH, it placed vocational training as a primary goal. The typed mandate in 1986 read: "To provide career oriented training in the theatre arts for disabled people." However, unlike NTWH, Theatre Terrific sought to develop a repertory group from the start and, like Graeae, set explicit goals to "sensitize the entertainment industry to look for persons with disabilities for roles as disabled persons."[21] Although Graeae also set itself the challenge of artistic innovation, no such claims can be found in Theatre Terrific's early mandate documents. The major contribution to the arts would be in terms of changing the culture of casting, and with it broader public perceptions. As the company's 1988 annual report outlined, for example, their mission would be "to enrich the arts and our community by increasing the participation, visibility and public acceptance of people with disabilities in the performing arts."[22] These concerns were evident in the company's development of two outreach initiatives: Direct Access, a student-focused performance group, and an integrated touring troupe to visit schools across the province.

Both of these initiatives involved members with disabilities moving out into various community settings to perform for diverse audiences, but in somewhat different measures. Direct Access, founded in 1987, brought together a disability actors' ensemble made up of members who had attended Lister's Creative Drama course.[23] Developing their own scripts and honing their performance styles, the group performed for local events such as conferences and conventions.[24] As the company newsletter explained in 1994, "Direct Access provides a framework within which students can polish their acting talent while acquiring the discipline, skills and teamwork required to mount productions."[25] In this respect, Direct Access served as a bridge between the company's many training workshops and its more professionally-oriented tours; some of the performers who developed their talents in the workshops and then Direct Access, such as Boby Lukacs and Ann Dusterville, moved on to join the casts of integrated touring shows.[26] Direct Access also provided more range for participants to experiment with their own voices and ideas, to write as well as to perform. Laurette Yelle, one Direct

Access performer and a woman with cerebral palsy, reflected in 1992 on the rarity and importance of the program at the time, particularly in comparison with the many chances to become involved with disability sports; "I always dreamed of getting into acting but I never thought I would have the opportunity. Besides, I was painfully shy. I wanted to get over it. During our first creative drama class, it was scary for me to do things in front of people, but it was enjoyable too. I took a public speaking class at the same time. (I never do anything half way.) When I joined Direct Access, it gave me an actual experience. What a rush it is to get an audience's reaction to you. It's like you and the audience make a connection somehow."[27]

The touring group, founded a year after Direct Access in 1988, integrated disabled and non-disabled actors, performing scripts commissioned from professional playwrights. The commitment to casting and programming choices that favoured integration of people with and without disabilities was driven by the company's research which had indicated that schools were most interested in productions around the theme of integration.[28] The tours crossed the province, lasted several months and reached tens of thousands of students in the public school system. The 1996 tour, for example, visited sixty-eight schools. Notable touring shows included Kico Gonzalez-Risso's *Syllabub* (1991), John Lazarus' *Good-Looking Friends* (1992), and Margaret Hollingsworth's *Ring of Fire* (1996), the latter two of which received Jessie Richardson Award nominations for their scripts. All of these shows examined some aspect of disability and raised questions for audiences about difference. *Syllabub* follows the story of Sylvia Bubble, a ten year old girl with cerebral palsy who is rejected by humans and opts to live with worms instead, creatures who appreciate her for her abilities. *Good-Looking Friends* tells the story of a group of friends at high school and the perils of labeling one another "disabled" or "uncool." *Ring of Fire* takes up questions of lying and truth-telling in a plot centered around a disabled boy who joins his cousin in a band only to discover that the cousin and his girlfriend intend to use him as "a freak."

For the casts of these shows, the experience of acting in front of a range of school audiences could be both energizing and challenging. As Boby Lukacs (an actor with a disability who performed in *One on One* (1988) as well as *Syllabub*) reflected, "I was so nervous when we started to perform in elementary schools. Would the same prejudices [that I had experienced as a child] appear? However, there seemed to be far more acceptance around and I learned to actually relax and enjoy myself in crowds. I think honesty helped to make the production real and touching."[29] As the many supportive and congratulatory letters from students and staff who witnessed the touring and Direct Access shows attest, audiences also gained from this production model.[30]

The company received many reviews for its touring works, some in the major dailies and others in small-town weeklies. Critical press generally included at least some mention of the company's mandate and earliest origins.[31] Also, like Workman Arts, this often included a reference that distinguished the company's work from therapy. As Sue Lister explained to *Globe and Mail* critic Liam Lacey in 1990, "I'm not a therapist ... I'm an actor, a teacher and a director. We're not going to cure anyone and we're not setting out to cope with anyone's personal stuff ... The theatre program is about developing actors."[32] Lister also made a point of highlighting the company's mission to change the culture of casting in the theatre and film industries. "There are lots of roles for disabled people and I think it is high time they were played by disabled people, instead of Raymond Burr sitting in a wheelchair. I feel the situation is a little like the situation with black people, when whites would blacken their faces to play black parts."[33] In this vein, many reviews also cited company members' success in finding roles on prominent television series and films, sometimes charting a narrative trajectory of inhibition to confident performance through work and training with the company.[34] While the recurrence of such narrative structures invites a critical analysis of media representation, it should also be recognized that the company's educational and outreach mission was being partly fulfilled.

Apart from putting the company's mandate into practice, the touring program and Direct Access provided critical financial support for Theatre Terrific. School boards paid for the touring shows, and so did audiences who commissioned Direct Access performances. In some years in the late 1980s, touring shows made up a substantial portion of the company's budget. As the company treasurer pointed out in the annual report, "Experience shows us that special projects [such as *One on One* and *Syllabub*] earn the most funding support."[35] While Lister and Hargrave failed to receive Canada Council funding in these early years, they did discover that a range of government departments sympathized with the company's outreach and educational ambitions and supported various facets of the touring and Direct Access programs. For example, from 1988 to 1992, the Secretary of State provided sizable annual grants to underwrite the touring shows.[36] Such support came at a critical moment as the company transitioned from its first two years of Employment Canada funding to develop a range of smaller grants and donations from government, foundations, corporations, and individuals. Casino nights were added to the fund-raising mix in the 1990s with company staff and supporters working bingo halls to keep the enterprise afloat. Added to this, various community institutions offered in-kind support, such as free or subsidized performance spaces and a small, functional office space, which would come to serve as the Theatre's administrative base, attached to the Jericho Gym (later re-named Jericho Arts Centre) in Point Grey. With a precarious financial base, seeking such support and fund-raising absorbed precious energy from staff, members, and the board.

By the 1990s, Theatre Terrific had nevertheless developed a format that could be repeated from year to year. At the centre of this lay the touring program and Direct Access, surrounded by a mixture of training programs offered at different sites across the metropolitan region, which fulfilled the training and vocational goals of the company. A diversity of instructors with professional experience offered classes. The company also organized annual productions using competitive auditions and integrated casts. The scope of this activity, which emphasized an inclusive approach while taking up disability themes, gained increasing local recognition. By the early 1990s, Theatre Terrific had become an accepted fixture in the Vancouver theatre scene and obtained membership with the Vancouver Professional Theatre Alliance in 1992.

Following Lister's departure in 1995, the company's activities continued apace, and the company moved toward a new era of professionalization. Drawing on a pool of local instructors, Theatre Terrific continued to run theatre training programs and create performance opportunities for students. However, the company also began to tackle adult-oriented issues in its productions, using its mainstage shows as a site for exploration and artistic innovation. *Breeding Doubts*, for example, written by Sandra Ferens, addressed the controversies associated with new reproductive technologies and genetic screening for disability. Apart from raising important issues for public debate, the production received wide recognition from audiences who chose it as one of the picks of the Fringe in 1995 as well as other theatre artists who nominated the script for a Jessie Richardson Award and the company for "outstanding ensemble performance."[37] A year later, acclaimed Alberta playwright Lyle Victor Albert developed his one-man show, *Scraping the Surface*, with the company. As noted in Chapter 2, it also received two Jessie Richardson Award nominations: one for outstanding performance by an actor in a lead role and another for outstanding original play or musical. Buoyed by this success and recognition, the company continued to develop, produce, and tour new works for local and regional audiences.

Surveying the company's newsletters over the 1990s, familiar faces recur, training programs grow, and the company staff, members, and supporters apply for numerous grants and engage in annual fundraising efforts. In the background, however, minutes from company meetings, changes to the mandate language, and individual statements and letters demonstrate that questions were raised by members, staff, and instructors about the teaching program and attempts to professionalize the company. Financial constraints and concerns fuelled much of this debate. Without comprehensive support for all of its programs, board and company members asked how they should divide their time, resources, and effort. The financial strains are worth noting because they demonstrate that the company was not formed or developed to take advantage of convenient funding opportunities. Rather, it had to press the boundaries of and make bridges between existing kinds of philanthropic, institutional, and governmental funding in order to survive. Further, the funding challenges demonstrate the tenacity of board members, staff, and company artists who persisted with the work in the absence of solid financial support. Instead of folding due to the pressures and the loss of Lister, the company and its board pressed forward.

Financial challenges continued to unsettle the work of the company through the mid-1990s during the tenure of three artistic directors – first Jamie Norris (1994–1998) and then co-artistic directors, Elaine Avila and Trevor Found (1998–2000). Writing in the fall 1996 newsletter, Norris noted that although the company had just received its first two Canada Council grants and its performers had also just received their first Jessie Richardson Award nomination for Breeding Doubts, "it must be acknowledged that there is still a long way to go before we can consider our own organization stable and financially secure."[38] While the basic elements of the training program, Direct Access, school tours, and annual performances that Lister had established continued, Norris raised questions about the balance between these activities and their sustainability. Expansion on all sides was proving challenging for a company with such a small paid staff. In the midst of his directorship, for example, Norris proposed splitting the company into two halves to create a vocational, educational company and a more professionally oriented theatre troupe.[39] This idea built on the growing professional and international ambitions of company staff. Norris claimed that while the classes remained a cornerstone of Theatre Terrific, the number of those attending, particularly people with physical disabilities, was dwindling.[40] Given that the classes fed Direct Access and the touring program with actors, this fact was disconcerting and challenged the assumptions lying behind the company's annual program.

It was in this context that Elaine Avila and Trevor Found assumed the Artistic Directorship from Norris in 1998, a time of perceived crisis in programs and funding. Both Avila and Found had worked closely with the company for several years, moving up through the ranks as instructors and then conceiving Theatre Terrific's innovative mainstage productions that attracted Canada Council funding under Norris' directorship. Whereas Norris had emphasized the importance of the classes to the company's operations and experimented with several models to retain them as a core company activity, Avila and Found began their directorship by delivering a respectful but nevertheless profound critique of their potential. If the goal of Theatre Terrific was to train actors to professional standards and affect public attitudes toward disability, they argued, then the class model could not be sustained. As instructors in the classes, they reported first-hand knowledge of their successes and challenges. The classes, they explained to the board, could be idiosyncratic exercises, which changed in focus from year to year with little vision or rationale; they described a lack of communication between instructors and staff and the recurring problems with finding accessible sites for classes and paying staff appropriately. While they felt proud of the classes and the way they had "helped many students tap into parts of themselves and discover creative abilities they never knew they had," they felt that the class model could not be repaired or developed further. To do so would involve recurring "low budget presentations intended for family and friends." Also, the school would "never increase its impact on the community at large and because of this lack of public persona, will always have difficulty attracting additional funding."[41] The answer, they argued, was a more streamlined professionally oriented troupe.

The vision document that Avila and Found composed as a blueprint for Theatre Terrific in 1998 presents a remarkable contrast to the vision notes written by Hargrave and Lister over a decade before. Whereas Hargrave stressed vocational training and Lister inclusivity and artistic outreach, Avila and Found conceived a "Dream School" which would comprise a small, repertory group, selected through competitive auditions, focused on artistic development and oriented toward major performances and international tours. Funding could come from traditional sources as well as arts councils. They claimed that by focusing efforts and honing the talents of a few, "we will transcend ... prejudice through theatrical presentations and workshops."[42] Although the full scope of this proposal would not be implemented, Avila and Found had already begun to put parts of it into practice. *Step Right Up!* (1999), their co-authored play about the changing meanings of disability in history, which received Canada Council funding, developed the talents of a small, four-person cast, in which only two actors with disabilities, Paul Beckett and Gord Molhoj, found a place.[43] Working with a few, or in this case, two disabled actors raised basic and unaddressed questions about whom the company should support. Avila and Found did not seek to explain in their vision statement how the company's future would include the many participants in the classes who had found them meaningful and worthwhile, as well as the community supporters and families of company members who donated to Theatre Terrific and volunteered in its operations. This core constituency in the company's development was simply elided in the vision document for a professional troupe.

Previews of *Step Right Up!* introduced the new company vision, but reviews questioned it.[44] Colin Thomas, one of Vancouver's leading critics, wrote a long introduction of the new Theatre Terrific and its artistic directors in the weekly arts-oriented paper, *Georgia Straight*. Part play preview, part company profile, he quoted Avila and Found at length explaining the company's new direction. Avila emphasized how the company had changed over time and that it had recently developed a more professional orientation. "When it was growing Theatre Terrific served all of Vancouver ... We found somewhere to put everybody in the city who had an interest in the arts at all." The new direction, she claimed, developed focus and could attract new talent. "What really excites me ... is that people with disabilities who I knew were out there – very talented people – are now coming out of the woodwork and saying, 'We like this new direction. It has a lot more respect for us as artists and we want to work with you.'"[45] Although Thomas' preview was respectful and appreciative, his review of *Step Right Up!* called the enterprise into question, criticizing the script as overly didactic and predictable, and criticizing the choice of assigning the playwriting to the artistic directors. The only praise came for actor Gord Molhoj and director Kate Weiss. Thomas charged that Avila and Found "stated their intention to raise their company's artistic standards, but their script keeps them mired in the mud of disability performance." Thomas did not spell out just what he meant by the "mud of disability performance," but given the then contemporary controversy in Vancouver's arts community over the critical reception of the touring disability dance troupe, Candoco (discussed in Chapter 5), it was not a neutral or casual comment. Disability performance for Thomas meant didacticism, predictability, and issue-driven theatre not artistic exploration. Whatever the merits of the review itself, this sort of dismissal of the form, which was in the process of changing as disability performance gained greater exposure, suggested a broader lack of understanding, not just among critics, but funding bodies and other theatre artists.

It is important to note that Avila and Found's vision for change coincided with major developments in disability arts and culture in Vancouver and internationally that would help create that exposure. They cited inspiration for their new vision from theatre artists in Australia and Sweden whom they had met at the inaugural HighBeam Festival in Australia in 1998, which they attended as representatives of Theatre Terrific. They hoped to bring Theatre Terrific into closer parallel with these international groups and to develop disability artistry. Avila and Found's tenure also coincided with the incorporation of the Society for Disability Arts and Culture (s4DAC – now Kickstart) in Vancouver, the group that would eventually produce the first Kickstart Celebration of Disability Art and Culture in the city in 2001. Just as s4DAC founders Geoff McMurchy, Bonnie Sherr Klein, and Catherine Frazee had participated in and learned from international disability arts and cultural festivals, so too did Avila and Found. Feeling inspired, they debated how Theatre Terrific might build on Vancouver's role as a festival city to sponsor some kind of disability art event itself, ultimately arguing that a major goal moving forward should be to tour *Step Right Up!* internationally with its first stop being the HighBeam festival in 2000.[46]

It is likely that Avila and Found understood that the radical shift they envisioned might not have been immediately attainable. They used the word "dream" in the title of their vision document, after all. As it turned out, the critical problem of funding could not sustain such a right turn. The first months in the Artistic Directorship had involved primarily pedestrian accounting matters, and the grant proposals they laboured over to support a tour for *Step Right Up!* to Australia did not succeed.[47] The company also experienced a major blow in 1999 when the BC Gaming Commission cut off funding. For the previous few years, gaming funds had made up a core component of the operating budgets, and their loss could not be easily replaced. With the deteriorating financial position of the company showing no immediate end, and the traditional program in limbo, the board made the decision in 1999 to place the company into dormancy while they tried to sort out a new direction.

While the archival evidence suggests that interpersonal tensions ran high at this moment of crisis in the company's history, it is not my purpose here to point fingers. Such crises are a common feature of enterprises in which resources are few and many have a stake in the outcome. More interesting in the broader context of disability theatre's trajectory is that the tensions suggest the company's profound value for its constituents who pulled through the lean period with a clarified and reinvigorated purpose. Perhaps most importantly, the crisis highlights the political contours of simultaneously trying to create artistic development opportunities for people with disabilities, foster theatre by people with disabilities, and produce disability theatre to challenge traditional aesthetic and social values. In tandem with their sense that talented Theatre Terrific performers needed greater professional development, the growing momentum of the disability art and culture movement in the city and around the world strengthened Avila and Found's resolve to provide professional caliber training and opportunities for talented candidates. However, if the company decided to put its chief effort into training a select number of students to existing standards of professional artistry, would this process unsettle or reify the non-inclusive practices upon which many of these professional standards are founded? Would this focus miss the opportunity to legitimize the experience and artistry of all the company artists? In short, would Theatre Terrific become another space in which the full range of artists with disabilities was not supported? More pragmatically, while the company might increase its eligibility for professional artists' grants, would it lose its power to attract community recreational and educational funding?

Ultimately Avila and Found moved on from Theatre Terrific and the company was dormant for a year and a half. The board assessed the company's position and began to search for a new artistic director. Interestingly, the advertisement which the board developed included a four page background document providing an outline of the past artistic direction of the company, identifying Avila and Found's tenure as the third phase in which the company moved away from educational and recreational programming to strengthen its role in the professional theatre community. Describing the future, the document suggested that it would be important to "include more regular classes and workshops within the community and [develop] a new mainstage production." The call also clarified the company's three-pronged mandate: "Provide theatre training for people and artists with disabilities; operate a theatre company which fosters quality performance from artists with disabilities; and give the theatre community a direct and positive experience of people and artists with disabilities, in order to provide opportunities to eliminate barriers that inhibit interaction between people with visible disabilities and those with no apparent disability."[48] In searching for a new artistic director in this way, the board signaled its own intention to return to core principles of the early company and away from the professional troupe model.

Theatre Terrific's next artistic director, Liesl Lafferty, came to the company with few expectations. She had been convinced to apply for the position by colleague and Theatre Terrific's acting artistic director, Sherry Bie. Bie had recently been appointed artistic director for the National Theatre School in Montreal and asked Lafferty whether she was "ready to change [her] life."[49]

Lafferty had no experience working with disability communities, and has explained that she "really had to start from scratch."[50] Lafferty nevertheless brought a wide-ranging professional experience as a dramaturg and director. Initially, Lafferty worked to resolve past funding problems and to put a structure in place that would allow for achievable programming goals. One enduring feature of this work was the establishment in 2001 of a two-month summer theatre training camp. This idea built on the earlier class model, but gave it direction and focus. In its second year, participating camp artists produced a Fringe Festival performance. Both the camp and the resulting performances became an annual feature of the company and helped in the short term to make up for the loss of regular classes. Bringing this kind of stability and predictability to the programming was a key strategy for winning back the trust of the BC Gaming Commission which had stopped funding the company during its dormancy. In 2003, through a United Way Community Innovations Grant, the company also took a "first, admittedly small, step toward again producing professional work of [their] own" by sponsoring absolut theatre company's *Spiraling Within*, a one woman show by Siobhan McCarthy which explored depression, anxiety, obsession, and bipolar disorder. A comparable step "signaling [their] return to professional theatre" was taken in 2004 when the company developed another comedic drama by Lyle Victor Albert, *Jumpin' Jack*.[51] Thus the movements forward were measured and built upon local momentum and opportunity. Reflecting on her experiences with Theatre Terrific after she resigned in 2004, Lafferty joked that she "learned a lot about accounting but little about people's actual diagnosed disabilities. It never really came up. We were too busy rehearsing and following the things that flowed."[52] Much of her tenure was spent working with board and community members to solidify a performance-training program throughout the Vancouver region and clarify the company's financial position so that it might again be eligible for a range of grants. In 2004, a successful Canada Council Flying Squad grant application recognized the company's artistic and cultural contributions while also offering capacity-building guidance. The board worked with Empyrean Consultants to determine effective strategies for capacity building and fund-raising.[53] This work led to increased media coverage, better use of volunteers, the company's first website, and a solidified committee structure for the board.

With rebuilt foundations, Theatre Terrific entered a period of growth and experimentation in 2005 under the artistic directorship of Susanna Uchatius. Uchatius was familiar with the company already, having been an instructor in its Summer Fringe camps. She had also taught theatre arts in a range of disability-oriented programs including the Down Syndrome Society and

Vancouver Mental Health Teams. With a BFA in theatre from Simon Fraser University, further performance training at the Banff Centre and University of British Columbia, and practical theatre, film, and television experience, Uchatius was familiar with performance and the local scene. As a parent of a daughter with a disability and someone who had worked with the Elizabeth Fry Society and underprivileged youth groups in Prince George, she was also practiced at advocacy and a vocal supporter of "marginalized groups' recognition as legitimate performers with an artistic voice."[54] Both in interviews and company newsletters, Uchatius cited the words of playwright and leader Vaclav Havel as a primary inspiration and blueprint for Theatre Terrific: "Theatre is a point at which the intellectual and spiritual life of the human community crystallizes. It is a space in which the community can exercise its freedom and come to understanding."[55] For Uchatius, including people with disabilities in this process is critical for the whole community. In this way, "theatre performed by people with a disability isn't recreation or respite" but, she argued, if approached with passion, commitment and courage, it could be critical, progressive, and democratic work.[56] For Uchatius, disability theatre could show "how multi-hued and integrated our society is."[57]

Strikingly, one of Uchatius' primary early initiatives echoed Avila and Found's "dream school" plan. In the fall 2005 newsletter, she announced "the first steps in a momentous journey," the creation of a "Professional Troupe of Actors with Disabilities." Following an audition process, an eight-person troupe was selected to represent "a broad range of disabled performers, each with something very unique to offer the ensemble."[58] The group had as its objective the creation of cutting edge theatrical work developed in a unique environment of disabled theatre artists supporting each other. Seed funding for the group came from the BC Gaming Policy and Enforcement Branch, the ArtsNow Innovations Program, and the Melusine Foundation. Like Avila and Found, Uchatius sought to expand the artistic capabilities and rigorous training opportunities for a core group. While this idea seemed to be out of reach in 1999, it would now be a recurring feature. What had changed to make this possible?

While there are no doubt many answers to this question, one critical aspect concerned the new opportunities made possible by the annual Fringe-oriented summer camps and the new "intensive program" of classes. Internal discussions within the company had also led to a more defined and refined mandate. "Our mission is to be a catalyst for growth and change by providing people with disabilities opportunities to participate in performing arts, thereby celebrating their gifts and enhancing their lives. Through its activities, Theatre Terrific encourages the broader community to become more inclusive, aware and educated."⁵⁹ Without identifying particular programs (as had earlier mandate statements), this new mandate language tied together the company's different elements, without prioritizing one over the others. Indeed, the company insisted that each of the company's elements fed the other.

In practice, the Summer Fringe program and performance opportunities as well as a more regularized series of training workshops helped the company to fulfill its educational mandate and draw a steady stream of potential performers. Most of the Summer Fringe productions have been developed collectively with the company's students through improvisational workshops around a theme. In 2004, for example, the company produced the *Error of Eros' Arrows* both for the Fringe Festival and Vancouver's second festival of disability arts and culture, Kickstart 2. With campy goddesses, troubadours, clowns, and Cupid, the play explored love's capriciousness. In 2005, Theatre Terrific's *Ugly* explored the limits of social distinctions between ugliness and beauty and garnered significant praise from *Vancouver Sun* reviewer Bryson Young, who rated the production a rare four and a half stars out of five. The production's poster had a tagline noting that while the word "beauty" has all the variety of beige, UGLY has infinite variations, most of which relate to the word's etymological connections with fear. Young was particularly struck by one scene in which each character turned to the audience and spoke a single line about what terrified them most. "When the actors speak directly to the audience about their fears of being different and ignored, the moment is magical because one senses the directness of the sentiment – it is barely 'acting' at all, and therein lies the power of the piece."⁶⁰ While Young's comments risked eliding the artistry of the performers, they also spoke to the power of engaging with performers whose work is grounded in the lived experience of disability. Company actor Candice Larscheid, whose angry turn in *Ugly* was an arresting highlight, has argued that while "in the 1980s the public did not want to deal with fear on a raw basis," the company has created a space where people with disabilities "share their rawness but in an artistic way that makes audiences stop, learn and take away."⁶¹ Subsequent Fringe shows have similarly attempted to express ideas that resonate personally for the ensemble. In 2006, for example, *slowrunning* investigated different relationships with time experienced by people with a range of disabilities. In 2007, for an over-capacity opening night crowd, the seventeen performers in *Workin'* "improvised their way through job interviews for BS Inc." and performed in several scenes aimed at exploring the importance and challenges of work life for people with disabilities.⁶² While Uchatius is generally listed as "writer/director" for the productions, she readily acknowledges the collective contributions of performers who identify key concerns and improvise around them during the development process. This improvisation, importantly, may or may not involve speech. One young performer in *Ugly*, a person who does not speak, was charged with painting a wall behind the performers during the two-week performance run. Each night, her live painting on set in response to the performance added a critical layer to the overall production's study of ugliness and beauty.

Both the company's mainstage professional and fringe festival productions under Uchatius have drawn from a common set of aesthetic sensibilities and development processes. Uchatius has described this process as a collaborative negotiation that privileges diversity as a critical creative element. For the professional productions, she runs open casting calls as classes in which she looks for people's willingness to work with a diverse range of others, including union actors and non-professionals, artists with and without disabilities. She argues that the company offers in turn respectful challenges and the promise of risk-taking. Most recently, she has insisted that the company is not interested in "doing things about disability, we're not interested in special interest groups; we're interested in doing universal human stories, in dealing with artists of all abilities."[63] At first glance, her language seems to disavow critical allegiances with disability arts and culture and the privileging of disability artists. However, while she highlights universal themes it is clear that, as for James Sanders and Realwheels, Theatre Terrific demands that "universal" explicitly includes people with disabilities.

Practically, audition notices have underlined the idea that the company will look for people with a range of disabilities. In the call for *The Glass Box* in 2008, for example, they did not require a memorized monologue (something that might have dissuaded many potential performers) and claimed to be looking "for all degrees of disability (developmental, mental health, physical) and for some able actors with the desire to work in an adaptive/exploratory ensemble creative process"[64] (see image 8.1). These notices have also let potential participants know the broad theme for the production. In the *Glass Box*, for example, those auditioning were told that the work would "delve into the research of sexuality; that vital human yearning that lies within all of us; often locked away, denied, neutered; yet fiercely desired."[65] The first professional show, *Naked Oranges*, explored the theme of exposed and raw emotions and drew on Jean Vanier's 1998 Massey lecture about becoming human.[66] The second, *doGs*, examined "the essence of belief" through the dialogue of nine diverse characters. In 2009, *The Secret Son* wove themes of classical tragedy and the more specific biography of Daniel Miller, a person with Down syndrome who they argue was disavowed by his father, playwright Arthur Miller (see image 8.2). In 2010, *Dirty White* investigated humans' earthy natures through a retelling of Ovid's *Metamorphosis* and its tale of the raven who changed from white to black. I will analyze some of their productions further in Chapter 8, but I list their major themes here to demonstrate how the company's focus shifted markedly from its school-touring days to explore more adult themes. No longer reliant on school touring funds, the company has garnered support for these productions from arts council and foundation grants. The diverse abilities and disabilities of their ensemble casts have led Uchatius to describe these productions as diversity in action.[67] In Larscheid's view, the company's greatest long term growth has been toward celebrating the idea that "we're all equal and we all have something to bring to the stage."[68] Thus, while they may turn on broad, universal themes, the company seems most interested in emphasizing the paradox that any pretense to universality must build from diversity, a concept that seems to have found growing support among funders, audiences, and critics.

Support for the company's direction must also be tied to the emerging awareness of the wider public and granting bodies of disability art's promise and possibilities following the Kickstart festival in 2001. Theatre Terrific had participated in this and subsequent festivals, and benefited from the greater attention to its work as well as to disability arts and culture more generally. The company's ability to work productively with other disability theatre companies in the city also suggests that the pressure to be all things to all people had subsided. The wider field was richer and more diverse and could accommodate a range of disability performers on different city stages. Where Connie Hargrave cited a lack of accessibility on Vancouver stages in the 1980s, in the new century, the city hosted touring international disability theatre companies, saw local theatre companies like Leaky Heaven Circus integrating performers with disabilities, and witnessed disability theatre companies emerge like absolut theatre company, Realwheels, and strong solo performers such as Victoria Maxwell, Siobhan McCarthy, Meg Torwl, Max Fomitchev, Jan Derbyshire, and David Roche. Within this wider context of disability arts and theatre, Theatre Terrific could and did begin to carve a niche.

Over a quarter century, it is not surprising that Theatre Terrific has changed, but just how and why it has done so is important. The experience of this single company both sheds light on the conditions attending disability theatre in Canada in its earliest phase, as well as the new possibilities emerging from a more active, diverse disability theatre community. Four points are worth stressing, particularly in comparison to the company histories examined in Chapter 2. First, funding mattered, every year. No matter the extent of artistic success or critical response, Theatre Terrific encountered challenges to obtaining long term, reliable funding. This had important implications both because it caused an episodic employment pattern for staff and it placed a considerable burden on board members who sought to raise funds. Beyond these serious issues, however, the struggle to secure funding also shaped the company's program. Artistic ambitions were both supported and undercut by the uneven response over time to Theatre Terrific's mixed program of vocational training, touring shows, and mainstage productions. Although a new balance in funding and programming seemed to be struck by about 2005, by the end of the decade instability reappeared when the provincial government threatened to cancel gaming funds as part of a sweeping cut to provincial arts funding. Like other BC theatre companies, Theatre Terrific faced the prospect of closing its doors before an eleventh-hour reprieve reinstated some of these funds. While the company's struggle to secure funds is not unusual in theatre at large or in disability theatre in particular, how its struggles have shaped its approach, outreach, and artistry have mattered.

Second, while funding has been an important ingredient informing the theatre's scope of activity over time, the emergence of a broader disability arts and culture movement has allowed the company to imagine a more professional and artistically innovative orientation. When Hargrave and Lister sketched out their visions of the company in the late 1980s against the counter-examples of the National Theatre Workshop of the Handicapped and Graeae Theatre, neither listed artistic innovation as a primary impulse. In 2000, Avila and Found, who had become deeply involved in the emerging disability art scene in Vancouver and abroad called for a "dream school" model, but without the necessary financial and company support. A decade later, under the Artistic Directorship of Susanna Uchatius, a performance ensemble, very close in design to what Avila and Found had imagined, operates at the centre of the company's annual program. This shift in direction suggests the extent to which the company's staff and members have sought to engage new ideas about disability art and expand them in the Vancouver context. Not only has Theatre Terrific been affected by the changing context, it has also been an important leader in the city. The disability arts and culture movement is in part an outcome of many diverse companies, Theatre Terrific prominently among them, finding common ground and working toward something larger.

Third, while many of the most successful disability theatre companies in Canada have only ever been led by one artistic director, operating with a relatively fixed mandate, the case of Theatre Terrific suggests the possibilities of a different theatre company model. One of the most impressive features of this company has been its ability to attract talent and commitment, even in times of great challenge; and this is in no small part because many hands have made it work – assisting in classes, on stage, and in fund-raising to keep some collective purpose alive even as many of its features evolved over time. This has been the result of a formalized structure which includes a multi-talented board guiding the company's direction, a strong artistic director position with wide latitude to shape and re-shape the company's direction, and a diverse and highly committed group of member artists and their families. Although the mandate has changed, as well as the artistic direction, Theatre Terrific's founding impulse to put disabled people on stage and allow them space to explore their artistic voices has endured. More than that, it has provided the inspiration to weather difficult storms.

Fourth, and finally, Theatre Terrific pursued its own distinctive approach to integration. Because it was founded and led in its early years largely by people without disabilities, it is reasonable to ask whether it should be considered a disability theatre company as such. Having considered various facets of this problem, I believe the answer is yes. The company has been focused consistently on re-framing the place of disability on stage and finding space in Vancouver's theatre scene for artists with disabilities. Furthermore, these same artists have proven to be the company's foundation as the core of the performing troupes and have taken on the leadership at various stages on the board. Boby Lukacs, for example, who joined the company initially through its training workshops, ultimately became one of its better known performers in the 1990s and also served on the board. As Theatre Terrific developed, one of its defining features became its positive outlook on integration at the heart of the company's operations. The company has shown leadership not simply as a theatre for disabled actors, but also as a company producing challenging theatre involving both disabled and non-disabled actors working together to explore something new.

CHAPTER FIVE

Scale-Jumping

Sit down with Canadian disability theatre artists who are involved in thriving local artistic communities and ask them how they came to work in disability arts. What or who was their source of inspiration? Which artists did they connect with, and why? Their answers recall a range of local events cross-cut by international flows of artists, ideas, and influences. The national frame matters comparatively little in these stories. Unlike other fields of Canadian theatre history, creating a nationally-based identity has had little part in the narrative until recently. In England, by contrast, the National Arts Council's dedicated funding and infrastructure initiatives for arts and disability and/or Deaf culture have helped disability artists build the field. Although the Canada Council for the Arts has supported individual disability theatre artists and companies over time and has announced its more focused plans to support disability arts in its 2008–2011 strategic plan, such coordinated, focused attention has not yet been a primary motivator for the field.

In the absence of targeted national guidance from funding bodies or nonprofits, disability theatre has emerged in a space linking local disability and theatre communities with an array of international counterparts and influences. The opportunity for this network has occurred in part because of the strong capacities provided by local disability theatre companies and organizations. Founded primarily on grassroots initiatives and the energies of individual artists and leaders, Canada's disability arts scene organized and gained force in the 1990s. This momentum also drew from opportunities that arose after 2000 to link complementary efforts and artistry across borders, to explore the dynamism of disability theatre in festivals and actor exchanges, and to put local groups from across Canada and beyond into conversation.

In 1991, Elaine Avila, an instructor working with Vancouver's Theatre Terrific Society at the time, made a trip to San Francisco to visit Theatre Unlimited – an innovative and established Bay Area disability theatre repertory company that has been operating since 1977. In two articles she wrote for her colleagues in the Theatre Terrific newsletter, she expressed the excitement she felt connecting with this group and articulated her dreams of facilitating exchanges with the company in the future. Her tone was both inspired and wistful. She sought to convey the energy she gained from her encounter, but also seemed resigned to the fact that no exchange could possibly take place; the practical barriers seemed insurmountable.[1]

A decade later, New Zealand disability artist and stand-up comedian Philip Patston returned home after performing at the first Kickstart Celebration of Disability Arts and Culture festival in Vancouver. Patston found it "impossible to articulate the experience of being in the company of more than 23 international and 44 Canadian performers with disabilities and 38 visual artists with disability."[2] Inspired by the talents he had encountered, he founded the International Guild of Disabled Artists and Performers in 2001.[3] Four years later, he became the creative director for Giant Leap, New Zealand's first international disability arts festival. Something happened in the time between Avila and Patston's journeys. Changes had occurred not only at the local level of disability theatre organization and artistry in Vancouver and other Canadian cities, but also at the international level. A new space of interaction and exchange, just on the horizon in the early 1990s, had become something more coherent and permanent by 2000.

An international dimension entered Theatre Terrific's work shortly after Avila's article was published. Alongside the company's central activities involving theatre training for persons with disabilities and touring shows to schools across BC, the company began to host disability artists from abroad to lead special workshops and sent representatives to international events. Disability theatre practitioners visited from Sweden (Kjell Stjernholm in 1999) and Australia (Jane Muras in 1999). In 1998, then co-artistic directors Trevor Found and Elaine Avila attended the High Beam Disability Arts Festival in Adelaide, Australia. For Found, the experience was revealing; "It became clear that Theatre Terrific is part of a global movement and there are many benefits to pursuing our work on an international level."[4] Found and Avila's recognition of a wider international disability arts movement suggested changes both within Theatre Terrific as well as abroad.[5] Theatre Terrific had not abandoned its core activities, but it had discovered another angle to its work and further points of contact with similar companies elsewhere. Found and Avila had also discovered that significant work was being done internationally that demanded their further attention. In this, they were not alone.

In the same year that Found and Avila traveled to the High Beam festival, Candoco – the London, England disability dance troupe – toured Vancouver (see Fig. 5.1). The visit was notable in and of itself; international tours to Canada by disability dance or theatre companies were not yet common. What was more important, however, was the reception of Candoco by local audiences and critics, reacting to a cutting edge performance that challenged aesthetic conventions, ideas of ability and normalcy, and just what dance and theatre were all about. While local disability artists found the performances inspirational, critic Michael Scott wrote a scathing review in the *Vancouver Sun*. Quite apart from his aesthetic concerns, Scott was revolted by the performance of non-normate bodies: "There is a horrific, Satyricon quality to Candoco that heaves up in the chest – nausea at the moral rudderlessness of a world where we would pay money to watch a man whose body terminates at his ribcage, moving about the stage on his hands."[6] Scott's hyperbole would go on to earn him an infamous reputation, an example in international disability and performance studies of "conservatism and normalizing tendencies in the dance establishment."[7]

Disability activists pushed back in the press. Margaret Birrell, executive director of the BC Coalition of People with Disabilities and Joan Meister, coordinator of the Pacific Disabled Women's Network, wrote a joint letter to the editor expressing shock at Scott's "deeply offensive review."[8] Local publicist, Kevin McKeown wrote that Candoco performer David Toole had read the review and exclaimed, "I think the bloke has told everyone more about himself than he did about our dance."[9] Although Victoria critic Adrian Chamberlain supported Scott publicly, Scott's review quickly became a symbol for the local disability arts community of the profound misunderstanding of their art and purpose.[10]

Scott's review nevertheless provided a rationale for coalition among disability artists, linking local practitioners and companies with a range of international colleagues. To its credit, at the base of the review, the *Vancouver Sun* carried an announcement for a public event, "What is Disability Art,

5.1
Candoco 1999 Vancouver
performance program.

Anyway? A Forum on Arts and Disability," co-organized by the Vancouver
East Cultural Centre, Theatre Terrific, and the newly formed Vancouver-
based Society for Disability Arts and Culture (s4DAC now known as
Kickstart). The event sought to initiate a discussion about disability arts in
the lead up to s4DAC's planned festival, Kickstart. It involved several leaders
in the local disability arts scene, notably future mayor Sam Sullivan, as well
as a cast of international participants, including Candoco performers, director Kjell Stjernholm of Moomsteatern (Sweden), and Jane Muras of No
Strings Attached Theatre of Disability (Australia). Burke Taylor, who would
go on to serve as the Vice President of Culture & Ceremonies for the Vancouver 2010 Olympic Games, noted in a letter to the *Vancouver Sun* that
Michael Scott had also been invited to speak, but declined.[11] Three years later
in 2001, when s4DAC produced the first Kickstart Celebration of Disability
Art and Culture, festival flyers invited audiences to come and see the art "that
Michael Scott loves to hate."[12]

Although much of this coalition-building and outreach occurred in
Vancouver in the late 1990s, other artists and groups across the country were
following parallel paths. Calgarian Pamela Boyd, founder of MoMo Mixed
Ability Dance Theatre, also cites her exposure to other disability arts companies both at home and abroad as a critical factor driving her artistry
forward. Ruth Bieber of Inside Out helped Boyd to attend the 2001 High
Beam Festival in which several Canadian disability artists participated, including Bonnie Sherr Klein and Geoff McMurchy. Boyd also visited London
and took in performances by the Amici Dance Theatre, a leading integrated
dance theatre founded in 1980, and had the opportunity to visit London's
Disability Arts Forum, an organization that promotes disability art and
artists. These international points of contact suggested models of practice
to Boyd and inspired her artistically. As a result, she has worked to build
MoMo's international connections and to sponsor artistic exchanges.[13]

While some disability theatre companies and artists reached out internationally for inspiration – to build connections and to strengthen capacities –
others left the country, citing its weak support of disability arts. For performer and playwright Alex Bulmer, the Canadian context could not compete
with the support she found in the UK. While collaborating with Rose Jacobson on the Picasso Project (described in Chapter 2), Bulmer re-located to
London.[14] Despite the fact that her play *Smudge* (2000) had been nominated
for several awards, including the Chalmers Canadian play award, and she had
significant professional arts and organizational skills and experience, Bulmer
was frustrated in her attempts to find a professional position that used her
talents in Toronto.[15] By contrast, as she explained to writer Diane Flacks in
the *Toronto Star* in 2009, in the UK she benefited from the Access to Work
program. This provided her with critical personnel and adaptive technologies to facilitate her work and these ensured that she would not be discounted
by potential employers due to her vision impairment.[16] She has since worked
part-time as a literary manager for Graeae theatre, the UK's leading disability theatre, and taught voice-work and inclusive theatre practices across
the UK. She also co-wrote *Cast-Offs* (2009), the ground-breaking six-part
comedy series commissioned by Britain's Channel 4. She hoped the show – a
mockumentary in the reality and survival television genre that features six
disabled actors – would be provocatively offensive and suggested that this
goal was another positive feature of her UK experience: "Over there, as a disabled person, you don't have to be so worthy!"[17] Bulmer argues that her work
and exposure to UK practices have been critical for her professional development and ability to imagine returning to Canada: "If I want to come back
and live here, I have this stuff under my arm – look at what I've done; you

know, here's my ammunition – under my big white stick."[18] As a longtime collaborator with Jacobson on the Picasso Project, Bulmer has stayed in touch with the Canadian disability theatre scene and shared her ideas and UK experience with Jacobson and others. In 2009, she also returned to Toronto to develop collaboratively and perform in the integrated theatre production, *The Book of Judith*, a mock-revivalist musical centred around inclusion activist Judith Snow.

These examples recount the experiences of different disability theatre companies and artists, operating in different cities and with different points of contact and connection, but all striving for inspiration, learning, and institutional models to build disability theatre. It is important to remember that Canadian artists have also contributed to the internationalization process and that Canadian disability theatre has not simply emerged as a derivative movement inspired by those who have toured festivals abroad. Given the range of disability arts festivals that have emerged across Canada, it is evident that Canadian disability arts festivals have been fertile grounds for a growing sense of disability arts community both among Canadians and with others around the world.

The Role of Festivals

Since 2000, Canadians have played an important role in organizing disability arts festivals with local, national, and international reach. These have raised the profile of disability arts in general and helped to connect discrete pockets of disability arts activity.

One of the first large-scale Canadian events of this kind occurred in Vancouver in 2001 when the recently formed S4DAC organized the inaugural Kickstart Celebration of Disability Arts and Culture. The Calgary SCOPE Society, Transition to Independence, and Stage Left Productions teamed up variously to produce two smaller-scale festivals in 2002, and Toronto's Workman Theatre Project and the Centre for Addiction and Mental Health co-produced the Madness and Arts 2003 World Festival.[19] Toronto is also home to the Abilities Arts Festival: A Celebration of Disability Arts and Culture, a multi-disciplinary festival that has featured local and international artists. It began as a project of the Canadian Abilities Foundation but became a separate not-for-profit organization in 2006. Since 2000, Toronto has also hosted Art with Attitude, an annual program initiated by Catherine Frazee and Judith Sandys at the Ryerson-RBC Institute for Disability Studies and Education, which has featured Canadian and international disability arts performers.[20] In 2002, the institute also began to host an annual cabaret-style Culture Cauldron of more informal, short "disability-inspired" works prepared in response to an open theme-based call.[21] Like the RBC-Institute events, each of the festivals noted above has been followed up with further installations. For example, S4DAC produced Kickstart 2 in Vancouver in 2004 and launched a third Kickstart that ran as part of the 2010 Cultural Olympiad. In 2010, Stage Left produced its ninth consecutive disability theatre festival. Although this activity collectively demonstrates the swell in disability arts activity and interest in Canada, the festivals also demonstrate interesting differences: they were initiated independently in Toronto, Calgary, and Vancouver; they are organized by different groups and leaders; and they draw their respective participants and audiences from a range of networks and communities.

Although links between the festivals are rarely drawn at a formal, organizational level, some common connections can be discerned. Consider first festival organizers and participants. For example, Catherine Frazee helped found S4DAC, Kickstart, Art with Attitude, and Culture Cauldron, she sits on the board of Abilities Arts Festival, and she also contributed to the panel discussions at the Madness and Arts 2003 World Festival. At the closing ceremonies of Kickstart 2, Frazee was presented with the first Joan Meister Award. Named after the woman who had been chair of the S4DAC board of directors since 1999, the award seeks to recognize outstanding contributions to disability arts and culture.[22] Several theatre artists have also been involved in more than one festival. Vancouver based solo performing artist Victoria Maxwell, for example, performed at Kickstart and Kickstart 2, the Madness and Arts 2003 World Festival, Art with Attitude, and Calgary's Balancing Acts Festival in 2004. Calgary's Inside Out Integrated Theatre and Vancouver's Theatre Terrific Society have performed in both Calgary and Vancouver festivals. Festivals have thus afforded opportunities for artists and organizers to convene repeatedly, building critical awareness of each other's work over time.

Although the primary focus of festivals has been to share artistic work with the public, many of the festivals have also aimed at providing formal opportunities for festival participants to develop networks and exchange ideas. Panels, symposia, lectures, and workshops have therefore been important parts of the various festival programs. These events have allowed artists and artistic organizers to meet with each other and share professional and artistic problems and strategies. For example, one of the three panels presented at the Madness and Arts 2003 World Festival featured artistic facilitators from groups that create artistic development opportunities by, for, and with people who have received mental health services. Each was invited to discuss best practices for funding, training, dealing with the media, promotion, conflict resolution, and networking. At Kickstart, participants could attend workshops exploring the global disability culture network or investigating funding strategies for disability arts. Panelists also considered different ways of discussing or describing disability in the media. For example, opinions about the terms "disabled person" and "person with a disability" varied as did ideas about the ethics of accessing pharmaceutical company or health care funding to support artistic projects. Although panelists disagreed, they and audience members had an opportunity to express and debate their viewpoints. Lectures and symposia have also allowed individuals to alert festival participants to new developments and opportunities in their field.

For disability theatre artists, festivals have been the primary means to meet with colleagues. Many of Canada's disability theatre companies formed and operated for many years without consorting with their counterparts elsewhere in the country, or beyond. Although each has a distinctive mandate and many have made different choices regarding company structures, funding policies, artistic programming, and training methods, each also faces a common set of challenges operating in environments which are broadly non-inclusive and ableist in attitude and practice. Disability arts festivals have provided opportunities for professional exchange on such issues along with providing prospects for artistic collaboration.

For James Sanders of Vancouver's Realwheels, for example, festivals have been pivotal opportunities for artistic development and building a sense of community. As he explains; "In Vancouver, the University of British Columbia, Simon Fraser University, and Langara College graduate hundreds of theatre students who go on to work with each other and form lively companies within the local theatre scene. By and large, however, these students and the theatre community they form are able-bodied. At a disability arts festival, disability artists have the opportunity to share ideas and be inspired by each other. I cannot express how important Kickstart has been for my artistic development."[23] Indeed, it was at a Kickstart workshop that Sanders first encountered the ES Dance Instruments which became central to his company's two major touring productions (*Skydive* and *Spine*). Lisa Brown has likewise described the founding impulse behind the Madness and Arts World Festival as the company's need to connect with artists similarly dedicated to re-imagining mental illness on stage and supporting artists who have received mental health services.[24]

International participation in Canadian disability arts festivals has also fostered a sense of community across national borders. The example of Patston mentioned above is not unique. While Patston returned to New Zealand after Kickstart emboldened to build new disability arts events and institutions, another participant, David Roche, a disability comedian and solo performer from California, elected to relocate. A multi-award-winning disability arts touring favourite who, over time, has performed at almost every international festival on the circuit, Roche connected with S4DAC leaders, immigrated with his family to BC, and subsequently joined the S4DAC board. Roche features prominently in Canadian Oscar-winner and S4DAC founder Bonnie Sherr Klein's documentary film *Shameless* (2006) about the community of disability artists with whom she has connected and found strength since becoming impaired after two strokes in 1987.[25]

Influence has also operated at a broader institutional level. When Germany's Theater Sycorax performed at the inaugural Madness and Arts World Festival in Toronto in 2003, they were inspired by the festival's novel opportunity to connect with other artists with mental illness experiences who are interested in re-imagining how mental illness is represented on stage. Company representatives met with Workman Arts festival personnel immediately afterward to investigate hosting the next festival. In 2006, they produced the second, expanded Madness and Arts World Festival in Münster, Germany (see Fig. 5.2). The third festival was produced in 2010 by Het Dolhuys in Amsterdam and as in 2006, Workman Arts contributed a production. In each of these examples, Canadian festivals have been the forging ground for a shared sense of community across borders.

One Canadian festival is particularly explicit and focused in its drive to connect Canadian performers and audiences with the global disability art and culture movement. Stage Left Productions' Balancing Acts Festival, Canada's longest-running annual professional disability arts festival, began with two installations in 2002 and has since taken place annually. Over time it has hosted Canadian disability arts festival stalwarts like Alex Bulmer, Jan Derbyshire, Inside Out Integrated Theatre, Victoria Maxwell, Siobhan McCarthy, and Alan Shain, as well as international disability theatre artist Mat Fraser. Stage Left Productions has offered the following explanation of its primary festival impulses: "Balancing Acts is the only professional multidisciplinary arts festival in Canada that is dedicated to advancing the concerns of the global disability art and culture movement – an international movement of disabled artists whose objective is to represent the lived experience of disability as complex, dynamic, and infused with a range of experiences that include hopes and dreams, self-worth and autonomy, sexuality and relationships, and social barriers to disability."[26] In its express aim of forging global links, Balancing Acts is exemplary of the kind of scale-

5.2
Madness and Arts World
Festival Program, 2006.

jumping common to Canadian disability theatre practice. The company has
built on its local community experiences and strengths to connect internationally. It has not been a seed planted by a national policy in support of
disability art nor has it limited the scope of its reach to national borders. It is
important to note however, that from 2008–10, Balancing Acts became a
commissioning body through the financial support of Calgary Arts Development and the Canada Council – Alberta Creative Development Initiative.[27]
With the specific aim of revitalizing disability arts and culture in Canada, this
initiative allowed Stage Left to commission "challenging, thought-provoking
performance work of high artistic merit from emerging and established professional disabled artists whose work aligns with the goals and principles of
the global disability arts and culture movement."[28] While this focused Canada
Council support points to an emerging role in fomenting Canadian disability arts activity, Stage Left's mandate nonetheless aims to develop a global
rather than a national culture.

General Canadian funding opportunities like the Canada Council Travel Grant to Professional Artists recognize the value of festivals for artists as a means to network and showcase their work to new audiences. Although the professional bias of the grant means that it does not serve many disability artists whose careers do not fit normative professionalization standards and patterns, some eligible grantees have used it to attend disability arts festivals. Festivals offer several alluring features to disability theatre and other performing arts companies. First, they provide media engagement, publicity, accessible venues, and targeted, interested audiences. Festival contexts also afford smaller theatre companies opportunities to perform in larger or more technically elaborate, centrally-located professional performing arts venues with strong reputations for innovation, high-quality programming, and commitment to diverse community interests. For example, Vancouver's Roundhouse Community Centre hosted both Kickstart and Kickstart 2. The Madness and Arts 2003 World Festival took place over ten days throughout the Harbourfront Centre with theatre events taking place in the Premiere Dance Theatre, the DuMaurier Theatre, the Studio Theatre, and the Brigantine Room. Since December 2002, Stage Left Productions has presented Balancing Acts: Calgary's Annual Disability Arts Festival at the Big Secret Theatre in the EPCOR Centre for Performing Arts. Each site has helped to raise the profile and status of disability arts within the local communities.

For all their generative work, festivals have also occasioned problems for disability theatre practice in Canada. Many of the problems and questions the festivals have raised are common to disability arts festivals elsewhere. Jayne Leslie Boase, general manager of Arts in Action and creative producer of the High Beam Festival, has offered a useful précis of the difficulties faced by those who try to sustain an international disability arts festival model. She argues that "financial, ideological and artistic fault lines have emerged that question the suitability of the international arts festival model to serve the needs of the disability arts sector."[29] Her critique goes beyond the broader complaint that annual festivals of whatever kind risk usurping the time, money, and other audience and performer resources of more sustained arts programing. Instead, she considers how producing a large-scale festival each year overly taxed the personnel of Arts in Action, wore out the good will of local assistance which had helped cut costs in the early days, and – in the face of growing insurance and expanded festival costs – stretched the organizers' financial and other resources to their limits. Further, the drive to serve both disability artists and artists with disabilities and the concomitant drive to meet both community and artistic needs and standards raised many problems. What kinds of publics were being solicited by the festival? Whose artistic and community needs did it need to serve most or best? Boase further describes how adopting a partnership model and audience development approach helped Arts in Action to move forward effectively and achieve their organization's more particular goals. In the Canadian context, however, Boase's broader insights are relevant for the number of ways that they resonate with those shared during the first focused meeting of disability arts festival presenters.

One of the few coordinated national-scale efforts in service of Canadian disability arts arose in 2006 at the behest of Stage Left's Michele Decottignies who, at that time, held a Canadian Arts and Heritage Sustainability Program capacity building grant which she received for her work as Artistic Director of Stage Left in Calgary. The grant aimed to help "individual arts and heritage organizations that do not have access to assistance from a Stabilization Project to improve their administrative, organizational and financial structures."[30] Because it was expressly aimed at her own professional development and capacity building, Decottignies set out to connect with other presenters across Canada who, like herself, had helped to support disability arts by producing festivals or other events dedicated to programing disabled artists. Following the terms of the grant, she hoped that these presenters could forge professional ties, explore possibilities for coalition, and work toward improving such efficiencies as: developing co-productions or sharing touring costs; determining best practices for serving artists with disabilities; or problemsolving around such recurring festival challenges as media relations or arranging travel and accommodation for specific disability needs. The meetings thus aimed to create a network which would provide a forum for professional support and questions. The range of responses to these discussions and goals, both positive and negative, suggests something of the current state of disability theatre in Canada and the need for stronger involvement from national supporting bodies.[31]

Decottignies had two models in mind when she initiated the network. The first drew upon her work helping Michael Green, artistic director of prominent Calgary theatre company One Yellow Rabbit, to establish the informal and successful Performance Creation Canada (PCC) in 2004. As its website explains, PCC invites artists, educators, administrators, funding institutions, presenters, agents, archivists, and critics to attend its meetings and is "dedicated to the nourishment, management and study of performance creation in Canada, and the ecology in which it flourishes."[32] From this practical experience assisting Green, Decottignies knew how Canadian grants in the arts might be encouraged to fund work which pushed boundaries in important ways not yet explicitly identified by the particular funding parameters. Thus, while disability arts might not have been noted as a target area for funding, Decottignies could point to the exceptional levels of disability arts activity and suggest ways that federal support would be warranted. The PCC was itself loosely modeled on the International Network for Contemporary Performing Arts (IETM), which also inspired Decottignies.[33] Both networks are expressly informal and broadly inclusive and both aim to build upon momentum in a vibrant artistic community. Recognizing similar momentum in the growing number of festivals and events featuring artists with disabilities, Decottignies hoped the gathering and information-sharing of presenters would similarly help to sustain and build disability arts activities in Canada.

After an initial period of outreach and organization, two national meetings occurred in Calgary (2006) and Toronto (2007), as well as in several regional centres, to gather people committed to the development of Canadian disability arts and cultures.[34] The people Decottignies invited to these meetings represented a diverse group, many of whom had not met before. Most of the participants came from Toronto, Calgary, and Vancouver, and included performers, producers, and scholars.[35] This group was not meant to represent disability artists at large, nor, due to financial restrictions, could it include every potential participant. All participants had firsthand experience of producing major festivals or events involving artists with disabilities and all had some sense of the joys, challenges, pitfalls, and problems attending this kind of enterprise. The mixture of people was meant to build new connections and consolidate emerging relationships while also testing the waters for the value of a network. For Decottignies, it seemed appropriate that such voices of experience should gather to share strategies and ideas for best practices while also perhaps finding ways of mutually supporting one another and the artists served by the various festivals and events.

This process would not occur without some friction, however, as participants drew together from sometimes quite different subject positions and held different views about the relevance, responsibilities, and purpose of disability arts. Realizing a network also meant recognizing the differences embedded within it. Networks run another risk – by connecting people they may be perceived to be excluding others. While some questioned whether the network was too exclusive even at these early stages, others suggested that the network might be too inclusive by involving members who came only recently to the concept of disability arts and culture. Arguments among early network participants arose concerning the decision to focus on presenters and the criteria for identifying someone as a presenter. Further, in between the two national meetings, Decottignies organized regional meetings in Calgary, Vancouver, and Toronto which invited local artists with disabilities and

disability arts activists to respond to the concept of the network and suggest
critical issues and areas of concern. While some artists saw strong potential
in the network for promoting disability arts in Canada, others questioned
why presenters should be taking the lead in organizing a network and wondered what place would be made for artists. In the absence of a comprehensive national disability network for artists and other nationally coordinated
supports for artists with disabilities, many such artists expressed wholly
understandable concerns that this network might just become another cultural, artistic, or political table at which they did not have a seat.

The presenters' network has not met since 2007 and it is unlikely to be
revived. Its brief history is an example of how institutions representing common goals depend upon a difficult dialogue between different disability arts
communities and members. It also suggests the problems of coordination,
effort, time, and money for groups that seek to reach beyond one city,
notwithstanding the fact that the network's important initial dialogue flowed
from a single Canadian Arts and Heritage grant given to one individual but
used to build connections among many. Although the presenters' network
was an experiment that may have run its course, in 2009 Decottignies began
organizing a separate and differently-oriented network of radical disabled
artists "concerned with disability arts practices as a unique mode of cultural
production, rather than with assimilation into the mainstream."[36] The more
precise terms and radical aims of this second initiative suggest how the company refined and distinguished its purpose following earlier discussions.

Another important network initiative also arose in response to an occasional funding opportunity, this time in British Columbia. In September
2006, a group of leading BC theatre and other artists with disabilities, disability arts allies, as well as cultural and arts organizers gathered to develop
"a collective '2010 Agenda'" which would address the group's needs for capacity-building and their desires to contribute to the 2010 Olympic/Paralympic
cultural events and its legacies.[37] The discussions at this meeting ultimately
led to the creation of the BRIAN initiative: the BC Regional Integrated Arts
Network. In 2007 the group, led by the Society for Disability Arts and Culture, received $50,000 from the 2010 Legacies Now: Strategic Investments in
the Arts to develop a strategic plan with a consultant for their network ideas.

Strikingly, the word disability is absent from BRIAN's title. While many at
the initial meetings explicitly identified as disability artists or disability arts
supporters, several others who were equally committed to the initiative
rejected the term and refused to self-identify as "people with disabilities." In
the face of these conflicting modes of self-naming, the BRIAN steering committee ultimately chose to develop the network around the concept and term

"integrated arts." Other Canadian artists with disabilities have also coalesced around this term. In each instance, the term has suggested a kind of thinking with and beyond borders. Who, the term invites you to ask, is integrating with whom and to what ends? For some the question and its answers are irrelevant and misleading. James Sanders has suggested that he finds the term neither exciting nor offensive.[38] MoMo, as we have seen, rejects it as confusing. Why, given the various levels of ambivalence the term engenders, did the BRIAN initiative settle upon the term integrated? The 15 August 2007 BRIAN draft strategic plan explains that "because the members of some groups participating in the initial planning meeting choose not to identify as 'people with disabilities' and because there was a clearly-expressed desire to include deaf people and those with various mental health issues, this core group, in naming the network, opted to use the term 'integrated arts' rather than the more politically-charged, though more commonly-used, phrase, 'disability arts and culture.' The term integrated arts is used ... to suggest inclusion and an unbroken continuum of human behaviour and expression."[39]

In addition to including artists with disabilities and disability artists, the group seeks to include "artists who may not be 'disabled,' but who choose to work with artists with a disability."[40] This addition acknowledges another important edge shaping the group discussions. What role might non-disabled participants play in the initiative? Is artwork that involves non-disabled artists or facilitators of equal or lesser value? If BRIAN generates further funding opportunities, will work generated in medical or therapeutic venues be eligible for funding? All of these questions press the limits of "integrated arts" currency.

Early debates in response to these questions among BRIAN's steering committee members have emphasized the initiative's focus on supporting, developing, and advocating for professional artists with disabilities and disability artists. Some members of the participating groups are wary of being connected with recreational arts programs. To this end, at a meeting held at the Vancouver Public library in May 2008, BRIAN members considered the idea of explicitly including the word "professional" in the mandate or title. The funding implications for privileging professionals are significant. For example, both the BC Arts Council and Canada Council focus their funding schemes on professional artists. BRIAN members hope to demonstrate to such funding bodies, however, that the term "professional" often excludes artists with disabilities who must contend with artistic training and career paths that are overwhelmingly non-inclusive in orientation and tradition.

Ultimately, it seems that BRIAN's deliberately broad explanation and language actively deploys the weaknesses of the term as strengths. In the context of BRIAN, the aim is not to produce a common position, forged out of a coherent viewpoint or political stance (as might be achievable in the context of a single company), but rather a critical mass of people engaged in the debates about arts and disability in BC. What remains to be settled is just how a critical mass will interact when a common purpose is important or when highly divergent political positions must come into contact. In seeking a deliberately open framing that transcends some of the politics of the disability arts movement, the term "integration" may contain stowaway baggage that will surface another day. Indeed, at the 2010 meeting held during the Paralympic Games, members considered the benefits and drawbacks of changing "integrated" to "inclusive."

By not forcing the issue of artistic collaborations and by grounding discussion in practical issues like event organization and the fight for central accessible high-end performance spaces and field development, BRIAN has proven useful as a way to shape regional disability arts without placing fences around it or forcing a particular vision of its artistry. The initiative owes a great deal to the background activity in disability arts and culture in Vancouver over the previous decades, but it must also be said that festivals, collaborations, and new moves toward organization also benefited significantly from the lead up to the 2010 Olympics. At a time when the province poured targeted arts dollars into a range of BC arts groups through the 2010 Legacies Now program, disability artists were well positioned to gain a considerable portion of the funds. The Theatre Terrific and Realwheels collaboration that fractured in its early stages and became an opportunity for both to clarify their distinct mandates, for example, began as a pilot project with a view to seeking larger shared Legacies Now funding. Here, a funding opportunity did not create the collaboration, but it did help suggest its feasibility. In addition to the strategic investment funds for Kickstart and the coalition of groups behind BRIAN, others have also gained Legacies Now funding, including Theatre Terrific twice and Realwheels for three projects. The sums were not insubstantial, averaging around $10,000 per project. At a time when the Canada Council was only beginning to develop a comprehensive strategy to support the disability arts field, these funds were highly prized.

These opportunities did not all lead to the same place. The result has been a peculiar evolution of the various forms of scale-jumping and artistic connections that I have outlined here. Earlier initiatives like Kickstart sought actively to engage the international disability community to foster local work and connections. The lead up to the Olympics and Paralympics incidentally shaped the local scene through funding opportunities and by shifting public understandings of disability. By the same token, disability arts groups took advantage of this enhanced funding and attention to build stronger local capacities, increase collaborations, and make BC and Canada hubs and beacons for international disability arts activity.

In their 2009 report from the field on behalf of the Canada Council for the Arts, Rose Jacobson and Geoff McMurchy argued that basic questions remain at the national scale. They wondered why disability arts lack a significant presence within Canadian cultural discourse and raised several pertinent questions: "Why [are there] virtually no statistics available regarding Canada's Deaf and Disability Arts sectors; e.g. number of individuals working as professionals, employed by cultural industries, trained and graduated from post-secondary arts programs, funded by arts councils? How will public and private funders, policy makers and others begin to track and confirm the presence and impact of this sector and the pioneers who contribute daily to Canada's cultural communities and industries? How can these same agencies accommodate, nurture and sustain the artists and practices which constitute Disability Arts?"[41] Further, the report pointed to arts service organizations as the "weakest link" in the access chain for Canada and beyond and argued that until they are supported by designated funding from arts councils, national and otherwise, nothing will change and indifference to access issues will continue. As evidence of the positive change that increased funding in these regards might effect, they cite carrot and stick efforts in the UK during the 1980s in which arts council clients were given incentives to improve their accessibility within a specific timeframe and penalized if they did not follow through by becoming ineligible for operating and program funding.

For many Canadian disability arts activists, institutional practices in the United Kingdom suggest possible goals for Canadian networks to pursue. Following intense debates and activism among a variety of different communities of artists with disabilities in the United Kingdom in the 1990s, the National Arts Council (England) introduced a monitoring committee, directory, and officer focused on Arts and Disability as well as dedicated funding for artists and organizations working to raise the profile of Disability and/or Deaf Arts and Culture.[42] Rather than hoping simply to be included in government funding schemes which target "diversity" – a category which all too frequently misunderstands or ignores artists with disabilities – these more specific government supports could provide the foundations necessary for sustaining disability arts festivals and disability arts over the long term.

In response to initial lobbying by many disability artists and their supporters across the country, the Canada Council explicitly recognized disability arts in its document "Moving Forward: Canada Council for the Arts

Strategic Plan 2008–2011: Values and Directions," released in 2007. For example, under the section entitled "Values and Achievements," the Council declared that its "historic commitment to diversity and equity and to inclusive policies reflecting Canada's rich and complex cultural reality – languages, cultures, racial groups, genders, generations, arts practices and regions – is one of its greatest achievements, and it must be reinforced, expanded (for example, in support of disability arts) and strengthened (to ensure that the Council can respond to evolving arts practices)."[43] The explicit reference to disability arts was tentatively welcomed by many disability artists, who were eager to learn more details about the Council's specific plans for achieving this goal. More formal discussions among Canadian disability artists were organized in 2010 and, a year later, a Deaf and Disability Arts Access and Equality Strategy was released. Although the outcomes of this strategy are difficult to assess yet, the possibility of greater support for access, disability arts development, and public engagement is promising.[44]

The promise of new funding opportunities raises new questions, of course. Will the artistic and social challenges of disability arts be fostered and maintained through new funding models and council recognition, or will it be institutionalized and normalized as only one further branch of identity performance in a multicultural Canada, a branch that does little to shake the ableist roots and history of the tree? Writing out of his experiences with disability arts over time in the United Kingdom, Paul Darke argues that the practice has lost the promising edge of its primary impulse, an impulse not rooted in trying to be part of the hegemony of normality but in trying to expose the fantasy of such normality:

> Disability Art was an art practice with a theoretical basis that was about revealing the 'hidden force of the effects of the majority culture's social uses', not just in relation to disabled people but all people. Too many of us have forgotten the theoretical basis of the Disability Art movement, and the success of a few Disability Artists has been at the expense of the many. As a result, Disability Art and Disability Artists have become, largely through no fault of their own, a tool of the 'hidden forces' used against disabled people to legitimise their (our) continued mass exclusion from not just art culture but culture more widely.[45]

Darke's cautionary remarks may resonate most for those artists and presenters who prize above all the socially activist theoretical basis for disability arts. Although the precise vehicle for Canada Council support has yet to be identified, disability artists may find themselves on the cusp of a new set of questions. Having received support and recognition, where does the future spirit of solidarity and activism among disability cultures come from and where does it go?

In Canada, attempts to articulate and connect disability theatre at the national and regional levels seem to draw primarily on pragmatism and a basic belief in Canadian interests in promoting multiculturalism, diversity, and inclusion. The presenters' network sought to improve efficiencies among presenters and promoted coalition as a means to lobby for greater funding, production resources, and professional support. In a similarly pragmatic vein, a founding impulse behind BRIAN was the need for coalition to capitalize on an unusual set of funding opportunities. Neither initiative embraced a distinctly Canadian or regional disability culture. While the Canada Council is moving forward with plans to investigate how it might better support disability arts, Jacobson and McMurchy outline several significant challenges that continue to impede full participation of disability arts in Canadian cultural discourse. More specifically, Canadian disability theatre functions within a broader inherited system of theatre architectures, design traditions, patterns for soliciting audiences, and performance training models that is largely non-inclusive. If anything may define the Canadian disability theatre context it is a shared sense of frustration among artists and companies across the country at the lack of a coherent national program to ensure that all Canadians have equal access to theatre training and opportunities both to create and witness theatre. This frustration, nonetheless, contains within it a fundamental belief that more inclusive practices are not just possible but critical for national culture. The means for articulating this belief draw in large part from a dynamic exchange between the local and the international. Cross-pollination of disability culture across national borders, through festivals, artistic collaborations, exchanges, and contact between like-minded artists has allowed international disability theatre practices to strengthen local capacities while also allowing Canadians to innovate and build momentum in the international field.

PART TWO

Performances

CHAPTER SIX

Re-Staging Disability Theatre

What are the salient features of disability theatre? Is there a distinctive and coherent disability theatre aesthetic? Is there pressure to have and articulate a coherent aesthetic as a strategy for artists in the field to receive financial and critical support? These questions cut to the core of debates that animate the field, and many Canadian artists have grappled with them in their work. In this chapter we will look at two relatively prominent productions by leading Canadian disability theatres, Stage Left Productions and Realwheels, which exemplify the tensions and possibilities put in play by these considerations. Both productions found audiences in mainstream theatre settings, sought standards of artistic excellence, garnered significant Canadian and regional arts council funding through which actors were paid, and experimented with new development processes involving artists and other collaborators with and without disabilities. Further, both productions received critical attention and both scripts have since been published. Despite these similarities, however, each approached disability theatre with a different and sometimes conflicting set of artistic ideals. By analyzing and contrasting the primary disability theatre features of these two strikingly different productions, we can gain a sense of the range of impulses driving disability theatre practices and contributing to a growing and diverse sense of disability theatre aesthetics in Canada.

Mercy Killing or Murder: The Tracy Latimer Story

From its title alone, Stage Left's December 2003 production of *Mercy Killing or Murder: The Tracy Latimer Story* announced its topicality and interest in provoking Canadian audiences. Like other Canadian professional political theatre that has centred around contemporary events, the production sought to redress an imbalance the artists perceived in media coverage of the criminal case that had captured national attention: a father's pre-meditated killing of nearly thirteen year-old Tracy Latimer, a girl with cerebral palsy, in 1993.[1] Drawing on extensive research and their own experiences, the company believed that the perspectives of Tracy and people with disabilities were largely unaccounted for in the widespread media coverage of her murder and the subsequent trial of her father, Robert. Instead, coverage was more typically focused on public sympathy for Robert as well as debates about euthanasia and the human rights of people with disabilities. In their published version of the script, Stage Left Productions offered this précis of the events around which public and legal opinion turned:

> On October 24, 1993, Robert Latimer took his young daughter's life. He thought about killing her for weeks and, after mulling over many options, he finally did kill her (by gassing her to death in the cab of his truck). He then put her body back in her bed and waited until she was found by his wife, Laura. He initially denied any involvement, telling his family and the police that Tracy had died in her sleep. But after an initial investigation clearly pointed to homicide, Latimer admitted that he had killed Tracy. He was arrested for first degree murder, not second degree, because the killing was premeditated. Under legal counsel, however, Latimer claimed that he had no choice but to kill Tracy because she was in 'constant, excruciating pain' due to having cerebral palsy. This 'necessity' defence went unchallenged in court and was widely reported in the media. But necessity, as a legal defence, does not exist in Canadian law.[2] After one trial and three appeals, Latimer was finally sentenced in 2001 to ten years in jail – the mandatory minimum sentence for second degree murder. The outcry against his sentence was unprecedented in Canada.[3]

Including Tracy's name in the title and emphasising the debate about murder or mercy killing, the production made clear that it would be tackling a critical, nationally divisive, and familiar topic for Canadian audiences. The play drew from verbatim trial and media accounts. It also included fictional material developed by six performers with physical and developmental disabilities, by a host of professional artists, some with disabilities and some not, and by community collaborators interested in giving voice to perspectives of people with disabilities on the case. Critically, therefore, the play referenced the details of Tracy Latimer's life, death, and the subsequent trial of her father. Another Canadian play which also drew from the debates surrounding the Latimer case – *Mourning Dove* by Emil Sher – was more symbolic in its title and created a "fictitious world" that did not cite the particular details of the Latimer case onstage.[4] For Stage Left productions, however, the details of the Latimers' stories provided the guiding questions for their artistic development process: "How did Robert Latimer stay out of jail for so long? Why was his necessity defence allowed in court when it does not exist in law? And why, when he clearly planned his daughter's murder, was he convicted only of second degree murder rather than first degree?"[5] Although each question cites Robert, it is clear that each also turns on the company's sense that Tracy Latimer had been belittled, dehumanized, and under-represented in the legal process. To counter this activity, the company aimed to develop theatre that attended to Tracy's humanity and privileged the voices of people with developmental and physical disabilities. Building an inclusive artistic process in this case required time, money, flexibility, and responsiveness.

Supported by the Canada Council of the Arts Artist and Community Collaboration fund as well as funds from the Alberta Foundation for the Arts, Stage Left Productions engaged in an extended period of research and collaboration to develop the script. The company's artistic director and one of the production's dramaturgs, Michele Decottignies, published a detailed account of this process alongside the script in the *Canadian Theatre Review* volume entitled "Theatre and the Question of Disability," which Decottignies and Andrew Houston edited in 2005.[6] Although I recommend this account as a rich resource, I do not want simply to reiterate its findings. Instead, and more importantly for our broader thinking about the range of ways that Canadians have engaged with disability theatre practices, I would like to analyze the most salient and distinctive features of the production process for re-imagining how people with disabilities might be included and represented in theatre.

As the company's chief critique of the media coverage was the sidelining of the voices of those with disabilities, much of this process focused on finding, supporting, and featuring such voices in their production. The company's methods in this regard were two-pronged: working with established dramaturgs who gathered relevant written and interview materials, and working with emerging artists with disabilities.[7] For these reasons, although she is listed as the production's writer in the credits, Decottignies' account of the script development process emphasizes its collaborative nature. In the production information associated with the published script, Decottignies' credit is immediately followed with references to dramaturgical support from Nancy Nassef, Jamie Popoff, Jennifer Repond, and principal researcher Shelly Hering. Significantly, also acknowledged were the "stories and advice directly from [disabled actors] Lee Davis, James Doyle, Jerry Gliwinski, Donald Norman and Tia Srivastava."[8] Apart from Tia Srivastava and Shari Evin, a young artist with cerebral palsy, whose critical roles I will consider further below, all were involved in the production explorations through to the final live performances.

Several specific choices in the development and production process were designed to ensure the disabled actors' full involvement. These included: making sure that the critical themes and ideas generated by the dramaturgical research team were made available in plain language for those collaborators who read with difficulty; organizing an "intense period of skills development" and focused actor training to address the waning confidence of some disabled actors as the show's scope and personnel grew larger; extending the final rehearsal period to integrate this training into the actors' specific rehearsal and performance processes; and supporting stress management techniques among actors, not least by providing them with taxi services to and from rehearsals to afford more rest. In production, actors with more limited literacy benefited from a coded system of drawings and symbols indicating blocking. A recorded script on CD helped one actor learn his lines while another actor was cast as a courtroom stenographer so that he could have a book prop containing his lines within it, alleviating any concerns he might have had about forgetting them. Inclusive practices in production also extended to scenography. "We made 'jury boxes' the disabled actors' main set pieces, so that they could sit down as often as necessary. We timed as many lighting cues as slowly as possible, so as not to trigger seizures, which can be induced by flashing lights in some with brain injuries or on specific medications. We repeated the shape of as many scenes as possible to reduce the amount of blocking they'd have to retain ... We played voice-overs that announced each scene, so that actors would know their place in the story."[9] All six performers were also involved in the making of two films related directly to Tracy Latimer and a third 1950s style mockumentary, which were integrated into the production. The first depicted a re-creation of her murder with Jamie Popoff playing her father and Shari Evin playing Tracy. The second offered a video montage in its final scene of Tracy Latimer played by Shari Evin and a disabled girl played by Tia Srivastava. The film work allowed both performers to have a critical role in the production even when health concerns prevented involvement in the live aspects of performance. All six performers were included in the work surrounding the film shoot as much as possible to prevent "hierarchies that would diminish the disabled artists and to foster a collaborative environment in which all could contribute equally."[10] Given the production's critical aim of challenging the relative absence of disabled people's voices in media, it is also important to note that the disabled actors undertook live and/or recorded radio and television publicity appearances in support of the production.[11]

Beyond these measures taken toward a more inclusive development process, formal features of the production also assert its ties to disability theatre aesthetics and practice. First, this was a production that pushed back at stereotypes. It did not present innocent, villainous, or helpless people with disabilities. Instead, the disabled actors played characters who were emphatically active, forceful, and critical of media representations of disability narratives. This is evident from the play's initial sequence of events. Entitled, "The Power of the Press," Act I begins with a voice-over collage of ten common media refrains concerning news of the Latimer murder. The scene is immediately followed by the entrance of a popcorn seller – who hustles her wares and passes out popcorn to people in the audience – and the arrival of three PWD (people with disabilities) characters: Donald, James, and Jerry. Two settle onstage to watch the play and another sits with the audience. The shared popcorn and seating arrangements ally the PWD and audience members as they proceed to watch three scenes together: the first, a retelling of the *Hunchback of Notre Dame* in the style of a silent movie; the second, enacted on stage with the aid of a mockumentary 1950s instructional film in which a husband and doctor convince a mother to leave her "mentally retarded" baby daughter in a secluded institution by emphasizing how the girl might grow up to become a sexually aggressive and promiscuous woman (demonstrated in a scene enacted onstage) and by touting the promise of sterilization and treatments; and the third, a soap-opera style scene between a wife, her injured husband on life support, and a doctor who lasciviously pursues the wife and drives her to cut off the husband's life support by explaining that the husband will "never be a man again" because he faces permanent disability. Following each scene the PWD shout their protests, deriding the scenes with such phrases as: "What kind of crappy movie is this?"/"Another dud!"/"That's just ridiculous."/"Who watches these shows?"/"Where the hell do these attitudes come from?"[12] Talking back to the work, Donald, James, and Jerry assert not only their frustrations but also their agency as critical spectators.

From their jury boxes, the PWD also protest loudly, express outrage and cite evidence to challenge many of the legal decisions made during the trial as it unfolds upstage (see Fig. 6.1). In Act II, scene 14 they address the audience directly:

6.1

Stage Left Productions' *Mercy Killing or Murder: The Tracy Latimer Story*, 2003.

JAMES: How did this happen?
LEE: How does a man who admitted to killing his own daughter stay out of jail?
DONALD: How did an ordinary farmer from Wilkie, Saskatchewan, convince two juries and a judge that he was acting in Tracy's best interests? (*Slides with the words "Prima Facie" on them are projected onto each platform.*)[13]

For the remainder of the scene, the PWD answer their own questions. They explain the concept of Prima Facie evidence as "lies that became true" and argue that Robert Latimer's untruthful claims that he had no other way out made the trial more about Tracy than him. Throughout the next scene –

"Scene fifteen: The Real Trial!" – the "Prima Facie" slide is reshown five times as the various witnesses' testimonies make arguments that frustrate and anger the PWD. After collectively shouting "Objection!" at each such moment they then proceed to cross-examine the key witnesses, as the stage directions indicate, "the way it should have been done."[14] PWD also have the final words in the scene. Arguing that Tracy was no more mentally or physically disabled than nine other students at her school, they proceed to list some of her favourite things and activities. Just as in their responses to the scenes about disability, these scenes emphasize the characters' individual and collective agency, critical engagement, frustration, and anger at the ways in which disability experience is represented and maligned.

While many scenes emphasize the agency of PWD, other scenes demonstrate how their voices and perspectives can be and have been actively ignored. In Act II, scene 2 entitled "The Wheel of Fortune," a slide with a six-square puzzle spelling "_URDER" is projected repeatedly onto the upstage right platform. When the PWD repeatedly ask to solve the puzzle they are not only absurdly ignored, but the host and all the other company performers "win" by suggesting answers like "altruistic filicide," "assisted suicide," "compassionate homicide," and finally, "mercy killing." Each is then projected until an "_URDER" is re-shown as the next puzzle. The scene closes with Donald asking "What the hell is going on here?"[15] Active ignoring is equally evident in the play's penultimate scene. Here reporters solicit opinions on the trial and verdict from several non-disabled "gossipers" but push past the PWD when they try to answer the reporters' questions.

One of the play's most disturbing scenes follows the "Wheel of Fortune" when some PWD (Donald, James, and Lee) move upstage behind courtroom podiums, a space reserved thus far for "experts." The characters proceed to describe and implicitly contrast six real-life examples of parents who have murdered their children: the first three examples related to parents who killed non-disabled children, the last three to parents who killed disabled children. As they describe each case in turn, projected slides upstage right show an image of the child or children, sometimes with and sometimes without his/her parents. In each case, the PWD note the jail time sentenced to each accused murderer and this information is also projected on the downstage left platform. The contrast between the life sentences given in the first three examples to no charges in the latter three builds the rhetorical platform for the characters' next scene. Here they compare Canadian statistics showing that the average annual number of Canadian murder cases in which parents killed their disabled children between 1990 and 1994 was thirty-four versus fifty between 1995 and 1998, when, as James notes, "the

Latimer case was prominent in the media." Lee closes the scene with the question, "Why the increase?"[16]

Another provocative feature of the play was its decision to include an actual image of Tracy Latimer. This was projected onto each of the platforms at the end of a video montage of Tracy as played by Shari Evin. The choice to include this image served two production goals. First, it forged a sense of solidarity between Tracy and the performers with disabilities involved in the production. Second, projected during the play's last scene, the images held the same space occupied earlier by the projected images of children who had been murdered by their parents, answering the production's title question with a forceful verdict: murder.

As the scenes described above suggest, the production did not step back from being critical, judgmental, and hard-hitting in its rhetoric and arguments. Instead, it hoped to provoke anger and greater questioning of Tracy Latimer's story by creating a forum in which PWD could speak back to the dehumanizing media and legal discourses that they argued frame how disability is understood and experienced in contemporary Canadian society. The diverse audience shared space, popcorn, and – in the final scene in which PWD encouraged everyone to light candles for Tracy – they shared a candlelight vigil with the actors. Audiences were thus aligned with the PWD perspective and shown, through the range of comic, absurd, and harrowing scenes, that this perspective is layered and complex rather than simplistic or merely reactionary.

Skydive

In stark contrast to the politically charged and edgy topicality of *Mercy Killing or Murder*, the Realwheels production of *Skydive*, arguably the most commercially successful and widely-known example of Canadian disability theatre, is a self-described "action-adventure-comedy for the stage" that since 2007 has had over 100 performances and been seen by more than 30,000 people in six cities (Vancouver, Victoria, Calgary, Montreal, Ottawa, and Kamloops).[17] Whereas Stage Left had innovated with an inclusive dramaturgical process and made formal alignments of audiences with an overtly political disability perspective, *Skydive*'s chief disability theatre innovation was to modify and use stage technology to create a play in which disability could be "strategically masked and revealed," rendering the actor's physicality as incidental rather than central to the plot.[18] This goal fit the company's founding mandate to "produce works that would serve as catalysts in changing the perception of disability and people with disabilities" while not creating a work wherein disability was the central theme.[19] The primary technology for this work was an ES Dance Instrument, an invention of BC choreographer Sven Johansson which Sanders had first encountered at the Kickstart festival in 2001. In the published version of *Skydive*, playwright Kevin Kerr explains the basic features of the technology:

> The ES Dance Instrument is essentially a long pole on a fulcrum, like a giant teeter-totter. Traditionally (if you can use that word to describe such an innovative device), a dancer sits on a bicycle seat at one end and is secured with a belt around the waist. At the other end is a counter-weighted wheel controlled by an operator. The dancer can be lifted vertically in the air as high as seventeen feet, be flown left and right along the horizontal plane, spun 360 degrees in a cartwheel motion, and pivoted to face left or right in profile to the audience (and thereby turning the cartwheels into somersaults and backflips). The entire instrument can also be tracked up and down stage allowing for the performer to occupy almost any point in the space above the stage and in almost any position.[20]

Driven by the goal of producing the appearance of flying for Realwheels artistic director and founder Sanders – an actor who became quadriplegic in 1990 – the company worked with a series of engineers, physiotherapists, and orthotic experts to adapt the instrument for his body.[21] Kerr described the net result of these efforts as a system by which "both performers, each with very different physicalities, were essentially equalized."[22] For their innovations, the production received the Canadian Institute for Theatre Technology's 2007 Award for Technical Merit as well as several Jessie Richardson professional theatre awards and nominations.[23]

Following the story of two thirty-something brothers, irresponsible slacker Morgan (Sanders) and frustrated housebound Daniel (Frazer), the play begins with the arresting sight of both windblown and free-falling from the sky with unopened parachutes on their backs, the sounds of wind and 80s metal music (Judas Priest's *You've Got Another Thing Comin'*) blaring behind them. The scene is without dialogue and transitions from the brothers' series of "well-executed free-falling positions" (the delta and the vector), to their mimicking of Michelangelo's Sistine Chapel "Creation of Adam" finger touch between God and man, to Morgan's checking of his altimeter and giving a thumbs up sign followed by both brothers pulling their ripcords – Morgan's working while Daniel's not – and finally the men's swift separation in time

6.2

Realwheels' *Skydive*, 2007.

and space (see Fig. 6.2).[24] Vancouver critic Jerry Wasserman described this opening scene as one of the most exciting of the 2007/08 season and Kerr has explained that its image was one of the first inspirations for the play.[25] Long-time friends and former Douglas College theatre school classmates, Bob Frazer and James Sanders had committed to developing a project with Kerr. Frazer had wanted an opening that would avoid the convention of actors groping for their marks in darkness before the lights come up and suggested they enter falling from the grid. Kerr had become taken with his idea of the characters falling through space and Sanders had mentioned his contact with Sven Johansson and interest in the theatrical possibilities of ES Dance instruments.[26] A slowed down version of the scene near the play's end follows the brothers as they narrate their actions and thoughts during the critical moments in which Morgan attempts to rescue Daniel and both fall, fatally in Daniel's case, to earth.

The three final scenes which follow are critical for investigations of how the play re-imagines and performs disability. The first, entitled "The Nightmare," is narrated by Daniel while hospital sounds play in the background and shadowy figures emerge from darkness to manipulate Morgan, laying him out on a gurney or operating table and then transferring him to a mysterious "somewhere else."[27] In the next scene, "Awakening," Morgan emerges for the first time in the production in a wheelchair with Daniel standing behind him. Although Morgan cannot see Daniel, he calls to him and they speak, Morgan wondering how to catch-up to his brother and Daniel reassuring him. Before fading to black, the final scene, "Night Sky," unfolds as follows: "*MORGAN takes hold of his wheels and turns his chair upstage to see* DANIEL, *but as he turns,* DANIEL *floats up into the space above. Music plays and* DANIEL *flies free above* MORGAN, *who wheels among the machinery. Stars fill the sky, with* DANIEL *floating among the constellations.* MORGAN *looks up into the sky at the stars."*[28] As Morgan wheels around, his now-empty brace remains attached to the instrument, exposing the means by which the actor had flown and maneuvered above the stage for the past hour and twenty minutes. Thus, these final scenes emphasize both the character and actor's range of physicality and the kinds of technology that support their movements; from his hyperkinetic airborne skydive rescue, to his being mysteriously man-handled by the shadowy clinical figures, to his first appearance onstage in a wheelchair in static conversation with his brother, to his final expert and dreamlike wheeling among the very machines that had held him aloft, the lights laying bare the bones of the technology while Daniel floats above. These transitions "masked and revealed" disability in strategic ways aimed at recasting disability in theatre. Morgan's different kinds of technologically and human-supported movements demonstrated how their combination can introduce a new spectrum of physicalities on stage. Moreover, unlike the longstanding tradition of productions in which able-bodied performers step away from their crutches, straighten out their bodies or step out of their wheelchairs and distance themselves from disabled characters to take a bow for their performance at the curtain call, Sanders remained in his wheelchair. These scenes and the curtain call stance pose a direct challenge to prevailing casting practices that would limit Sanders to roles in wheelchairs. The production's emphasis on innovating with technology to re-imagine theatrical physicality and movement demonstrates how theatre itself is reinvigorated by pushing the kinetic possibilities for bodies of all kinds.

In between these enactments of the brothers' skydive and its aftermath are loosely connected scenes charting their shared childhood memories (misadventures involving Steve Austin toys, Scouts, and Morgan's ill-fated dream band "Hawk Rider") and banter about their current life circumstances (raunchy dating stories, failed career attempts, the plight of their ailing mother). Morgan casts himself as Daniel's therapist and prescribes several fixes for his problems, among them lucid dreaming and the ultimate skydive, "a deep tissue massage for your soul."[29] He is given to mispronunciations (*pie-lates* for pilates, agrophobia for agoraphobia) and to over-confidence in his delivery of nonsensical advice for his more uptight and anxiety-ridden brother. In short, his character is relaxed and funny, delivering a smattering of shocking personal tales and woefully misguided philosophies synchronized to a soundtrack of crowd-pleasing 80s pop tunes. His jokes and concerns are banal and

have broad appeal; he does not discuss physical disability directly throughout the play. These choices are aligned with Realwheels' vision of how theatre
can best serve the goal of normalizing disability.

In a 2009 interview, Sanders described the physical accommodations
(ramps, lifts) made for him when he returned to acting school after his spinal
cord injury but noted that attitudes toward him shifted and he struggled with
others' assumptions that "he would now be asked to play characters with a
disability, and by that I mean the characterization of disability, which at that
time, seemed to be based in anger and fear."[30] Against this trend, Sanders
hoped instead to develop "theatre as a mechanism to establish a natural character fighting with universal issues, represented by a performer with a
disability, that will enable a greater awareness of the common concerns that
all people share and, by doing so, offer a deeper understanding of the disability experience."[31] The strategy of playing a winsome, adventurous, comic
character whose physical disability emerges late in the plot, coupled with the
dynamic and broad range of physicalities he performed on stage, allowed
Sanders to test his two-pronged disability theatre strategy. First, *Skydive*
invited audiences to connect with him "as a natural character fighting universal issues" and then revealed his disability to normalize disability as part
of human experience.

Did the strategy work? Realwheels hired research company Ipsos Reid to
conduct an impact study of the 2009 Vancouver Arts Club and Montreal
Centaur Theatre productions. Trained interviewers approached 380 patrons
exiting the shows and asked them to complete a five-minute questionnaire
designed to measure the production's impact on how audience members
viewed disability. One third of the combined audiences in both cities felt the
production changed how they viewed people living with disabilities, leaving
two thirds, however, who cited no significant change. More positively, poll-
sters did note that *Skydive* "had an impact on specific views of people with
disabilities," especially in terms of encouraging a sense that "people who are
quadriplegic can lead full and productive lives."[32] While the overall results did
not demonstrate a landslide turn in audience opinion, they did offer up some
interesting insights. The exit interviews showed that 97 per cent of attendees
liked the show, with Montreal audiences citing the play's technical aspects,
originality, themes of brotherhood and dreams, humour, emotion, and new
perspectives about people with disabilities as part of their assessment. Strikingly, however, fewer than one-in-ten thought the play was about disabilities
and of those who did, more focused on Daniel's emotional disability than
Morgan's physical disability. Interestingly, although 65 per cent of the audience reported *Skydive* as the first play they had seen with a connection to

disability, those who had seen other plays about disability all felt it offered something new. Was its decentralization of disability issues the most novel aspect for these audience members? The data are unclear on this account but the complex results suggest that *Skydive*'s approach of masking and revealing disability did less to create a forum for overhauling public attitudes toward disability than it did to develop a forum in which a disability theatre artist could showcase his artistry, physicality, imagination, and talents – arguably a more subtle means for pressing audiences to shift their expectations of actors with disabilities.

Disability Theatre Aesthetics and Practice in Canada: Coalition and Debate

These two quite different productions begin to suggest the range of disability theatre practice in the country. Realwheels sought to deepen audiences' understanding of disability by masking and revealing disabled characters and performers strategically to give a sense of disability as one critical perspective in the human spectrum. By contrast, Stage Left emphasized the distinctive perspectives of people with disabilities on a controversial case of critical importance for all Canadians. Whereas Realwheels' approach sought to normalize disability experiences by insisting that they have a place in theatrical explorations of universal issues, Stage Left's sought to foreground how the perspectives of people with disabilities offer distinct and valuable counterarguments to mainstream media coverage of critical cases involving people with disabilities. Can disability theatre practice contain these two distinct approaches, one seeking to normalize disability experience and one looking to mobilize its radical and socially transformative potential?

Few people in Canada have been as eloquent on the topic of Canadian disability arts aesthetics as Catherine Frazee and it is well to approach this more specifically theatre-oriented question first with reference to her sense of the diverse artistic approaches at play in the broader movement. Citing other strong Canadian arts movements that have sought to engage with the "social realities of our times," she argues that Canada's disability arts movement also seeks to upset the "cultural apple cart:"

It does so by speaking back against dominant narratives that report our bodies as broken, our lives as tragic, our status as inferior and our humanity as diminished. It does so by giving us a language in which to talk about our lives and what we share. It does so at times by raising a voice of unremitting reproach for the shabby conditions of disabled people's lives. It does so at times by offering a generous entry point for rapprochement, as openhearted citizens on both sides of the border of disability seek to establish relations of mutual respect and civility. It does so at times with the beguiling charms of table turning – staring back at the *normals*,[33] displacing their gaze with our own. It provokes and stimulates us with the roller-coaster force of the unsettled, the unfamiliar, the uncomfortable – opening audiences to the thrill of discovery, revelation and awe and, perhaps most importantly, the displacement of the fear that can hold us captive in small and restrictive categories.[34]

Frazee's insistence on the value of different tacks within the disability arts movement helps to explain how connections may be drawn between the two contrasting productions described above. Frazee's rubric reveals the value in *Mercy Killing or Murder*'s "unremitting reproach" for the dehumanizing way in which Tracy Latimer's death was accounted for by some media and legal discourses. There is a critical place within disability theatre, therefore, for the production's deliberately one-sided focus on Tracy Latimer and the ways in which her perspective and the perspectives of people with physical and intellectual disabilities have been suppressed or discounted. Frazee's commentary also values the kinds of points of rapprochement afforded by *Skydive*'s "normalizing of disability" and its challenge to pre-existing aesthetic traditions that would seek to exclude disability from the gamut of universal issues and experiences. Both productions provoked audiences to rethink how disabled bodies are cast as passive, tragic, or broken by emphasizing the agency of characters with disabilities and, by extension, the performers with disabilities who played them. The PWD from Stage Left spoke back to popular entertainment narratives about disability as well as the more specific disability-related legal testimony and media questions. Sanders played a comically flawed yet winsome non-disabled and disabled character and upset the convention for how disability performances are traditionally unmasked at the curtain call. The artistic decision to reveal within the show the apparatus that had supported Sanders' performance demonstrated for audiences how disability can stimulate theatrical and technological innovations that smash "small and restrictive categories" of how bodies of all abilities might animate the stage. Thus, although they did so from different directions, each production invoked disability to unsettle standard theatre practices for representing disability.

These Canadian productions' commitment to shaking up theatre traditions and their connections to Frazee's articulations about disability aesthetics resonate with US disability studies theorist Tobin Siebers' more recent investigations of the topic:

> Disability aesthetics refuses to recognize the representation of the healthy body – and its definition of harmony, integrity, and beauty – as the sole determination of the aesthetic. Rather, disability aesthetics embraces beauty that seems by traditional standards to be broken, and yet it is not less beautiful, but more so, as a result. Note that it is not a matter of representing the exclusion of disability from aesthetic history, since such an exclusion has not taken place, but of making the influence of disability obvious. This goal may take two forms: (1) to establish disability as a critical framework that questions the presuppositions underlying definitions of aesthetic production and appreciation; (2) to establish disability as a significant value in itself worthy of future development.[35]

Both productions highlighted the influence of disability and played with traditions for representing disability using the two main goals Siebers outlines. First, Stage Left organized the PWD downstage and aligned with audiences as they generated a critical framework for assessing the role of disability in the scenes from the *Hunchback of Notre Dame*, the 1950s maternal melodrama, and the soap opera regarding the husband in a coma. The jeering and popcorn-throwing in these opening scenes formed a basic foundation for their subsequent direct critiques of media and legal discourse concerning Tracy Latimer's story. Second, the production valued the involvement of people with disabilities and adapted its artistic development and production process to help the PWD characters satisfy professional standards of artistic merit. Likewise, *Skydive* also adapted stage technologies and built the production to mask, reveal, and emphasize Sanders' status as a performer with a disability. It is chiefly through this effort that *Skydive* also addressed Siebers' first goal of using disability to create a critical framework through which to query pre-existing aesthetic standards for theatre production and appreciation. Developing a production in which he played a central character that moves from being non-disabled to disabled allowed Sanders to speak back to casting practices that would invite him only to play characters in wheelchairs. Although they did so from different directions, each production forged new patterns and standards for developing theatre involving disability artists.

The question of standards is one that returns again and again in disability arts discussions. Theatre reviewers, arts council jurists, audiences, and practitioners struggle to know what modifications, if any, need to be made when assessing disability theatre. In the Canadian context, Frazee has also shown leadership by positing standards for disability arts practice, all of which seem relevant to the more specific analysis of Canadian disability theatre. In a panel address to the Kickstart festival in Vancouver in 2001, Frazee urged disability artists to reject normative and frequently oblique standards of excellence and place importance instead on: *authenticity* of voiced experiences; *engagement*, demonstrated through focus, commitment, risk-taking, and sincerity; and *transformation* through shifting knowledge and perception, changing experiences from "oppression to emancipation," and in presenting "a distillation of raw emotion to new language and forms." Fundamentally, Frazee called for the recognition of *audacity* – for "speaking back to power, pushing the boundaries of existing forms and exploring new forms, bold or insolent heedlessness of restraints of prudence, propriety or convention, challenging and stretching mainstream notions of grace, beauty, lyricism or craftsmanship, confronting the dominant narrative and reinventing ourselves." While other standards for excellence might privilege refinement, praising a "polished performance" for example, Frazee pointed to some assumptions and limits behind this term by arguing that it is "less a reflection of artistic merit than a question of artistic confidence and access to resources (editors, staging, costumes, opportunities to refine work through workshops and peer collaboration)."[36] These artistic standards offer robust means for assessing works that might vary widely in form due to their connection with different kinds of disability experience and artistic practice. Committed to involving and artistically innovating with disability artists throughout their development processes and productions, both *Mercy Killing or Murder: The Tracy Latimer Story* and *Skydive* can claim strong levels of authenticity and engagement on this scale. Their processes also allowed the artists to transform these experiences in generative and audacious ways, creating rich juxtapositions of scenes featuring disability voices and perspectives to redress their relative absence in mainstream coverage of the Latimer trial in the first case and re-imagining casting practices and the physical possibilities for a quadriplegic performer in the second.

The fact remains, however, that these very different productions made distinctive choices in terms of their engagement with wider public audiences. The casting choices and production process developed by Stage Left committed it to a single city performance model. Realwheels' streamlined cast, portability, and commercial orientation meant that it could and would travel. Stage Left, like so much disability theatre, was not reviewed in the mainstream press; Realwheels was ... and in all of the cities in which it performed. Perhaps the most important distinction between the productions concerns the political topicality and thrust of the works themselves. Stage Left's more radical politics struck directly at pressing human rights concerns for Canadians with disabilities and created a pointed critique by allowing people with disabilities to question directly verbatim trial excerpts and media accounts related to the Latimer case. The production went beyond inviting audiences to think critically about how disability is represented in art by also demanding a critical re-assessment of how people with disabilities are excluded from full participation and representation in Canadian media and legal discourse. In short, its theme was of particular interest to people with disabilities and its mise en scène aligned audiences to characters with disabilities from beginning to end. By contrast, Realwheels did not privilege disability experience throughout the narrative but masked and revealed disability strategically in service of a narrative more interested in comedy, adventure, and exploration of such universal themes as brotherhood, family dysfunction, and the morass of middle age. With disability as an element of the narrative rather than its focus, the production invited audiences to re-examine disability as a critical factor in any narrative with a pretense to universal relevance. The production's mise en scène, its masking and revealing of disability, also challenged audiences to reconsider how non-disabled and disabled bodies might claim space, embody roles, move, and animate the stage. Whereas Stage Left drew from the perspectives of people with disabilities to highlight the socially and politically disruptive power and generative potential of attending to the ways that disability is silenced and marginalized within mainstream society, Realwheels demonstrated how disability experience could play a critical role in developing a mainstream, professionally oriented, "action-adventure-comedy" with broad appeal.

Arguably, these contrasting goals can seem to be working at cross purposes. Stage Left used innovative theatre techniques to develop and produce a forum in which lead characters played by people with disabilities, all of whom were paid for their work but none of whom had professional theatre status at the time, could share critical ideas connected with the disability rights movement in an affectively powerful and inclusive artistic framing. Realwheels followed more mainstream professional artistic development processes and protocols but innovated with technology to create a more inclusive theatre framing that received professional theatre award nominations and strong audience support in several Canadian cities. Both productions used disabled and non-disabled performers, but in *Skydive* the performer with a disability was a professional theatre artist while in *Mercy Killing or Murder: The Tracy Latimer Story*, none of the PWD performers were professional artists at that time. I note the differences in professional status not as indicators of artistic merit but as a means to distinguish the company's different artistic approaches. These distinctions raise critical questions about the place of existing professional standards and overt allegiance to the disability arts movement in disability theatre. Do either of these features qualify one production as more connected to disability theatre? Different attitudes among disability theatre practitioners to these questions have given rise to tensions in the Canadian disability theatre scene and it is important to note how these shape the contours of the field.

It is not my aim here to air every argument that I have encountered during the course of my research. Instead, I would like to address critical issues around which some of these debates have turned and suggest what seems to be at stake in each. Debates such as these need not be viewed negatively; rather, they attest to the commitment many have to seeing disability theatre flourish in Canada. The first issue concerns how strongly or explicitly the theatre in question connects to the aims of the disability movement. Does disability theatre need to be overtly linked to the emancipatory project of this movement and raise, as in the case of the Stage Left example, pressing human rights concerns for people with disabilities? Is the lack of overt engagement with disability issues a reason for diminishing Realwheels' contributions? Some might argue that yes, the work's attempts to include disability experience within universal themes risks folding disability theatre into mainstream theatre aesthetics without fundamentally challenging the ableist ideologies upon which these rest. Why become involved with aesthetic traditions that value universality when these traditions have so often devalued human variation and diversity? Why seek the critical acclaim of a theatre establishment that has long-rewarded representations of disability that were patently not connected to disability experience or activism? In the other direction, however, artists who hope to transform the landscape of current professional theatre practices argue that overtly political theatre does not allow them to reach all kinds of audiences and some appeal must also be made to those audiences, whose membership may or may not include people with disabilities, who do not currently seek out politically challenging theatre. In a parallel fashion and while recognizing that theatre needs to serve audience members with disabilities, some argue that it is equally critical to begin challenging assumptions and practices at professional theatres that do not yet actively court patrons with disabilities, whether through inaccessible theatre architecture, infrastructure, programing, or pricing. Since those who seek out overtly political art and those who do not often gather in different spaces, is it advisable or counterproductive to generate theatre that targets each differently? Will doing so risk entrenching the divisions between audiences, divisions that are often informed and reified by the accessibility issues noted above? I can see value in several directions as long as one does not usurp the other as the only acceptable contributor to the Canadian disability arts scene. If all available theatre funding and opportunity goes to those who are not overt in their political challenges, critical opportunities for more radical art and dialogue may falter. If all efforts are directed at this more radical stream, critical dialogue with some strains of mainstream practice and the opportunity to "upset the applecart" from within may be lost.

As the arguments above suggest, the concept of professionalism in disability theatre is both vexing and of paramount concern to those involved in the field. The problems of inaccessibility at many professional theatre venues and training programs in the country and the challenges many disability artists face when trying to forge a professional career while also living with a disability, make existing standards for professional designation inappropriate for many. Most disability theatre artists would argue for greater flexibility in the rubric for such designation and would also demand full accessibility at all levels of theatre training and practice. Consensus in this regard suggests that the debates about professionalism turn most around the more mercurial concepts of talent and artistic achievement. Frazee's standards go a great distance to articulate ways in which disability theatre holds great social and aesthetic value. Indeed, her standards seem valuable for most theatre. However, what can disability theatre artists do to ensure the form generates enthusiasm from audiences? As solo performer Victoria Maxwell has argued, "as a disability artist, I only do a service if the pieces I offer are good theatre. If what I present is mediocre in quality, I only reinforce tokenism, the image that disabled and disability artists can get an 'A' for effort but not for talent – the very stigma I am trying to eliminate."[37] A key challenge for each of the companies and artists producing disability theatre in Canada is to find a particular way of being "good" within current standards of assessment and critique and to demonstrate talent.

Beyond presenting attributes of what Frazee and Siebers have constructed as a disability aesthetic, the approach to this aesthetic and the motivation of artists to mobilize that aesthetic for different ends suggests a basic fault line in contemporary Canadian disability theatre. The following chapters consider how different Canadian theatre companies have approached disability aesthetics – attempting both to be "good" and demonstrate talent – while also exploring how they wrestled with the problems of audience and public engagement.

CHAPTER SEVEN

Staging Schizophrenia

> For a lunatic is also a man that society does not wish to hear but
> wants to prevent from uttering certain unbearable truths.
> Antonin Artaud, "Van Gogh: The Man Suicided by Society"[1]

Mental illness has a long and varied cultural history, in which theatrical representations have played an important role, reflecting dominant cultural perceptions but also constituting them. As a result, it is important when investigating mental illness representations onstage to ask questions about context: What cultural norms and forms do plays reflect or interrogate? Who creates mental illness representations and how? Who performs mental illness and for whom?

Vincent is a play about schizophrenia written by Terry Watada. Workman Arts (WA), introduced in Chapter 3, originally commissioned and produced the play to be part of a 1993 provincial conference investigating strategies for handling mental illness in a post-institutional era. The company has since toured and remounted *Vincent* over ten times at such venues as Ottawa's National Arts Centre and Toronto's Harbourfront Centre (see Fig. 7.1). In 2006, the original cast and crew toured the show to Germany for the second Madness and Arts World Festival. As I suggested in Chapter 3, Workman Arts' formal connections to disability theatre came late in their development but *Vincent* helps to suggest some of the disability theatre aesthetics at play in their work. Like *Mercy Killing or Murder: The Tracy Latimer Story* and Friendly Spike Theatre Band's *The Edmond Yu Project*, *Vincent* drew from real-life events to highlight an issue of critical importance in the lives of people with

7.1
Workman Arts, *Vincent*, performed in Toronto,
Madness and Arts World Festival, 2003.

disabilities, in this case people diagnosed with schizophrenia. The play's
development process followed the company's approach described in Chapter 3: bring company members together with a professional playwright to
create work that has both artistic and social impact. Performed by a series of
company members and professionals over time, *Vincent* has become the company's most enduring and performed work.

Most of the wa's works have relied on innovations in form to give
audiences a direct experience of some aspect of mental illness or stigma.
The central formal innovation of *Vincent* is the liminal presence/absence of
the play's eponymous protagonist, Vincent, a man diagnosed with schizophrenia. At no point during the play does he appear onstage. In various post-
performance discussions, this aspect of the play has attracted considerable
interest and provoked audience discussion. At an early re-mount of *Vincent*
at the Workman Arts, for example, I heard post-performance panellist and
community-outreach worker Bob Rose note regretfully that the audience

never heard from Vincent but "again heard only the voices and words of others."[2] Correcting Mr. Rose, an unknown audience member pointed out that, although Vincent's character was never visually present onstage, his character could be heard in the production's two brief voice-overs. In a sense, the truth of both assertions points to a central tension underlying Watada's play: Vincent is simultaneously present and absent, both known and unknown.

In *Vincent*, Watada develops a strategy for representing schizophrenia that emphasizes the border between Vincent's presence and absence. His approach is formally akin to the representational mode called negativity. In *The Act of Reading: A Theory of Aesthetic Response*, Wolfgang Iser suggests that negativity can only be defined in terms of its salient features and operations.[3] To this end, he outlines the position of reception in the play of negativity: "Negativity, in the true sense of the term, however, cannot be deduced from the given world which it questions, and cannot be conceived as serving a substantialist idea, the coming of which it heralds. As the nonformulation of the not-yet-comprehended, it does no more than mark out a relationship to that which it disputes, and so it provides a basic link between the reader and the text."[4] Thus negativity, as Iser and Sanford Budick later suggest in *Languages of the Unsayable: The Play of Negativity in Literature and Literary Theory*, involves the limit between presence and absence, the border at which something begins to be present by making us aware of its absence. Negativity draws attention to the limits of knowledge, awareness, and understanding. As Petra Kuppers has argued with reference to her own artistic work in mental health settings, emphasizing unknowability is a particularly valuable strategy for disability performances which engage with the many layers of stigma associated with mental illness. In mental health contexts, she notes, "it is too easy to allow the spectator to see the performers as 'mad' and to see the traces of that 'madness' evidenced on their bodies."[5]

Investigating the play of negativity in Watada's dramatic text and in the performance texts from the WA productions of *Vincent* presents a useful opportunity to extend Iser and Budick's theories beyond literary analysis and account for actual audiences. WA's productions of *Vincent* offer an unusual opportunity to examine actual audience responses because the panel discussions with the audiences that followed early performances were recorded and a summary of these responses has been maintained in the company's archives.[6] The volume and quality of these summarized responses allow us to refine our understanding of negativity in light of a range of audience responses. Moreover, they demonstrate the play's ability to create a space for listening to what has been unsayable in this particular cultural and historical context. In what follows, I explore how negativity operates in *Vincent* and make connections among the text, the context, and the range of audience response.

Developing the play in association with Workman Arts, Watada sought to emphasize the limits in society's ability to speak knowledgeably about schizophrenia. *Vincent* therefore explicitly avoids more stereotypical and homogenizing representational strategies, which offer stable visual, linguistic, and spatial cues that distinguish the character diagnosed with schizophrenia as recognizably "other" than normal. Cultural theorist Sander Gilman argues that western culture has typically understood mental illness through exteriorizing the aesthetic terms that render mental illness sufferers visibly, expressively, and linguistically Other. Gilman's historical and aesthetic investigations of mental illness representations have identified a tradition of representing schizophrenia in ways that devalue and stigmatize schizophrenic experience.[7] It is precisely this tradition that *Vincent*'s representational choices aimed to counter.

Based on the fatal 1992 shooting of Dominic Sabatino – a man diagnosed with schizophrenia – by a Metro Toronto police officer, *Vincent* recounts a similar shooting by Police Constable Woods. The play tells the story of Vincent's struggles with mental illness, the side effects of medication, homelessness, poverty, his family, and the law. Throughout the play, only three characters are present on stage: Frank Carbone (Vincent's younger brother), Vincent's Mother, and Police Constable Woods. These characters are seated on stage and, as spotlights bring them individually to view, they answer the unheard questions of a formal police inquiry. When, in accordance with the stage directions, a character "steps forward" out of his or her seat, she or he then seems to address and respond to the unseen and unheard Vincent. In such scenes, characters may also interact with each other, sometimes in scenarios that imply Vincent's presence and participation:

(*Lights come up. Frank and Mother step forward. Frank addresses Vincent.*)
FRANK: (*angry*) Vince what are you doing here?
MOTHER: Frankie, be nice he's your brother.
FRANK: Ma, be careful. He wants something. Vince, when was the last time you took your meds?
Four months ago!? That's crazy![8]

Thus, in the silent gaps between the other characters' speech, Vincent's voice is implied but not heard. Bob Rose's suggestion that Vincent's experience is characterized only through its absence seems accurate.

Yet, as the unknown audience member noticed, both scene one and the final scene of the play offer Vincent's voice through voice-over. Each of these scenes includes Vincent's voice in recorded altercation with Frank and P.C. Woods. Their argument suggests the critical action that forms the impulse for the play: Vincent swings a baseball bat at both Frank and Woods, shouting "[G]et the fuck outta my head! Get out!" and "[F]ucken leave me alone. Leave me alone! I want you to get the fuck outta my head"; Frank begs the police not to hurt him and reminds them that Vincent is sick and needs help; Woods warns Vincent repeatedly to "[P]ut that baseball bat down."[9] In scene one, this brief argument is played along with a montage of sound, which includes street traffic, chaotic music that includes Don McLean's song "Vincent (Starry, Starry Night)" about Vincent Van Gogh, and breaking glass. The audience listens to the sound while the stage is in total darkness. Not until the music and sound have faded do lights come up on stage.

In the final scene of the play, the same sound montage is played with four significant changes to heighten the tension: sirens are also heard; Frank's speech becomes "For God's sake don't shoot him!" rather than "don't hurt him"; Frank also shouts "Don't shoot! He's sick he needs help"; and finally, at the end of the original dialogue, a gun shot rings out.[10] After the climactic gunshot, a reprise of McLean's song is played in full and the lights come up. As in scene one, this series of sounds is played over an unlit stage in a darkened auditorium. Vincent repeats the lines heard in the opening sequence. In both instances, Vincent's speech addresses something unseen and unheard rather than any characters introduced in the play.

The conflict heard in the first scene presents an enigma: to whom is Vincent speaking? Because he always refers to Vincent in the third person, Frank does not directly engage with Vincent in these voice-overs. In contrast, P.C. Woods directs his imperatives – "Put that baseball bat down," for example – directly at Vincent and ignores Frank's pleas. Vincent's own voice, however, engages directly with neither Frank nor P.C. Woods. Rather, he argues with an unqualified someone to get out of his head. Thus, in scene one, the urgency of Vincent's exclamations and expletives draws attention to his own unexplained conflict, while their incongruity with the surrounding dialogue separates their logic from that of the other characters' interchange. Between the opening and final scenes, characters reflect on Vincent after his death and explain the opening scene's action from their own perspectives. In the play's final scene, only Vincent's experience remains unexplored, as the audience again hears the voice-over. Because Vincent does not describe his experience further and simply re-exclaims imperatives to an unidentified addressee is in his head, his own unexplained conflict remains the sole enigma of the production.

Watada represents schizophrenia by combining Vincent's tacit but disembodied presence in the stage action with his aural presence in the voice-overs. Both modes of representation limit the spectator's sensual experience of the character. Hearing the voice-overs in darkness, the audience does not see Vincent, and watching and listening as the characters address Vincent and imply his presence and responses, the audience neither sees nor hears him. Because of these sensual limitations, each manifestation of Vincent's figure has a tacit dimension; the manifest text implies his character through a series of lacunae. That audiences experience Vincent as a whole character is evident from the audience responses. In fact, the commentators quoted earlier differed only in their qualitative and quantitative assessments of Vincent's presence; neither described or experienced a total absence. Thus, synthesizing the comments of Bob Rose and the unknown audience member, we discover a mode of representation that relies less on absence than on a play of negativity, a presence implied through absence.

Literary theorists Iser and Budick suggest that negativity operates as a language of the unwritten or unwritable, the unspoken or unsayable. In their formulation, such language is thus not merely absent but has an implicit presence whose expression is suppressed.[11] The play of negativity disrupts this suppression by drawing attention to it. As Iser and Budick explain, "What allows the unsayable to speak is the undoing of the spoken through negativity. Since the spoken is doubled by what remains silent, undoing the spoken gives voice to the inherent silence which itself helps stabilize what the spoken is meant to mean."[12] Ultimately, Iser and Budick stress the power of negativity to transform not simply because it lures absence into presence. By constantly subverting that presence, negativity "changes it into a carrier of absence of which we would not otherwise know anything."[13] Thus drawing our attention to the dynamism of negativity, the play of its transformative power, Iser and Budick also help to distinguish negativity from nihilism and nothingness to assert instead negativity's "function of marking a threshold in the ways of knowing, acting, and speaking."[14]

Watada's characterization of Vincent works precisely to assert such a threshold. Because the spectator's sensual experience of Vincent's voice and visual presence is limited, his character is conditioned only through the interplay of presence and absence. In a 1993 WA document entitled "Notes from the Playwright," Watada, in a manner that engages negativity's play, explains the need to break from traditional ways of describing people diagnosed with schizophrenia: "I immediately decided that the central character, Vincent, should not be seen on stage. Society tends to demonize the schizophrenic and makes him inhuman somehow. However, through the interaction with family members and the police, I hoped a portrait of a human being, filled with hopes, dreams and anguish would emerge."[15]

Because it necessitates the play of negativity, Watada's text positions Vincent's experience at the limits of the sayable. The portrait that Watada hopes will emerge, therefore, relies on key audience actions: their active recognition and engagement with Vincent's absence and their attentive listening to his silence. Engaging audiences in these ways, Watada's choices seem driven by the same impulses Budick and Iser associate with negativity: "[O]ne cannot speak for the unsayable. It can only speak for itself. To say otherwise is to become imprisoned in one's own ventriloquism or gimmick. By the same token, there is no adequate substitute for listening to the languages of the unsayable. No one can fully do such listening for anyone else."[16] Driven by a need to recognize the humanity of and difficulties faced by those who live with the diagnosis of schizophrenia, Watada's choices create space and time for listening to what is unsayable. In *Vincent*, negativity directs our attention to the limits in our ability to speak knowledgeably about schizophrenia. Iser and Budick suggest that negativity must be experienced rather than defined or explained.[17] Any attempts at definition are axiomatically incomplete; to explain negativity would mean that one could master it discursively, thus ending the experience of negativity. For example, a representation of Vincent that relied on the coherence of his visual and aural presence to represent schizophrenia would again encounter schizophrenia only through discourses of the knowable: medical, legal, or aesthetic definitions of schizophrenic experience. For Workman Arts members and Watada, such discourses label and dehumanize by suggesting that a stable, visible, and accessible experience exists "out there" to be represented. These discourses are dehumanizing because each has historically drawn from the assumption that those experiencing what has been labelled as schizophrenia lack the human faculty to represent themselves and must rely on the advocacy and interventions of professionals or those who stand apart from this experience. Rejecting these stable definitions, Watada's representational strategy engages negativity instead. Negativity functions to emphasize the limits of knowledge in the face of heterogeneous, ambiguous, or unfamiliar experience; it stands in opposition to representational strategies that objectify, dehumanize, devalue, or romanticize.

In *Disease and Representation: Images of Illness from Madness to AIDS*, cultural historian and theorist Sander Gilman demonstrates how the anxiety originating from the social stigmas associated with mental illness has historically engendered a need to make plain the illness and clearly distinguish its sufferers from a healthy public. He describes the connection between anxiety and the impulse to label and devalue deviance: "The banality of real mental illness comes into conflict with our need to have the mad be identifiable, different from ourselves. Our shock is always that they are really just like us. This moment, when we say, 'they are just like us,' is most upsetting. Then we no longer know where lies the line that divides our normal, reliable world, a world that minimizes our fears, from that world in which lurks the fearful, the terrifying, the aggressive. We want – no, we need – the 'mad' to be different, so we create out of the stuff of their reality myths that make them different."[18] Drawing from a broad historical range of medical illustrations, as well as high and popular art, Gilman demonstrates a long representational tradition in western culture that emphasizes the physical, expressive, and linguistic differences of people with mental illness to render them as safe and "Other." It is a history and continuing representational pattern with which many WA members are familiar.

Many members cite feeling alienated by representations that emphasize physical differences between those with mental illness and those without. In their experience, such divisions are more socially and culturally constructed than rooted in actual mental illness experience. In an interview, one WA member, who also sits on the Canadian Mental Health Association Board, argued that it is important to consider the role of representation in shaping illness experience: "These kinds of alienating representations are confusing because they cloud the experience and make it hard for actual sufferers of the illness to identify their problems and seek help."[19] In order to rectify this difficulty, this member identifies the importance of examining the historical roots of contemporary meanings for the category of schizophrenia. "The term schizophrenia and the range of symptoms associated with it is still a matter of great debate. In some ways the term itself is confusing because its literal translation, 'split mind,' does not adequately describe the experience and frequently leads people to misrepresent the illness as a split personality."[20]

In *Disease and Representation*, Gilman also focuses upon the historical construction and indeterminate aspects of the nosological category "schizophrenia."[21] Distinguishing schizophrenia from most other psychiatric illnesses, Gilman calls schizophrenia a "label in search of a structure; it is a category applied to a rather large group of symptoms with an almost equal number of etiologies proposed for it."[22] After outlining the mainstream and secondary debates connected with the category's history, Gilman concludes, "No composite theory of schizophrenia can be proposed and perhaps none will ever be generated, certainly not one that will unify all of the views ... Thus the best we can do is to understand how the various concepts have evolved historically – and how, on one level or another, they relate to each other."[23] To this end, Gilman traces the importance of language in the diagnosis, representation, and stigmatization of people with schizophrenia over time. After outlining traditional patterns of representing schizophrenia, Gilman discovers language to be a central factor defining madness in late-twentieth-century perception; "One of the most striking qualities ascribed to the stereotype of the 'Other' is his or her altered language or behavior. Whether they are perceived as the sympathetic Other or as the fearsome Other, the mad have always been perceived as possessing a special quality of language. Indeed, the very essence of the stereotype of madness can be summarized as a disruption of cognition and language. Whether this disruption is seen as threatening, as prophetic, or merely as inchoate, it is a quality that is inherent to our perception of insanity."[24]

Gilman goes on to demonstrate how the "special quality of language" attributed to the mentally ill is typically labelled as "bizarre," an aesthetic term used to bind and define the world of the mad within the discourse of aesthetic representation. Gilman outlines how the term "bizarre" has historically been used in madness representation to contain mental illness in a mad world, a separate world incapable of comprehensible self-expression, an illness that can only be expressed by art itself.[25] The logic underlying this idea is founded on anxiety and accomplished through the principle of exteriority: "Thus we use the stereotype of the bizarre language of the schizophrenic as a means of defining our own sanity."[26]

Yet, to display the gaps between these representations of madness and its reality, Gilman cites the World Health Organization's 1973 International Pilot Study of Schizophrenia, which found that "only 10 percent of those patients examined actually showed the classic thought (and therefore, language) disorders associated with 'schizophrenia.'"[27] While Gilman's questions about the stability of this representational stereotype are important, his reliance on medical discourse from the 1970s to assess the falsity/genuineness of the stereotype neglects his earlier assertion of the historical boundedness and instability of medical discourse itself. More useful to the analysis of *Vincent* is Gilman's attention to the mechanism by which anxieties about the unknown are displaced onto representation and language.

Gilman demonstrates how representations of the bizarre language of the mad work more to promote the artist's distance from the experience of madness than to explore the experience of madness itself. He points to mental illness representations as products of a principle of exteriority, a clear demarcation between normative language and the language of the bizarre; "When later images of madness label the language of madness as bizarre, they draw a line between their own creation of texts that define madness and mad texts. The line is clear. We who stand apart from the world and language of the insane, who define ourselves as 'mentally healthy,' are in no danger of having our language, the language that marks the bounds between ourselves and the insane, labeled as 'bizarre' … This is an arbitrary line that defines the difference perceived (and represented) between the pathological and the normal."[28] The principle of exteriority which follows is a syllogism: if the artist is able to represent madness and the mad cannot represent themselves, the artist is, therefore, not mad. The artist's capacity to represent madness necessarily divides him/her from the world of the insane.

Vincent, however, rejects this representational strategy and offers, instead, speech that does not clearly distinguish normal or mentally healthy linguistic patterns from the "bizarre" patterns of the mentally ill. Throughout the play, Frank, P.C. Woods, and Vincent's Mother address and respond to the unheard Vincent in ways that suggest their shared patterns of language. Even in his construction of the voice-overs, Watada characterizes Vincent through his use of imperatives, the same linguistic pattern evident in the dialogue of P.C. Woods and Frank. The only difference between the characters is the relative ambiguity of Vincent's impulse to speak compared with the obvious directedness of the others' imperatives. By collapsing the distinctions between the characters' respective speech patterns, Watada breaks from traditional representational strategies. Yet, while Watada does not distinguish Vincent's language as "bizarre" or linguistically unintelligible, he does limit the audience to a disembodied manifestation of his speech. Thus, by offering only limited access to Vincent's language, Watada passes over the mode of exteriority in favour of the play of negativity. He creates a space for audiences to listen to Vincent's silence rather than to some form of bizarre speech.

Whereas Vincent's aural presence is limited, visually he is wholly absent. Just as Watada's use of negativity avoids reifying stereotypes of schizophrenic speech, so his choice to imply Vincent's presence without providing visual cues also works to avoid stereotypical visual representations of madness. For examples of the stereotypes Watada sought to avoid, we may turn to Sander Gilman's *Picturing Health and Illness: Images of Identity and Difference.* Analysing a broad range of historical and contemporary illness illustrations, Gilman studies the visual depiction of people with a range of illnesses. He demonstrates links between these images of illness and cultural fantasies about illness. Using madness as a "test case" through which to assert the cultural influences on representation in medical iconography, Gilman discovers an arsenal of images that link mental illness with ugliness and sanity with beauty.[29] Where representation of somatic illness relied on physical signs, representation of mental illness has tended to rely on "'ugliness' [as] a symbolic reflection of the imagined inner state of the patient."[30] Examining images from medical literature, as well as high and popular art, Gilman contends that the currency of such images is founded upon their interdependence: "The images of 'health' and 'illness' thus employ a level of artistic intertextuality that is vital to any understanding of their impact. Art quotes art."[31] Refraining from such quotation, Watada asserts neither Vincent's beauty nor his ugliness. In so doing, he disallows the comfortable distance and exteriority afforded by clear visual distinctions between illness and health. The power of this disembodied representation derives from its refusal to accommodate the association of mental illness with ugliness through either acceptance or rejection.

In *Vincent*, Watada rejects linguistic and visual coherence, clarity, and wholeness in favour of ambiguity and seeks to alert the audience to Vincent's attenuated presence. He further challenges stereotypical representational modes that clearly mark the person with schizophrenia as Other, by spatially aligning the audience with Vincent's experience. The stage directions in *Vincent* construct the performance and audience spaces to emphasize Vincent's simultaneous presence and absence. In the WA productions, the audience is aligned with Vincent's disembodied but implied presence through the convention of having characters address Vincent as though he were in the audience's space. Each time the characters "step forward," they address Vincent. When they sit back in their chairs and the lights change, they explain their version of events to the audience or engage in dialogue with each other. For example:

> (*Frank enters stage and moves forward. He acts as if talking to Vincent.*)
> FRANK: Vince! Look at me when I'm talking to you. What is it with you? Your life's a mess ...
> (*Frank sits down again. Attention shifts to mother.*)
> MOTHER: I wanted to help him so much, but there was nothing I could do. I tried everything. Now I feel ... empty.
> (*Lights go to black*).[32]

Since the characters directly address the audience in two modes, the audience's alignment with Vincent is unstable. In the first mode, they are temporally positioned in the character's flashback encounter with Vincent and spatially aligned with Vincent's presence. In the second mode, the audience seems to share the same place and moment as the characters while they recollect events. Oscillating between these two temporal and spatial orders, the audience is aligned with Vincent's disembodied and silent presence only to be reminded subsequently of his absence. Through these aural, visual, and spatial instabilities, Watada engages the play of negativity.

While Watada's characterization of Vincent is explicitly organized not to reiterate cultural stereotypes about the appearance and linguistic patterns of people with schizophrenia, the question remains, what aspects of his character's "portrait" do emerge? To answer we may consider the many textual references that parallel Vincent with the painter Vincent Van Gogh. Until 2002, the poster design associated with the WA's productions of the play used Van Gogh's painting *La Nuit Étoilée* (1889) as background. Vincent's mother recalls taking him as a child to see a Van Gogh exhibition, which led to his fascination with the artist's work: "His favourite painting was *Starry Night*. He would have traced the swirls with his fingers if we let him! He liked the fact that his name was the same as Van Gogh's. He might of [sic] been a painter himself if he had the chance."[33] Frank also refers to Vincent's artistic ability. Finally, the use of Don McLean's song "Vincent (Starry, Starry Night)" in both the opening and closing scenes of the play draws a further parallel, as the song was written in honour of Van Gogh's own struggles with mental illness.

Beyond these allusions to Van Gogh, we could also explore the scenes in which Vincent's voice is implied by the dialogue of the other characters. In the scene two example mentioned earlier, it is clear that Vincent has explained that he has not taken prescribed medication for four months; in scene one, we see and hear Frank react angrily to Vincent's telling him that he bribed a baseball pitcher to let Frank have a home run. While such evidence is useful insofar as it alerts us to such character traits as obstinacy, independence, or duplicity, all such assertions of character emerge only in relief, mediated through the interpretation of other characters. Much of the play's action is thus predicated on Vincent's direct unknowability for the audience. Because it emerges in relief against the diegetic world physically introduced onstage, Watada's portrait ultimately seems less concerned with providing the details of Vincent's character than with stressing its ambiguities, limited accessibility, and attenuated expression.

To this point, my identification of negativity at play in *Vincent* has not explicitly addressed the particular institutional and historical circumstances that provided the opportunity and impetus for the play and shaped the range of audiences who attended its performances. WA Artistic Director Lisa Brown commissioned the play from Watada in 1993 to open a conference discussing forensic mental health issues in the wake of de-institutionalization. She suggested that Watada's use of negativity in *Vincent* was at least partially

influenced by his knowledge of this intended audience.[34] Watada was familiar with the company mandate and development processes. His play was
developed, therefore, in close consultation with artists familiar with mental
illness labels and experiences. Knowing that the play's original intended audience would include many individuals who would be either professionally or
personally familiar with a wide range of people with mental illnesses, the
playwright was keen to avoid stereotypes that would be rejected by those
familiar with lived experiences of being diagnosed with schizophrenia.

In June 1993, the Mental Health Centre Penetanguishene and the Ontario
Ministry of Health presented a conference in Midland, Ontario, called
Working with the Mentally Ill in a Post-Institutional Era. The conference
offered research and practical information for professionals working in the
forensic mental health system and criminal justice field. After discussions
with conference organizers, Brown had committed wa to giving a special
presentation on the opening night of the conference. Hoping to draw on
Watada's playwriting experience, as well as his familiarity with the wa's
objectives, she approached him to develop a script. The wa was then developing Watada's second play, Tale of a Mask, for production later in 1993.
While the presentation in Penetanguishene was as yet unspecified, it was
expected to engage issues relevant to the main questions of the conference.
In an era of mental health reform that was moving to a more community-
focused mental health system, conference organizers were keen to anticipate
changes in quality of care.[35] Most importantly, they wondered how offenders
diagnosed with mental illness would be affected by the structural reforms.
The professionals working in the forensic mental health system and criminal justice field who attended the Midland conference hoped to explore
two key questions in the wake of these reforms: "Can we anticipate vast
improvement in the quality of care and treatment in community-based settings, or will what we believe to be progress result in the further abandon-
ment of the severely mentally ill in our society? And how will mentally
disordered offenders be affected as we shift in focus and structure to a post-
institutional era?"[36]

Speakers at the conference included a police chief, social workers, police
officers, psychiatrists, psychologists, community health workers, a health
economist, psychiatric nurses, a criminal prosecutor, a Presbyterian minister, and the director of the mental health facilities of the Ontario Ministry
of Health. Although some of the keynote speakers were internationally
known experts in their various fields, most of the conference attendees were
local professionals familiar with Ontario's mental health system. As such,
most attendees of the conference were aware of the widely publicized

Toronto shooting of Dominic Sabatino, a tragic event that had captured public attention and focused local argument about the treatment, management, and individual rights of people diagnosed with schizophrenia living in the community.

That Watada knew of the public discussion related to the shooting and to changing health policies is evident from the over thirty newspaper articles clipped and noted in the *Vincent* production archives and the WA resource information for Penetanguishene. Lisa Brown was responsible for amassing much of this material, as she had a particular interest in the discussion. She had worked for many years with Sabatino in her former capacity as a psychiatric nurse at the Queen Street Mental Health Centre.[37] Many of the clippings are written upon and include Watada's marginalia, including his questions arising from the often extreme opinions expressed in the articles. While these opinions form a complicated debate, across the articles there is consensus on the order and immediate context of the actions that led to and included the shooting.

At the time of the shooting, Dominic Sabatino had had an eight-year history with schizophrenia and had stopped taking his medication approximately four months earlier. Prior to the shooting, he had lived in a series of hostels in downtown Toronto and he had been previously convicted of minor offences. Since his diagnosis of schizophrenia, he had been in and out of the Queen Street Mental Health Centre and the Mental Health Centre Penetanguishene more than fifteen times, usually not for more than fifteen or thirty days each time. On the day before the shooting, he had returned to the home of his mother and brother, Joe Sabatino, to request financial aid. After they refused him, Dominic returned the next day and chased his brother out of the house and down the street, swinging a baseball bat. At an intersection one kilometre from the family home, a police cruiser containing constables Peter Zemeckas, Kristine Brubacher, and James Davis cut Dominic off. Dominic smashed the cruiser with the bat and lunged at Brubacher, who carried a baton. At this point, Zemeckas shot Dominic in the upper body. Although he was rushed to hospital, Dominic died half an hour later.[38]

Beyond these basic actions, however, accounts of events varied, most notably in their assignation of blame for the tragedy. June Beeby, executive director of the Ontario Friends of Schizophrenics, blamed Ontario's mental health policies and diminished crisis services for severely ill people with schizophrenia. She advocated new laws that would compel people diagnosed with schizophrenia to take medication and authorize forced treatment in the event of non-compliance.[39] Steve Lurie, executive director of the Metropolitan Toronto Branch of the Canadian Mental Health Association, saw the event as "another example of the continuing difficulty of the authorities in dealing compassionately and effectively with the mentally ill." He advocated "training and support programs for police officers" that could be provided by the Canadian Mental Health Association.[40] Norm Gardner of the Metro Toronto Police Services Board advocated the use of pepper spray or oleoresin capsicum, substances which can debilitate suspects within five seconds but may not be lethal. In response, a *Toronto Star* editorial rejected the possible police use of pepper spray as "no substitute for qualities such as patience, common sense and discretion."[41] Many family members of people diagnosed with schizophrenia expressed frustration with mental health policies that prevented hospitalization except when individuals posed a clear danger to themselves or others, a proviso many found too vague for effective prevention of shootings such as Sabatino's.

For mental health workers at the maximum-security psychiatric institution in Penetanguishene and the other professionals invited to the Midland conference, Sabatino's shooting would have encapsulated several key concerns: the poverty attending de-institutionalization, the criminalization of the mentally ill, the problems for family and community care, the challenges of policing people with mental illnesses, and the question of forced medicalization outside of institutional care. Recognizing its centrality to the aims of the conference, Lisa Brown shared her collection of newspaper clippings and directed Watada's attention to Sabatino's death, as well as to the similar fatal Toronto police shooting of another man diagnosed with mental illness, Lester Donaldson.[42] As Watada explains in his notes, Brown suggested that a "play around the shooting of a schizophrenic outpatient by the police was timely."[43] For the conference attendees seeing the play, the parallels between Sabatino's death and the events depicted in *Vincent* would have been striking.

The initial production was successful in inspiring discussion about the conference and issues brought up in the play. Since its 1993 debut at the Midland conference, the WA has regularly remounted *Vincent* for a range of different audiences. Originally directed by Ines Buchli, the first production starred Tom Free, Denise Naples, and Jeff Clarke. *Vincent* went on to tour provincially, inter-provincially, and internationally, playing in a range of mental-health care facilities, professional theatres, and community centres.[44]

A panel discussion has followed most performances of *Vincent*. The specific individuals who have comprised the panel have varied, but it has usually included a police officer, a close relative of someone diagnosed with schizophrenia, a community-outreach worker, a mental health care professional, and as often as possible, someone who has been diagnosed with schizophrenia. The company has recorded most of these discussions and they provide a valuable opportunity to consider the range of responses to the performance. This range and the volume of discussion suggest the play's power to focus attention on the contemporary experience of schizophrenia.

Across the panels, several issues emerged as common themes for questions and discussion. Addressing the clinical background of and social stigma attached to mental illness and schizophrenia, panellists and audience members discussed the degree to which violence occurs among people diagnosed with schizophrenia; the diagnosis, causes, symptoms, onset, prognosis, and possibility for relapse of schizophrenia; the percentage of the people with mental illnesses within the general population; the types of medication available and their relation to earlier forms of medication; the impact of culture and ethnicity on mental illness; and patterns of denial and non-compliance with medication among people diagnosed with schizophrenia. With regard to the violence associated with the victim's behaviour and with the police response, questions were asked about how police de-escalate violent situations; how many police officers typically are involved in any such situation; what the appropriate means are to defuse such situations and whether the police have the right to shoot; what the police shoot at and whether they shoot to kill; and how much danger the violence of a mentally ill individual poses for the average citizen. Participants commented on the need for dialogue between the police and people with mental illnesses; on the importance of a consensus in defining the situation; and on the use of other professionals by the police. With respect to the impact of schizophrenia on families, questions focused on the fear, pain, lack of awareness, and state of denial of the families; on access to services; on the failure to reach out for support; and on the family's right to have siblings/children receive treatment. Others asserted the freedom of choice of people diagnosed with schizophrenia and pointed out the effect of dysfunctional families on such individuals.

Questions for the medical community, mental health community, and police focused on the qualities of professional behaviour. Asking about professional barriers or limitations, many suggested that budget cuts were having significant impacts and that greater financial support was needed from the government. Others discussed the legal implications of treatment, the need for more research into mental health care concerns, the inadequacy of legislation guaranteeing people with schizophrenia freedom of choice, the lack of coordination between social and police services, the lack of advocacy and mental health promotion in government, the stasis of systemic services, and the need for more mobile crisis teams.

In response to criticism levied against professionals, many panellists and audience members suggested that police were not to be blamed, as many already worked with clinical teams; a twenty-four-hour crisis line, a self-help group, and a drop-in centre were all available; efforts were being made to look for other possible forms of intervention; services were being developed; other alternatives were being explored; and steps were being taken to resolve crises. Some participants criticized the professionalism of the police, describing them as authoritarian; others suggested that the media sought to embarrass police. With reference to the police-training program, many suggested that police needed more sensitivity, humanity, and understanding of the experience of being mentally ill. Many wished there had been a stronger process probing the shooting.

Because part of the WA mandate is to promote public awareness of mental health problems and related issues, the show's initial success and that of its subsequent remounts was partially measured by the community discussion and education generated by these post-performance panels. While it is impossible to attribute most of these questions to specific individuals, particularly in the case of those questions raised by anonymous audience members, the records of post-performance questions give some sense of the production's effects. With an average of ten questions and at least half an hour of audience and panel discussion following each show, the sheer volume of these responses suggests *Vincent*'s power to solicit further inquiry and to focus community discussion on problems related to schizophrenia. Such power may be taken as evidence for the negativity at play in the text itself.

Iser and Budick draw our attention to negativity as a threshold at which something begins its presencing. However, to offer the post-panel discussions as evidence of negativity within the text, we must account for the real, contextualized presence of audience members in reception. Did performances of *Vincent* highlight the presence of the unsayable by drawing audience attention to its absence? The conflicting interpretations of Vincent's figure within the play offered by Bob Rose and the unknown audience member are evidence of the possibility of multiple readings. So, too, the extensive questioning and discussion *Vincent* generated for the post-performance panels suggest its power to encourage a multifaceted investigation of mental illness. In his avoidance of cultural stereotypes about mental illness, Watada does not build on what is known about the experience of what has been labelled schizophrenia. Rather, he focuses attention on the barriers to such knowing. Iser and Budick stress negativity's power to transform, to make us aware of an "absence of which we would not otherwise know anything."[45] Bob Rose's wish to hear more of Vincent's own voice suggests that the production encouraged greater listening to a language of the unsayable.

CHAPTER EIGHT

Disruptive Spaces: The Clinic

SOPHIA LOREN: Stop the stupid questions.

CLEOPATRA: I can't. We need to determine your worth as a sexual being.

SOPHIA LOREN: My worth?

CLEOPATRA: To see if the accident has affected your sexual worth.

SOPHIA LOREN: Why?

CLEOPATRA: To calculate the monetary worth of the sexual experiences you will never have because of the accident.

SOPHIA LOREN: I don't think I can do this …

CLEOPATRA: Oh please, I was 15 and had no choice. Get tough Cookie Lady![1]

How do clinicians determine "sexual worth?" By contrast, how do individuals? What assumptions about disability and impairment underlie an idea like "sexual worth?" These questions informed the dramaturgical process behind Theatre Terrific's 2009 production of *The Glass Box* in Vancouver and Victoria, British Columbia. In the play, actors Kyla Harris, Watson Choy, and Theatre Terrific artistic director Susanna Uchatius each played the role of a sexual icon: Cleopatra, Brad Pitt, and Sophia Loren, respectively. In the framework of a celebrity game show, the characters tried to win points by answering private questions about their sexual experiences, attitudes, inhibitions, and aspirations. In a neatly defined cube of clear onstage light, they opened themselves up in the "glass boxes" of clinical encounters and celebrity tell-alls, an ever-present three ring binder onstage providing the clinical questions that linked the two spheres (see Fig 8.1). Many of the questions in the binder were ones Harris had actually had to answer for insurance claim purposes when, at 15, she had become paraplegic following a diving accident on a school trip.

While actual clinical questions formed the primary framing device in *The Glass Box*, a clinical experience of a different kind provided the critical background for the company's second major 2009 production, *The Secret Son*. In

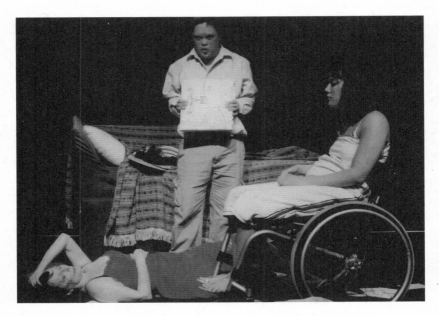

8.1
Theatre Terrific's *The Glass Box*, 2009.

the lobby area outside the performance space, the company invited audiences to read material about Southbury Training School, a state-funded Connecticut institution built in the 1930s as a residential facility for people with "mental retardation" which is currently run by the Connecticut Department of Developmental Services.[2] This display drew from public criticism of the institution to highlight the conditions of patients' lives over time. It referred, for example, to a legal action pursued in 1984 by plaintiffs alleging civil rights violations against patients at Southbury. To connect the clinical settings explored and criticized in the display with the production itself, however, audiences needed to have either encountered its promotional materials or read the program. In each of these contexts the company explained the link between their play and the institution: Southbury Training School was where Daniel Miller – the son with Down syndrome whom they assert playwright Arthur Miller publicly disavowed through most of his life – lived from the early 1970s to the early 1980s.

The Secret Son wove together several narrative threads. One followed the story of a fictional author, explicitly not Miller but a bespectacled, articulate, white, male playwright interested in re-imagining classical tragedy nonethe-

8.2

Theatre Terrific's *The Secret Son*, 2009.

less, who sat centre with a typewriter on the uppermost level of the stage (see Fig. 8.2). From this perch, he tapped out the events of an invented classical tragedy loosely based on the Agamemnon and Oedipus myths. These events were enacted below by the 12 other cast members. The final thread that encircled all of this, however, was the complicated, controversial, and puzzling relationship between Arthur and Daniel Miller, which was introduced in the lobby display, promotional material, and program.

With the tag line "The Story Arthur Miller Didn't Want Told," *The Secret Son* invoked Miller's own decisions regarding Daniel. Playwright Susanna Uchatius explained what inspired her to weave these threads together: "I was reading Ted Hughes' translation of *Agamemnon*, a rich, poetic, Greek tragedy of family horror. The same day I picked up a copy of *Vanity Fair* magazine. Therein, was the most astounding tale of one of the world's greatest playwrights, Arthur Miller. His last child, Daniel, was born with Down syndrome. Miller refused to accept him as a son and insisted, against his wife's wishes, to have him institutionalized, effectively erasing him from his life. The striking similarity of these two powerful men to value their public honour over their own flesh and blood was a lightning bolt."[3] Uchatius, herself a mother of a child with developmental disabilities, was driven to explore the moment in which Miller decided against having Daniel live in his home in favor of placing him in an institution. For her, the moment had echoes of several themes from Classical tragedy, notably pride, honour, and family sacrifice.[4]

In her *Vanity Fair* article, Suzanna Andrews argues that Arthur Miller did not mention Daniel "in the scores of speeches and press interviews he gave over the years. He also never referred to him in his 1987 memoir, *Timebends*. In 2002, Daniel was left out of the *New York Times* obituary for Miller's wife, the photographer Inge Morath, who was Daniel's mother." The article also cites the general lack of attention paid to Daniel in the obituaries following Miller's own death.[5] *The Secret Son* begins with this apparent disavowal. Uchatius was frustrated by the lack of critical attention paid to Miller's decisions regarding Daniel both during the playwright's lifetime and after. She believes Miller would have "had the skills and resources to maintain a connection with Daniel and yet something made him stop. Did this child make him feel less than?"[6] This separation of father and son and the public erasure of Daniel from Miller's life are what interested Uchatius and the ensemble of Theatre Terrific performers who helped develop the project.

The Secret Son begins with the name "Arthur Miller" spoken by the anonymous author sitting in front of his typewriter atop steps above the main performance space. The author goes on to list key dates in the playwright's life: "Author: Arthur Miller. Remarkable. Born 1915. 1938: Marries. 1947: Tony. 1949: Pulitzer. 1953: another Tony. 1955: *Death of a Salesman* has been playing non-stop somewhere for the past 59 years. *All My Sons*, not as much. Sons. Fathers and Sons."[7] At this moment, a young male actor playing the character of Daniel, begins to slap a ball into his glove repeatedly as he softly sings of ballgames. The author reasserts himself, shouting, "Miller," and continues with his list, "Author. 1956: Marilyn Monroe. 1961: divorces. 1962: Marries Austrian photographer Inge Morath. Rebecca is born. 1966, [Pause]. 1966: No entry. Nothing remarkable in 1966. No bumps, no ripples. Nothing. Chorus: (whisper) Shhhhhhhhhhh."[8]

Thus, the year of Daniel's birth is hushed in this account. While he remains visible onstage for the rest of the play, moving with the chorus and often in tandem with another actor, the character of Daniel does not hold centre stage again until the play's end. The play within the play has come to its tragic conclusion, the death of all the noble family members, and the author exclaims triumphantly, "It's finished!" The stage darkens except for a spotlight on Daniel who pounds his baseball mitt and declares, "I'm not finished. I'm here. My name is Daniel Miller. I'm 42 years old. I love you Dad."[9] The moralizing tone of the production is therefore not light nor is its allusion to Miller's own choices indirect.

Both of these productions clearly drew from a critical perspective on clinical encounters involving disability. I would like to explore these encounters in the context of this particular company's attempt to re-imagine the clinical encounter in ways that subvert and question medical authority as well as disability stereotypes. While *The Glass Box* seeks to highlight normative assumptions behind particular clinical questions about sexuality, *The Secret Son* confronts and re-imagines the place of disability in tragedy, casting Miller as a misguided tragic figure who fell when he consigned Daniel to a separate life in an institution. Although they do so differently, both productions create space for artists with disabilities to "speak back" to the medical model of disability which informed the actual clinical encounter.

Many people living with disabilities routinely negotiate critical questions of privacy, identity, personal agency, and quality of life through clinical encounters. Indeed, disability studies scholar Lennard J. Davis argues that people with impairments have been "isolated, incarcerated, observed, written about, operated on, instructed, implanted, regulated, treated, institutionalized, and controlled to a degree probably unequal to that experienced by any other minority group."[10] In a similar vein, disability scholar Helen Meekosha argues that it is the "impaired body that is medically, technologically and culturally disciplined."[11] As we noted earlier, a growing disability studies discourse seeks to uncover and challenge the ideology of ability that has thus far informed clinical negotiations and the medical model in which they are rooted. Given the ubiquity of clinical encounters in the lived experience of disability, it is not surprising that many Canadian disability theatre artists have explored them in their work, from Workman Arts' *Tripping Through Time* to Friendly Spike Theatre's *Angels of 999* to MoMo's *The Matilda Stewart Show*.

Theatre Terrific's productions of *The Secret Son* and *The Glass Box* also turned on problems associated with actual clinical encounters. In each case the encounter suggested a node where the regulatory systems which construct disability affect the artists' lives. Although the premise for *The Glass Box* was connected to actor and visual artist Kyla Harris' personal experience, it is one that would resonate for many women with disabilities. In their analysis, Catherine Frazee, Joanne Gilmour, and Roxanne Mykitiuk explain the ways in which law shapes disabled women's experience in the clinical encounter: "For many women with disabilities, the clinical encounter is not an experience of privacy or trust, nor one in which information about their conditions and needs is truly heard. Rather, the gaze of the health-care professionals is often focused exclusively on the impairment, reinforcing a medical model of disability that locates disablement within the individual. This is not to suggest that the material reality of embodiment should be ignored in the health-care encounter, but, in this context, it needs to be situated and understood within the broader social, economic, and political landscape that constructs disablement."[12] While *The Glass Box* plays with questions drawn from the clinical encounter, Harris also situates these in a broader context of disablement. She is particularly concerned in her artworks to challenge pervasive representations of people with disabilities as asexual. She has described feeling frustrated at having to field the question, "can you have sex?" routinely from strangers: "It's appalling, hurtful, and intrusive, but I try to muster my patience because if they can learn something from me, then hopefully they'll not be as ignorant and curious next time. I explain that just because I am in a wheelchair doesn't mean I am no longer a sexual being. Yes, I can have sex."[13]

Following a workshop they did together, Uchatius and Harris had a conversation about disability and sexuality that inspired them to create the play.[14] The play was not the first artistic exploration of disability and sexuality undertaken by Harris. In 2007 she had worked with photographer Sarah Murray to create an exhibit called "Access Sex" which was shown in Toronto and Vancouver. The playwriting experience was new, however, and Harris found the process took her surprisingly "close to the bone," as they began by writing about themselves and using their own stories to create characters who each take a journey through sexuality in the play.[15] In the invitation to the public reading of the play as part of the 2008 Magnetic North Festival in Vancouver, this element of personal disclosure was promoted. "Inspired by the true life and sex stories of the performers. *The Glass Box* blends and refracts the experiences and perceptions of three disparate, sexually active people: a 55 year-old, straight, able-bodied woman, on the verge of a latent but powerful sexual awakening, a 23 year-old woman in a wheelchair, in full ownership of her bisexuality and a 38 year old Downs syndrome man who has a fully satisfying, albeit solo, sex life."[16] Thus, although each actor played a sexual icon, each also told intimate stories connected to their own sexual experiences and ideas.

The eclectic mix of individuals sharing such personal stories is suggestive of the company's commitment to showing "diversity in action."[17] Rather than offer a solo performance in which a single actor speaks and performs his or her own story, the company's aesthetic tends toward explorations of more universal themes – sexuality in this case – which incorporate a range of perspectives drawn from lived disability experience. This strategy has ties with an emerging scholarship concerning disability and sexuality which holds, as Michael A. Rembis argues, that "a multiplicity of voices will be needed to rearticulate and reconceptualize (dis/abled) sexualities."[18] In *The Glass Box*, the question was not limited to "can you have sex?" Rather, each performer answered the question of how they have sex, how they have had sex, and what they wish they could change in response to both questions. Each also connected his or her experiences to the sexual icons with whom they wanted most to identify. Countering their own stories with those of sexual icons provided the characters with useful foils; if not being seen as sexual beings is a struggle for some people with disabilities, then being seen as icons of hypersexuality is often the lot of celebrity figures. Harris' impersonations of the sexually powerful Cleopatra contrasted sharply with her extremely vulnerable telling of her first sexual encounter with a boyfriend. This story included a poignant moment in which her mother came in briefly from a nearby room to help with a catheter as Harris suddenly had to pee. It also offered a hilarious account of her surprises concerning the actual mechanics of having sex. This mixture of comic and serious tones ran through the entire sixty-minute show. In another amusing scene, Cleopatra used the binder to outline the "Rules for Dating in Rehab," text that played once again on her own clinical experiences: "Rule 1. Dating starts with self-confidence. Don't let your new interest keep you from your regular physical and occupational therapy sessions. Remember a new relationship will allow you to show your abilities. Don't aim low but be realistic about your chances."[19] In the context of the play, those actual clinical discourses were demonstrated as absurd and comic. This was nowhere more evident than in Cleopatra's questioning of Sophia Loren: "Are you able to reach orgasm? … Up to this point, can you show me a graph of the height of your orgasm?" Playing up the ridiculousness of charting sexual experience in this way was one strategy of undermining a clinical discourse that measures sexual experience against standards of "normal" human function. This strategy of sharing, comparing, and contrasting the three disparate characters' sexual experiences demonstrated the vast range of nuanced sexual perception and activity that gets missed by such measures and questionnaires.

Critiques of clinical practice from a disability studies perspective often interrogate the idea of normal at play in the kinds of clinical standards and calculations taken up in *The Glass Box*. Rosemarie Garland-Thomson has coined the term "normate" to suggest the figure constructed in contrast to the disabled person "through which people can represent themselves as definitive human beings."[20] In his investigation of the medical case narrative from a disability studies perspective, Leonard Cassuto suggests that the standards, measurements, and quantifications generated by clinical practice contribute to the reified vision of Garland-Thomson's "normate." To explain this connection, he links the term to the rise of clinical practice in the twentieth century: "Centred on 'the gaze' – in this instance the hierarchical scrutiny of the patient by the doctor – clinical medicine quickly standardized and quantified this objectifying, 'calculating' practice. As new diagnostic hardware was invented in the early twentieth century, precise measurement became standard in medical education, consultation and practice ... This collection of averages created a quantifiable idea of the normal."[21] As Cassuto suggests, clinical practice may be interrogated as part of a broader social system that informs the "normate" or, as Lennard Davis argued above, enforces normalcy by regulating its other. For Davis, it is a system that has "ended up segregating and ostracizing [individuals with impairments] through the discursivity of disability."[22] *The Secret Son* production cast Daniel Miller's experience at Southbury Training School as a concrete example of the segregation and ostracization that Davis describes.

While *The Glass Box* invoked specific clinical interpellations to undermine their authority and highlight their place in an ideology of ability, *The Secret Son* did not introduce any clinics or clinical encounters onstage. In fact, the idea of the clinic and its role in Daniel's segregation from his father and family life framed the production chiefly through the lobby display and other supporting materials noted earlier. Apart from Daniel Miller's fictional shout to his father at the play's end, there were no enactments of specific scenarios drawn from Miller's family history either. Instead, the play explored traditional aesthetic and social norms at play in canonical Western tragedy from a disability theatre perspective.

The Secret Son took up both of the goals that Tobin Siebers, as we saw in Chapter 6, has argued drive disability aesthetics: (1) to establish disability as

a critical framework that questions the presuppositions underlying definitions of aesthetic production and appreciation; (2) to establish disability as a
significant value in itself worthy of future development."[23] In the first vein,
the production invited audiences to consider how Western tragedy has long
invoked disability to achieve its effects. Few plays are more central in the
Western theatre canon than those of Aeschylus' *Oresteia*, Sophocles' *Oedipus
Rex*, and Arthur Miller's dramatic oeuvre. Weaving narrative threads from
these works, *The Secret Son* investigates connections between western tragedy
and the ideology of ability. How might both be denaturalized and examined
for their "blueprints?" After first invoking Miller's decisions concerning
Daniel, the play follows the fictional playwright's creative process; as "The
Author" writes "The House of Seikilos" (a play within the play he composes
from above), a disruptive chorus challenges his artistic choices, particularly
as they relate to the place of disability in the narrative. Through these
metatheatrical features, *The Secret Son* considers tragic form to emphasize
how plays are imagined, constructed, and thus remain open to deconstruc-
tion and re-imagination from a disability theatre perspective.

Like *Oedipus Rex*, "The House of Seikilos" turns on a past event involving
disability with tragic consequences.[24] Where Sophocles' Oedipus was left as a
baby to die on a hillside with impaired feet, the Oracle in "The House of Seikilos" explains that the General's current failures in battle are due to his failure
to comply sixteen years earlier with an edict that "All malformed babies / On
day of birth / By father's hand / Their blood must flow / Or all battles / To
the enemy go."[25] To avoid the pain of infanticide, the General had banished
his baby boy born with leg impairments and tricked his wife into believing
their servant's unimpaired baby girl was their own. Years later, this daughter
is about to turn sixteen and the General brings an artist from a conquered
village back to his palace to paint her portrait. This artist, played by an
actor in a wheelchair, is eventually revealed as the lost son. Like Aeschylus's
Agamemnon who sacrificed his daughter Iphigenia to secure sailing winds
for his fleet, the General feels pressure to sacrifice his child and comply with
the Oracle in order to secure victory for his flailing army. Like Agamemnon's
wife, Clytemnestra, the General's wife feels betrayed by his actions. Ultimately, and as is so often the case in tragedy, when the truth of the artist's
identity emerges at the climax it is too late to prevent disaster; all in the noble
family are dead, leaving a final tableau of death and destruction. It is against
this tableau that the Author shouts triumphantly from above, "It's finished!"[26] In this production, his elation contrasts sharply with the misery
onstage. Further, his sense of triumph is undermined by Daniel Miller's last

words insisting that he is not finished. Tragedy here is demonstrated as a form that strains to resolve the problems it raises through excessive violence and false endpoints.

Using some of the most familiar tropes and features of tragedy, the production was particularly concerned with reconsidering the place of disability in the form. Its work thus contributes to a growing body of scholarship and theatre practice that interrogates and re-imagines the place of disability in Western theatre. In the influential *American Theatre* 2001 article "We are not a metaphor," Victoria Ann Lewis – in conversation with Kathleen Tolan and a host of leading disability theatre practitioners and scholars – invited all theatre artists to engage creatively with the lived experience of disability rather than use the tired metaphors "shaped by the old cautionary and sentimental models of representation [that] have filled the stage for generations, from the stigmatized Oedipus and Richard III to Tiny Tim, the special child who manifests innocence and goodness in the world." [27] Failing to challenge such metaphors, they argue, perpetuates cultural stigma surrounding disability and inhibits more meaningful engagement with specific lived experiences of disability. Disabled figures abound in Western tragedy and Lewis has further argued that these types of characters have typically illustrated "the 'moral' or religious model of disability depiction, in which the physically different body is explained by an act of divine or demonic intervention." [28] Disability in these cases is mobilized theatrically as a fateful or symbolic tragic flaw or fated tragic endpoint, tropes that persistently charge disability with moral meanings. By contrast, however, as in the case of Realwheels' *Skydive*, *The Secret Son* complicates the idea of disability as an unquestioned metaphor in tragedy. As Carrie Sandahl has noted, disability theatre does not insist that theatre avoid disability as a metaphor altogether. [29] Indeed, in an art form in which things introduced onstage are arguably ineluctably read as signs for something else, such a proposition would seem to miss the form's chief creative opportunities. Rather, the call is for fresher metaphors that engage more fully with the complexity and range of disability experience.

The Secret Son did not include disabled characters as single-note metaphors for innocence, evil, or something else. Rather, disabled characters were multidimensional and active on stage. The character of the artist, for example, had racy love scenes, debate scenes with the General, scenes that highlighted his visual art and musical talents, and a moving recognition scene with his mother. The character of Daniel spoke the details of his specific biography and also joined the chorus as it moved about the stage to observe and critique the Author's play. In each of the narrative threads, disability experience was included as part of a broader investigation of family, art, and tragedy.

Casting choices, as in most disability theatre, were pivotal in this work.[30] Like most Theatre Terrific productions, the performance ensemble comprised artists with a wide range of disabilities. While the cast also included a few non-disabled actors, disabled actors took the critical roles of the artist and Daniel. Thus, the layers of narrative did not examine disability experience in a single register or through a single figure but rather through a poly-vocal layering of diverse perspectives. The critical role of the chorus was performed by actors with a diverse range of disabilities and abilities. Like the People with Disabilities (PWD) who spoke back to stigmatizing and dehumanizing narratives about disability in *Mercy Killing or Murder: The Tracy Latimer Story*, the chorus in *The Secret Son* continually challenged the Author as he wrote his tragedy from on high. Their commentaries and attitudes added a metatheatrical dimension to the work, inviting audiences to reflect on how the playwright used disability to build his tragedy. In this way, the diverse ensemble served as a counterpoint to the production's framing of Southbury Training School and the processes of social segregation and ostracization that, they argued, it suggests. It offered a counter-discourse in which people with a range of disabilities were competent actors and interpolating agents on a public stage.

Carrie Sandahl has distinguished new disability theatre plays as those which aim to "explore the lived experience of disability" rather than follow more traditional patterns of using "disability as a metaphor for nondisabled people's sense of outsiderness."[31] Following this rubric, both *The Secret Son* and *The Glass Box* contribute to new disability theatre by grounding themselves in the lived perspectives of people with disabilities. More specifically, both plays created opportunities for disability artists to speak back to the ideology of ability at play in the clinical encounter. Each drew from an actual clinical experience but expanded upon it to incorporate a range of disability artists' creative responses. The clinical questions in the binder were asked of each character in *The Glass Box* to demonstrate how such questions assume an idea of normal sexuality that misses the richness of experience shared onstage. The references to Daniel Miller's experience at Southbury Training School that framed *The Secret Son* invited audiences to brush common features of western tragedy against the grain. *The Secret Son* explored tragedy from a disability theatre perspective, unsettling a longstanding western aesthetic tradition in which disability is used ubiquitously as a signifier for something else, a metaphor for innocence or brokenness, for example, or the uncomplicated evidence of a tragic end. Interweaving narrative elements from canonical western tragedies, casting a connection between these and the ideas at play in the Miller family's history with Southbury Training School, the production queries the relationship of tragedy and the clinic. What role does theatre play in shaping ideas about disability experience? What blue-prints does it provide that permit a society to build edifices and rationales for the segregation and ostracization of people with disabilities? How might including disability artists' voices in these narratives challenge such blue-prints, unsettle the ideology of ability at play in clinical encounters, and re-imagine disability as a valued human condition?

CHAPTER NINE

Performing Paralympia

This book was completed in large part during the excited atmosphere of the 2010 Vancouver Winter Olympic and Paralympic Games, an event which more than any previous Canadian games highlighted disability in sport and society. The association originated in 2006 when, from his wheelchair, Vancouver mayor Sam Sullivan accepted and waved the flags during the Olympic and (a month later) Paralympic closing ceremonies in Turin, Italy (see Fig. 9.1). The optics of these ceremonies and Sullivan's address created enormous attention internationally and raised the expectation that the Vancouver games might engage with disability at a new and heightened level. Unlike Calgary, which did not host the Winter Paralympic Games along with its 1988 Winter Olympic Games, Vancouver hosted both in sequence using largely the same venues. Rick Hansen, world-renowned disabled athlete and philanthropist, carried the torch in both the Olympic and Paralympic opening ceremonies. Although CTV, the official Canadian broadcaster, planned not to air the latter ceremonies live, a storm of public criticism reversed the decision, at least for the local market.

Alongside the athletes' performances ran a whole series of cultural events with a strong showing of disability art. As in prior games, a cultural Olympiad paralleled the preparations and events, featuring work of local and international artists with disabilities and disability artists. Starting in 2002, the province of BC also partially financed a 2010 Legacies Now program, an independent nonprofit organization aimed at "strengthening arts, literacy, sport and healthy living, accessibility and volunteerism in communities across BC leading up to, and beyond, the 2010 Olympic and Paralympic Winter Games."[1] Money from this source supported numerous disability and arts initiatives. Attending the many events sponsored by the Cultural Olympiad and Legacies Now in the city, I found it difficult not to reflect upon the connections between art and sport, as well as the relationship between disability theatre and mainstream productions that took up disability themes. If these games were going to be different, if Vancouver was an active centre of disability theatre in the country, then how would things play out at this particular and unusual moment?

After investigating the many theatre companies and artists for this book, I wondered more particularly how disability would be put on stage. Research had demonstrated the growing momentum of disability theatre in the country but had also highlighted differences between groups and practices and underlined the fact that in most cases disability theatre practice continued to be a struggle and a political challenge. The games atmosphere did not alter this sense. It was a challenging time for many local disability artists who had not supported the city's hosting of the games and sought to protest what they saw as government cuts to critical social programs in favour of spending on the games. Further, the Paralympic Opening Ceremonies theme of "One Inspires Many" and mainstream media's focus on narratives of superheroes and personal overcoming in their Paralympic coverage produced feelings of unease and conflict among disability artists who wanted to celebrate the athletes but also push for an expanded set of narratives to complicate these worn and problematic standards. Although it is a rich field for further study, it is not my purpose here to look at all the contradictions and controversies at play in the Paralympic Games. Instead, I would like to consider how the watershed moment of Canada's first shared hosting of the Olympic and Paralympic Games also produced a critical moment through which to reflect on disability theatre practice in the country. It was a time in which theatre and disability intersected in both generative and problematic ways, the latter most notably in relation to striking choices in three productions from Vancouver's 2009–10 theatre season: *The Miracle Worker, Rick: The Rick Hansen Story*, and *Spine*. Read together, these choices suggest important dimensions of the contemporary social and artistic space of Canadian disability theatre practice.

The October 2009 run of the Vancouver Playhouse's mainstage production of William Gibson's *The Miracle Worker* (see Fig. 9.2) preceded the

9.1
Vancouver Mayor Sam Sullivan flies the Paralympic
flag during the closing ceremony of the 2006 Winter
Paralympics in Turin.

games by several months. Although it was not affiliated with the Cultural
Olympiad, the decision by BC's premier regional not-for-profit professional
theatre to run *The Miracle Worker* – a play redolent with themes of overcoming, perseverance, hope, and inspiration – helped it fit in with a city
increasingly wrapped in the rhetoric of Olympic and Paralympic inspiration.

9.2

The Miracle Worker, Vancouver Playhouse, 2009

The production promoted the tagline, "before she touched the world, some-one touched her," and recounted the story of famed teacher Annie Sullivan's earliest encounters with Helen Keller and her family. Both Helen and Annie, in William's play as in the women's real-life history, have disabilities, yet in this production, neither role was performed by an actor with a visual or hear-ing impairment. The choice was not unusual in the sense that it merely repeated the trend evident in the play's production history: in 1959 Patti Duke and Anne Bancroft played the Broadway roles, respectively, of Helen and Annie, and reprised these in the 1962 film version, performances for which both actors won Oscars. The Playhouse's casting choices also anticipated the controversial casting of non-disabled young film star Abigail Breslin as Helen Keller in the 2010 Broadway revival.

Interestingly, while in New York, the October 2009 announcement of Bres-lin's casting was met with an outcry from the Alliance for Inclusion in the Arts, an advocacy group seeking full diversity in the arts, and the story prompted articles exploring the controversy in the *New York Times*, review-ers from Vancouver's major dailies and weeklies did not raise the issue at all.[2] Further, while the New York production ultimately hired 10-year old visu-ally-impaired actor Kyra Ynez Siegel to be Breslin's understudy – either because they had always planned to do so or responded to public pressure – neither of the talented young women hired to play Helen at the Vancouver Playhouse, Margot Berner and Emma Grabinsky, claimed to have a disabil-ity.[3] By all accounts, both were remarkably strong actors and together they were nominated for the prestigious local Jessie Richardson Theatre Award "Outstanding Performance by an Actress in a Lead Role, Large Theatre." Another actor in the production, Jennifer Clements, also received praise for her turn as Helen's mother, Kate Keller. In a talkback session following one of the evening productions, an audience member asked Clements about how her experience differed from her 1993 Richmond Gateway Theatre perform-ance as Annie Sullivan. Clements remarked that she has since become a mother and this shaped her understanding of Kate Keller in new ways. Life experience had added an enriching dimension to how she would approach her work in this enduring and popular play. It is striking that the public dis-course surrounding the Vancouver production did not query the absence of people with visual and/or hearing impairments in its casting choices, partic-ularly in a city with a lively disability arts scene and in which people with disabilities have been mayor (Sam Sullivan) and local heroes (Rick Hansen, Terry Fox). In New York, protests were led by the Alliance for Inclusion in the Arts but in Vancouver, local disability arts organizations became involved with the production from a different angle.

That the production continued a longstanding pattern of reviving tried and true plays with central disabled characters and casting talented non-disabled actors who could turn in praise-worthy work is not in itself remarkable. The more uncommon features of this production's run were its efforts to support audiences with vision and hearing impairments. Two evenings featured ASL Sign Interpreted Performances, something not entirely new on the Vancouver scene. But what was more groundbreaking was that the company partnered with the Canadian National Institute of the Blind (CNIB) and Kickstart to provide audio description (AD) services free of charge to audiences who called in advance to reserve them. The media call for the 17 October event, which also included a Gala and balcony fundraising party and auction in support of the Playhouse and CNIB, explained the significance: "For the first time in British Columbia, this performance will feature descriptive audio services, enabling people with vision loss to listen through headphones to a narrative description of what is happening on stage. With this event, Kickstart Disability Arts and Culture, Canada's pioneering disability arts organization, is launching *SeeHearNow*, a service which enables people with vision loss to take in the set, lighting, costumes and physical action along with the rest of the audience."[4] Beginning in 2008, Kickstart had decided that it would lead the introduction and practice of AD in Vancouver and Canada. Citing many positive responses from participants at *The Miracle Worker*, Kickstart provided further AD during other Cultural Olympiad events and, in September 2010, "launched the first full season of live Audio Described theatre in Canada (under the name EarSighted), partnering once again with the Vancouver Playhouse and 4 other theatres, describing 15 productions in Metro Vancouver, Richmond and North Vancouver."[5] As one positive review by Linda Weber cited on Kickstart's website explained, "Most importantly, the AD allows me the independence and choice to attend a live theatre production without having to rely on a sighted companion."[6] Thus, instead of publicly challenging casting and artistic production choices in *The Miracle Worker*, the organization embraced a partnership with the Playhouse and, later, other professional theatres, to promote better accessibility for patrons with visual impairments.

The choice illuminates one of the key questions facing disability theatre practice in Canada at this moment: what should accessibility mean in theatre? Building more opportunities for audience members with disabilities to witness theatre – mainstream, disability, or otherwise – is an important step in generating a critically-engaged, informed, and invested audience and artistic community. While disability theatres have often been proactive in addressing accessibility issues, disability themes and disabled characters are ubiquitous in contemporary mainstream theatre practice and it is strange that people with disabilities are so often unable to participate in these productions because of inaccessible theatre architectures, scenographies, programming, and pricing. To borrow phrasing from theatre phenomenologist Bert O. States, if there are to be so many great reckonings about disability in commercial, popular, and mainstream theatre rooms, it is imperative that people with disabilities be able to access and respond critically to these stories, interpretations, and performances.[7] Moreover, this kind of access, engagement, and investment in theatre of varying kinds (disability activist or not) may be critical for fomenting an interest in theatre practice among potential artists with disabilities. In this respect, Kickstart's decision to partner with the Playhouse and promote AD in a major, professional, regional theatre space is an important step toward inclusion. Although the program was not launched in conjunction with disability theatre, it did afford blind and vision-impaired audience members an important opportunity to engage more fully with a well-known play about a disabled heroine that has drawn audiences for fifty years and provided star-turns for well-known non-disabled actors. Allowing patrons with disabilities to increase their familiarity with this kind of performance tradition is certainly worthwhile. The challenge will be to make sure that these inclusive practices for theatre audiences do not depend on full endorsement of the participating companies' artistic production practices. It will be important that initiatives like this keep momentum even if they lead to heated public discussion of inclusive casting choices or inclusive hiring practices in general.

The issue of accessibility brings us back to the quote from Rick Hansen with which I began this book: "You can get into theatres now, but can you also get on stage?" Initiatives like Kickstart's for disabled audience members are important but, Hansen reminds us, holding the stage is critical. For this reason, the second problematic instance from the games where theatre and disability intersected relates to the production: *Rick: The Rick Hansen Story* (see Fig. 9.3). In 2007 the Rick Hansen Foundation approached the Manitoba Theatre Centre to create a show about Hansen's life for the 2010 Cultural Olympiad. The show's study guide explains the rest of the development process over its three-year germination period: "With playwright Dennis Foon and production director Deco Dawson engaged to respectively write and conceive *Rick: The Rick Hansen Story*, a proposal to develop an innovative, multimedia production was accepted by the Cultural Olympiad. At this point, the Rotary Okanagan International Children's Festival came on board as a third partner."[8] Not only would March 2010 mark the twenty-fifth anniversary of Rick Hansen's four-continent Man in Motion World Tour, the

9.3

Rick: The Rick Hansen Story, Vancouver, 2010.

play's official Vancouver opening would also coincide with the opening ceremonies of the Paralympic Games. The production targeted youth from ages
eleven and up and alternated playing for school and public audiences at the
Granville Island Stage. Publicity and the production study guide emphasized
the production's innovative and "vibrant multimedia component from film-
maker Deco Dawson."[9] The flexible white scenic spaces allowed projected
film images to suggest that the characters were in cars, beside rivers, outside
a high school, and in the back of a pick-up truck: pivotal sites from Hansen's
youth. Foon explained his decision to focus on this period: "How do you tell
the story of a living legend? Rick Hansen has done so many amazing things
– wheeled 40,000 kms around the world, created an amazing foundation, and
a spinal cord research centre. He's larger than life. So I decided to look at what
made him. What happened to him as a teen growing up in Williams Lake,
BC, and the accident that changed his life – and the life of his best friend,
Don, who was with him at the time but landed without a scratch. This is the

story of how Rick overcame this incredible challenge – and helped Don over-
come his."[10] As Foon's last line suggests, the narrative focused on overcoming
and inspiration. This focus meant that the play emphasized Rick's successes
as an athlete in his youth prior to the car crash in which Hansen suffered a
spinal cord injury and became paraplegic, a scene also taken up in the narrative. This emphasis built the platform for the problematic choice of the
production: casting talented, award-winning, Vancouver-based, non-disabled
actor Kyle Jespersen. My aim here is not to undermine the strength of the
actor's performance, something praised by many, but rather to query the
implications of this casting choice. What does it mean for actors with disabilities and for youth audiences with and without disabilities to see a
non-disabled actor playing such an icon? Further, what does it suggest about
the current status of disability theatre in Canada if this particular production did not draw from any of its precepts or practices? Clearly the
production had strong artistic, creative, and financial resources and it had a
significant period of development. Why did it not explore ways of casting an
actor with disability experiences akin to Hansen's? This was a production that
sought to innovate technically and formally. Artistically, this might have led,
like *Skydive* before it, to innovative ways through which to represent the
character before and after the injury. Seeing actors with disabilities onstage
in this narrative of a national hero could have been positively meaningful
to the children and youth with disabilities who attended the production. It
also could have been a significant professional opportunity for artists with
disabilities. In short, why did this production not help get people with disabilities on stage? Why does there seem to be a disconnect between different
kinds of disability activism? At what moment will disability theatre practices become legitimate tools for disability activists and professional artists?

If the argument against casting actors with disabilities in professional productions like *The Miracle Worker* and *Rick: The Rick Hansen Story* hinges on
a perceived dearth of talented performers with disabilities, one can counter-
argue by questioning both the reasons for such scarcity and the parameters
of talent. One line of questioning is practical: what are the best strategies for
training actors with disabilities in theatre? Programs organized by Picasso
Pro, Theatre Terrific, Workman Arts, Stage Left, MoMo, Inside Out, and other
groups noted in this book have involved theatre professionals in their training programs and many have created progressive streams for committed
students to advance to more professional levels. Each of these programs has
come up with inclusive strategies to address the particular needs of participants. Some examples of these include holding classes in accessible spaces
and near accessible transit routes, building flexibility into the progression

through classes so that students need not quit the program if impairments or illnesses flare up, being proactive in finding potential students, and working with students' attendants to facilitate regular and consistent participation. However, the risk associated with these programs, which are in many cases feeding grounds for the company's productions, is that they isolate disability theatre. Could such programs gain from greater partnerships with external professional training programs? Do the more professional aspects of these programs take pressure off of government-funded training institutions to create accessible performing arts training? In their 2009 report to the Canada Council, Jacobson and McMurchy argued for the importance of gathering statistics about the accessibility of post-secondary theatre and other arts training programs across the country and also presented a long list of ideas for theatre trainers and producers to address accessibility.[11] This evidence would be critical for gaining understanding about how artists with disabilities have been supported or denied training opportunities and for thinking proactively about how training programs can best be organized to develop future talent. Gathering this information would also be vital in helping to understand access in more radical ways than just inclusive built environments or accessible course-planning. As James Sanders noted when he returned to his prior theatre training program post-injury, attitudinal barriers can be as or more inhibiting than physical ones. For this reason, the second line of questioning to consider with regard to the development of talented disability theatre artists is philosophical: what preconceptions about theatre and aesthetic traditions resist inclusive casting, training, and production practices? If government-funded theatre training institutions in the country accept as their responsibility the provision of educational opportunities free of prejudice to all Canadians, then investigating the ways in which their training methods might preserve ableist ideologies seems an important task.

Disabled characters and themes have figured prominently in the Canadian repertory, from classical to contemporary and from mainstream to alternative programing. As Canadian theatre has long included disability as a theme and trope, initiating or amplifying the involvement of disability theatre artists could go a long way toward unsettling or redressing stigmatized understandings of disability. In the US, Carrie Sandahl has described watershed moments when disabled theatre artists and entertainment industry professionals gathered to discuss exactly this kind of question: in 2005, the Disability Theatre initiative teamed up with New York City's Public Theatre to host an open conversation between disabled theatre artists and 150 entertainment industry professionals; and in 2006, industry professionals met again with representatives from the Disability Theatre Initiative, Disability/Arts, the Non-Traditional Casting Project, the Screen Actors Guild, and the Dramatists Guild at HBO Headquarters in New York.[12] Although there have been smaller initiatives of this kind in Canada, a large scale version such as those described by Sandahl would be timely, particularly in view of the third and final Paralympic moment I would like to explore here.

While *The Miracle Worker* and *Rick: The Rick Hansen* story drew from disability-themed work, the final production that I would like to consider relates to the disability theatre produced parallel to the Paralympic Games. Many performances during the games, including the Paralympic opening ceremonies, featured artists with disabilities. Kickstart was reinvigorated as an organization in no small part due to the funding opportunities associated with the games; in addition to providing AD for a number of Cultural Olympiad events, it produced the Kickstart Disability Arts and Culture Festival 2010 during the Paralympic Games. The theatre entry in this event was a single performance of local Jan Derbyshire's one-woman comedy about bipolar disorder entitled *Funny in the Head*. Beyond this show, however, and outside the Kickstart Festival, by far the largest-scale disability theatre produced during the games was *Spine*, a co-production by Realwheels and the University of Alberta (U of A) Department of Drama (see Fig. 9.4). Written by Kevin Kerr, directed by Bob Frazer, and starring James Sanders, the production re-united the creative team behind *Skydive*. *Spine* had been commissioned by the U of A Department of Drama, where Kerr was the Lee Playwright-in-Residence, and also featured the talents of U of A BFA acting students. The production immediately followed internationally renowned Québecois director Robert LePage's *The Blue Dragon* in the inaugural season of the newly built Fei and Milton Wong Experimental Theatre at the Simon Fraser University Woodward's building in downtown Vancouver. While LePage's show ran in advance and alongside the Olympic Games, *Spine* did the same during the Paralympics.[13] Both productions were technologically innovative and demanding and both received mixed critical reviews. I cite the parallels between the productions not to compare their content but to give a sense of the prestige of the venue, its significant technological capacities, and the media draw of the programming affiliations with the games promoted by the Cultural Olympiad. How did disability and theatre intersect in this heightened context?

Perhaps one of the most striking features of *Spine* was its deliberate avoidance of straightforward heroic narratives. On the Cultural Olympiad website, Sanders explained that the production aimed to promote a more realistic view of disability, as opposed to what he described as mainstream media's tendency to feature "triumph over adversity stories." "A character may be unable to walk, or unable to speak, but they're really good at mathematics, or track and field, or something that's superhuman so the community accepts them … They're able to do things that normal people wouldn't be able to do. That's a horrible way to represent it … People with disabilities just don't have these superhuman qualities. We're just regular people."[14] Sanders played James, a recently unemployed married man in mid-life crisis who near the top of the play makes an ill-advised sexual advance on his personal care attendant, prompting him to wonder self-disgustedly who he has become. The play's title and tagline invited audiences to question, "who at your very core, are you?" It was critical for Sanders, Kerr, and Frazer that the central character's problems not be solely about disability: "We wanted a main character who was complex, who was trying to figure out his relationship with his wife,

9.4
Realwheels' *Spine*, Vancouver, 2010.

with himself. He's making all these mistakes, and it's not his disability that's the problem. It's his personality."[15] James becomes a rehabilitation centre mentor to a young woman named Carmela who has recently suffered a spinal cord injury through an art experiment with her art collective, "The Precursors," a technologically savvy and innovative group that works "off the grid" and aims to empower the underprivileged. Carmela and James' live scenes were juxtaposed with screened archival film footage of Sanders himself from his early post-injury days at a Vancouver rehabilitation centre, contrasting the middle-aged character onstage with himself 20 years earlier. This was one of many ways that technology complicated concepts of identity throughout the play. The fourteen member cast also invented Second Life avatars, which they performed with wildly inventive costumes, interfacing with each other in ever-more complex ways. When I attended the show, spectators who were familiar with Second Life snorted with the laughter of recognition at the many scenes of awkward avatar exchanges. The more poignant scenes concerned Carmela and The Precursors rekindling their former friendships and artistic collaborations. Played by BFA student Carmela Sison, the character spends most of the play in a wheelchair although, as in the *Rick Hansen Story*, the play also includes scenes of her walking before the injury. At one point all cast members are in wheelchairs on the stage but most often it is just Carmela and James. In interviews Sanders praised Sison's research and commitment to learning how to live in the wheelchair as part of her preparation for the role. In their descriptions of approach, Sison's methods seem much like those of Kyle Jespersen's 2010 preparations to play Rick Hansen; both spent extended periods in wheelchairs and spoke with people who had direct experience of spinal cord injury. What then, apart from the casting of Sanders himself, distinguished this work as disability theatre?

The chief answer to this question steps outside the concerns of casting alone to consider also the artistic process and impulses guiding the enterprise. Sanders has explained Realwheels' mandate to promote "a deeper understanding of the disability experience, the lived experience, a show don't-tell approach."[16] *Spine* began in part from Sanders' experience that many people with disabilities "use video games to temporarily escape from their bodies ... which was an interesting and universal basis for the piece."[17] The play builds on this idea of how humans in the fictional year 2152 negotiate reality through technologies. What happens, the play asks, if you create an avatar that you like better than yourself? Where will your identity rest? While the question moves well beyond disability, disability remains in the show. Sanders insists that they "represent it and speak out about some of the issues. But it's the landscape upon which universal issues are discussed – questions of identity and questions of what's real. It just so happens that we have characters with disabilities telling sections of the story."[18] Playwright Kerr and the collaborative ensemble wrestled with these questions during the development period. Sanders did too, with the additional struggle of having to make inaccessible rehearsal systems adapt to his needs. In an interview with Peter Birnie of the *Vancouver Sun*, Sanders emphasized his frustrations with the Edmonton snow and inaccessible on-campus accommodations which forced him to stay offsite and rely on taxis for travel: "It's something that I think really needs to be addressed within theatre in Canada … I need an accessible rehearsal space and dressing room, I need a bed to get on and off of when I change in and out of my costumes, and I need the schedule to allow for the extra time that it takes me to get to and from the theatre."[19] Sanders' call echoes those expressed in the McMurchy and Jacobson report to the Canada Council about building accessibility into professional Canadian theatre practices in Canada. Strikingly, however, it is clear that the co-production valued Sanders' artistic involvement enough to persist with the process through to production. Further, accessibility concerns became less of an issue when they arrived at the Milton and Fei Wong Theatre, a space that has been built with the mandate that a disabled person can do any job in the theatre, from hanging lights to performing.[20] While not wholly successful, the production's twin commitments to push past accessibility barriers in the artistic development process to include a disabled artist and to draw from his lived disability experiences in the artistic explorations of the play's central themes mark the show as disability theatre.

Why bring these three disparate productions into dialogue about disability theatre in Canada? In many ways they are as remarkable for their differences as their similarities. One was the season opener for a mainstream large Vancouver theatre, another was aimed at children and youth, while another was a co-production involving student actors. Nonetheless, each invoked disability in ways that suggest the challenges, practice, and reach of disability theatre. Comparing their critical reception by one prominent reviewer, Peter Birnie – who reviewed them all in the city's major daily newspaper, the *Vancouver Sun* – affords a useful glimpse into some of the key issues facing contemporary Canadian disability theatre practitioners.

Birnie described the *The Miracle Worker* as luminous, "a production rich with reminders of how great theatre gets made."[21] Most of his praise went to director Meg Roe for her refusal to "settle for less than the best" from her cast and artistic team, particularly in view of the challenges posed by Gibson's play: "By today's standards, Gibson created something of a clunker. Overly earnest with righteous purpose, *The Miracle Worker* is riddled with such clumsy devices as having Sullivan hear haunted voices from her own horrible childhood, or read her letters out loud to advance the exposition. Its sense of time and place, looking back to Alabama circa 1887, gives the Keller family's "Negro" servants precious little to do, thankfully, Roe opens these small roles so Marci T. House and Hamza Adam can do more than merely mug."[22] Emphasizing how Roe moved beyond the script, Birnie also highlighted clever scenographic features as "one of many such sweet little notes in a satisfying symphony of pure theatricality." It is striking that Birnie attends to the more limiting features of the servant roles and admires the production for its ability to push past the weaknesses of the script.

By contrast, for *Rick: The Rick Hansen Story*, Birnie's praise was emphatic for both the play and production: "Everything about *Rick: The Rick Hansen Story* feels just right. A straightforward script, strong performances and a superb stage design make this little gem a shining example of theatre for young audiences."[23] Birnie also praised the production for its lack of "phoney emotion," and argued that Kyle Jespersen had "clearly done his homework about paraplegia" to turn in "an exhaustingly convincing portrayal of what it means when one's legs don't work." Again Birnie reserved the highest praise for the set: "Finally, it all comes down to Deco Dawson and his astonishing production design to make this a landmark piece of theatre. William Chesney's set is a complex grouping of panels and platforms carefully structured so it can be transformed by Dawson's video projections into, well, anything – a forest road, a gym or, across the floor of the stage, a fast-flowing creek … That's where Rick Hansen comes close to drowning, in a remarkable scene that sees Jespersen falling from his chair and flailing in seemingly deep waters. One word comes to mind to describe this moment, and indeed the whole show: Wow!"[24]

In sharp contrast to the superlatives of these two reviews, Birnie's review of *Spine* was largely negative. While in his preview Birnie had cited Sander's aims and concerns, his review did not revisit these but rather suggested that the play was unwieldy, message-oriented, and clumsy. Birnie twice invoked disability to depict the play as substandard, calling the play "crippled by its excesses" and worse than an "elephant designed by a committee of blind people." While Birnie found Dawson's set for *Rick: The Rick Hansen Story* superb, in the case of *Spine*, Robert Shannon's elaborate wheelchair inspired set was said to be "cumbersome." These throw away lines might be dismissed as just that, but Birnie argued more pointedly that "since Realwheels advocates on issues of disability (lead actor James Sanders is quadriplegic), *Spine* is obligated to include plenty of exposition about the hard row to hoe when you're in a wheelchair." Birnie went on to suggest that the play's primary problems originated in its script and divergent plot lines, but it would be difficult for a reader to conclude that he did not view the disability content of the play as holding it back. Otherwise, why the invocation of disability as metaphor, or the criticism of advocacy?[25]

This chapter is neither an indictment of Birnie (the fact that *The Miracle Worker* garnered several Jessie Richardson Vancouver theatre nominations and awards and a survey of concurrent reviews of the productions suggest his review responses were more typical than outlier) nor does it aim to suggest that *Spine* rightfully deserved top-notch reviews.[26] Having attended the production, my own assessment was that *Spine* offered many memorable, fun and compelling scenes but these were set within an over-complicated narrative structure that made uneven use of its ample innovative stage technologies. What is striking about the review responses, however, is their thorough lack of engagement with disability theatre, arts, and culture precepts. While Birnie offered passing references to the belittling features of Gibson's play for actors of colour, no mention was made of the production's comparably belittling casting decisions related to actors with disabilities in a production focused on disability. This kind of omission helps to raise questions about current relationships between disability and mainstream theatre practices in Canada. Some of Canada's most talented and creative artists were involved in each of the productions cited above. In the cases of *The Miracle Worker* and *Rick: The Rick Hansen Story*, why did this creative energy not flow toward rethinking disability representation? What will it take for talented and creative artists to break from the longstanding patterns for demonstrating artistic virtuosity through non-disabled performance of disability? What if both *The Miracle Worker* and *Rick: The Rick Hansen Story* had started with the precept that it is important, especially in light of the plays' narratives, for people with disabilities to take the stage and for audiences to know that they are doing so? How might artistic innovation have imagined the place of disability onstage? Finally, young people were involved in each of the three productions described here, either onstage or in targeted audiences. What messages did each send to potential and emerging Canadian performers about how disability might find a place on future Canadian stages? Will Canadian artistic laurels continue to be held in reserve for non-disabled performers who do stage turns as disabled persons or will new generations innovate with more creative ways to feature, support, and recognize Canadian disability theatre artists? In other words, what will this next generation reject as "phoney" – non-disabled mimicry of disability, however credible it seems, or theatre that mines disability for effect while upholding a system that inhibits disability artists from taking their turn on stage?

CHAPTER TEN

Conclusion

Although first canonized as part of the Canadian dramatic tradition, David Freeman's *Creeps* is also one of the oldest and most celebrated Canadian disability theatre exports.[1] The play is the only non-US entry in Victoria Ann Lewis' recent disability theatre anthology, *Beyond Victims and Villains: Contemporary Plays by Disabled Playwrights.*[2] Prepared first as a script for the Canadian Broadcasting Corporation in 1965, the play had its premiere stage production at the Factory Lab Theatre in Toronto in 1970 and a revised version was premiered as the inaugural production for Tarragon Theatre in Toronto in 1971. It won the first prestigious Chalmers Canadian Play Award in 1973 and, following an off-Broadway production, also garnered Freeman a Drama Desk Award for best new playwright.[3] It has gone on to be staged internationally and has returned to its roots with a staged reading at the Tarragon Theatre in 2009.

Freeman, who has cerebral palsy, explains that the play "was born of my own frustration, working in a Toronto sheltered workshop where I sanded blocks, folded boxes, and separated nuts and bolts. It deals with people who have the courage to take destiny in their own hands."[4] Set in a workshop's washroom where men with disabilities gather to vent their frustrations and seek privacy from a female supervisor, Lewis argues that the play "prematurely bear[s] witness to wrongs that would not find political analysis and advocacy until later in the decade."⁵ *Creeps* offers, according to Lewis, a world of disabled characters through which Freeman is able "not only to present a variety of disabled character types, but also to theatricalize the lived experience of disability as a collective, social process, not an individual destiny."⁶ Written and produced well before most of the disability theatres described in this book began, notes at the play's outset assume that actors cast in the roles will be non-disabled and need guidance about how to perform disability. In the intervening decades, an expanding number of disability theatre artists and playwrights from Canada and beyond have been seeking to follow Freeman's example, but also with the aim of galvanizing and developing a disability identity.

Plays matter, as *Creeps* exemplifies, but theatre involves more than plays. It is a collaborative art form which often requires large and sustained investments of time, labour, and funds. Since the late 1980s, a broad range of Canadian theatre artists have organized, connected, made distinguished efforts, and contributed in countless ways to the emergence of disability theatre. They have founded companies, drawn up mandates, re-invented old scripts, and commissioned new ones. They have developed training programs, formed ensembles, challenged casting practices, and pressed the boundaries of convention and form. Disabled artists have taken the stage as actors, directors, designers, and other artistic personnel. There has been no one way to do this, and part of the purpose of this book has been to explain the sheer diversity that may be found within the commonly held label of disability theatre, itself connected to disability arts and culture, and disability identity and politics.

Looking across time and space in the institutional and artistic development of English-language disability theatre since the mid-1980s, several conclusions can be drawn. First, most companies have faced similar core debates over the balance between training and artistry, amateur involvement and professionalism, fundraising and partnerships, disability identity and politics. No two companies have addressed these issues in the same way, and in many respects the debates will be on-going, but the choices made have helped to shape development processes as well as artistic outcomes. Second, companies have emerged locally, but also increasingly in connection to active disability and artistic communities. Part of the reason why Toronto, Calgary, and Vancouver stand out as hubs of disability theatre in the country is that festivals in these cities have provided space for interaction, exchange, debate, and inspiration. Such festivals have also forged critical links to the international field at a time when national connections have generally been weak and difficult to sustain. Third, although more recent focused interest by the Canada Council points to the fact that disability theatre in Canada may be "on the verge of institutionalization," as Michele Decottignies aptly puts it, it is well to remember that, in the past, the strengths of this field have been found in regional contexts with connections to an international movement.[7]

Just as *Creeps* challenged common ideas of disability, a growing body of original plays and performances by disability companies has contributed to an emerging disability theatre aesthetic. This aesthetic challenges conventional representations of disability on stage, impacts the development process, and seeks to re-construct the social meanings of disability. A wide spectrum of approaches exists, each differently charged by disability politics and aesthetic considerations, at times seeking to place disability within universal stories or to rupture prevalent ideas and insert disabled voices and performances into public debate. *Creeps'* inclusion in Lewis's anthology serves as an influential early outlier representing Canadian output at the time; however a similar Canadian play anthology is now easily imaginable. It could include, for example, Alex Bulmer's award-winning *Smudge, Mercy-Killing or Murder: The Tracy Latimer Story* (Stage Left), Kevin Kerr's *Skydive* (Realwheels), *Spiraling Within* (McCarthy), *The Edmond Yu Project* (Friendly Spike Theatre Band), Terry Watada's *Vincent* (Workman Arts), *Help UnWanted* (Inside Out), *The Matilda Stewart Show* (MoMo), Uchatius' *The Glass Box* (Theatre Terrific), as well as solo works. While such an anthology would help connect the ideas of these works, it is important to note that it would not cap the growing movement they collectively represent. Rather, as critical responses to recent performances during the Paralympics in Vancouver suggest, the challenges posed by disability theatre to mainstream practice seem yet to have wholly "upset the applecart" of theatre tradition, like Catherine Frazee has called for in disability arts practice.[8] This is certainly a movement in progress rather than a fait accompli.

Although it was not the governing principle of a recent theatrical production about his life, Rick Hansen's call for disabled actors to get on stage resonates with most of the companies and artists explored here. As we have seen, many disability theatre artists have found different ways of balancing competing impulses to provoke or entertain, empower or educate, contribute to the mainstream or fight institutionalized discrimination, build community or contest its borders. What is clear, however, is that taking a turn on stage matters. Delivering the 2000 John F. McCreary Lecture entitled "The Art of Disability" at the University of British Columbia, Kickstart co-founder Bonnie Sherr Klein explained, "It's our turn to tell the story. It's our turn to tell who we are, where we come from, what the journey is about."[9] Speaking specifically about disability theatre, Inside Out's founding Artistic Director, Ruth Bieber is similarly plain: "The heart of our message to the public speaks of our desire to challenge convention, to take our rightful place on stage and tell our own stories."[10]

Notes

PREFACE

1   Tobin Siebers, *Disability Aesthetics* (Ann Arbor: Univesity of Michigan Press 2010), 20.
2   Erin Hurley, *Theatre & Feeling* (London: Palgrave Macmillan, 2010).
3   Robert Rae, "Disability, invisibility and theatre: which nation are we staging?" *International Journal of Scottish Theatre* 2, no.1 (2001), http://erc.qmu.ac.uk/OJS/index.php/IJoST/article/view/78/html.
4   Simi Linton, "Disability and Conventions of Theatre," http://www.similinton.com/about_topics_2.htm.
5   Catherine Frazee, Kathryn Church, and Melanie Panitch, eds. *Out from Under: Disability, History & Things to Remember* (Toronto: School of Disability Studies, Faculty of Community Services, Ryerson University, 2008), 4.
6   Ibid., 5.
7   Council of Canadians with Disabilities, "Social Policy," http://www.ccdonline.ca/en/socialpolicy/.

INTRODUCTION

1   Andre Picard, "Vancouver Airport Wins New Hansen Prize," *Globe and Mail* (12 June 2004).
2   Sharon L. Snyder, Brenda Jo Brueggemann, and Rosemarie Garland-Thomson, "Introduction: Integrating Disability into Teaching and Scholarship," in *Disability Studies: Enabling the Humanities*, eds. Sharon L. Snyder, Brenda Jo

Brueggemann, and Rosemarie Garland-Thomson, (New York: Modern Language Association of America, 2002), 8.

3   Petra Kuppers, *Disability and Contemporary Performance* (New York: Routledge, 2003), 4.

4   Snow Personal Interview, 28 May 2008. More recently Snow explained in a blog entry, "Disability is not real in a concrete sense. Disability can only exist where people have a social agreement about the way some people's bodies and/or minds exist in the world. In particular the culture 'already knows' that there are ways that people should never be in their bodies, minds and emotions … The good news is that we don't need the concept of disability at all. With some work, self reflection, dialogue and change of action disability as a concept and as a practice can disappear." Judith Snow, *Judith Snow Inside Her Third Cycle of 30 Years* (blog), 1 February 2011, http://thirdcycle.blogspot.com/2011/02/february-1-2011.html.

5   Paul Anthony Darke, "Now I Know Why Disability Arts is Drowning in the River Lethe (with thanks to Pierre Bourdieu)," in *Disability, Culture and Identity*, eds. Sheila Riddell and Nick Watson (Harlow, England: Pearson Education, 2003), 132.

6   Bonnie Sherr Klein, quoted in *Arts Smarts: Inspiration and Ideas for Canadian Artists with Disabilities* (Vancouver: Society for Disability Arts and Culture, 2002), 41.

7   *Arts Smarts*, 39.

8   Colin Barnes and Geof Mercer, *Disability* (London: Polity, 2003), 102.

9   Yvonne Peters, "From Charity to Equality: Canadians with Disabilities Take Their Rightful Place in Canada's Constitution," in *Making Equality: History of Advocacy and Persons with Disability in Canada*, eds. Deborah Stienstra and Aileen Wight-Felske (Toronto: Captus Press, 2003), 119–36.

10 Michael J. Prince, "Canadian Federalism and Disability Policy Making," *Canadian Journal of Political Science* 34, no. 4 (December 2001): 791–817.

11 Sally Chivers, "Barrier by Barrier: The Canadian Disability Movement and the Fight for Equal Rights," in *Group Politics and Social Movements in Canada*, ed. Miriam Smith (Peterborough: Broadview Press, 2008), 321.

12 Theresia Degner, "Disability Discrimination Law: A Global Comparative Approach," in *Disability Rights in Europe: From Theory to Practice*, eds. Caroline Gooding and Anna Lawson (Oxford: Hart Publishing, 2006), 90.

13 Aldred H. Neufeldt, "Growth and Evolution of Disability Advocacy in Canada," in *Making Equality: History of Advocacy and Persons with Disability in Canada*, eds. Deborah Stienstra and Aileen Wight-Felske (Toronto: Captus Press, 2003), 11–32.

14 Richard K. Skotch, "American Disability Policy in the Twentieth Century," in *The New Disability History*, eds. Paul K. Longmore and Lauri Umansky (New York: New York University Press, 2001), 375–92.

15   Neufeldt, "Growth and Evolution of Disability Advocacy in Canada," 24.

16   Doris Zames Fleischer and Frieda Zames, *The Disability Rights Movement: From Charity to Confrontation* (Philadelphia: Temple University Press, 2001), 33–48; Neufeldt, "Growth and Evolution of Disability Advocacy in Canada," 24.

17   Catherine Kudlick, "Disability History: Why We Need Another 'Other,'" *The American Historical Review*, 108, no. 3 (June 2003): 763.

18   Carrie Sandahl and Philip Auslander, "Disability Studies in Commotion with Performance Studies," introduction in *Bodies in Commotion: Disability & Performance*, eds. Carrie Sandahl and Philip Auslander, (Ann Arbor, MI: University of Michigan Press, 2005), 8.

19   Tobin Siebers, *Disability Theory* (Ann Arbor: University of Michigan Press, 2008), 3.

20   Ayesha Vernon, "The Dialectics of Multiple Identities and the Disabled People's Movement," *Disability and Society* 14, no. 3 (1999): 394.

21   *Arts Smarts*, 42.

22   Sandahl and Auslander, "Disability Studies in Commotion with Performance Studies," 6.

23   Frazee quoted in *Arts Smarts*, 41.

24   Barnes and Mercer, *Disability* (Cambridge: Polity, 2003); Barnes, Colin, Mike Oliver, and Len Barton, eds. *Disability Studies Today* (London: Polity, 2002); Sheila Riddell and Nick Watson, eds. *Disability, Culture and Identity* (Harlow, England: Pearson Education, 2003).

25   Tom Shakespeare and Nicholas Watson, "The Social Model of Disability: An Outdated Ideology? Exploring Theories and Expanding Methodologies," in *Research in Social Science and Disability* 2 (Stamford, CT: JAI Press, 2001), 9–28.

26   Mairian Corker and Tom Shakespeare, eds. *Disability/ Postmodernity: Embodying Disability Theory* (London: Continuum, 2002), 15.

27   Tobin Siebers, "Disability Aesthetics," *Journal of Cultural and Religious Theory* 7, no. 2 (Spring/Summer 2006): 3–4.

28   Ibid., 33.

29   Ibid., 22.

30   Kuppers, *Disability and Contemporary Performance*, 5.

31   Ibid., 50.

32   Sandahl and Auslander, *Bodies in Commotion*, 5.

CHAPTER TWO

1   For more on Pourquois Pas Nous? see *The Enchantment*, directed by Gille Blais, produced by Colette Blanchard and the National Film Board of Canada, 1994.

2   Rose Jacobson and Alex Bulmer, "The Picasso Project: A Report from the Field of Disability Arts," December 2004, http://www.picassopro.org/resources.html.

3 Rose Jacobson and Geoff McMurchy, "Focus on Disability & Deaf Arts in Canada," January 2009, http://www.picassopro.org/resources.html.

4 Ibid., 23.

5 Ibid., 4.

6 Michele Decottignies and Andrew Houston, eds. "Theatre and the Question of Disability," *Canadian Theatre Review* 122 (Spring 2005): 1–97.

7 Ted Dinsmore, "Play's Cast is Blind But You'd Never Guess," *Toronto Star*, 16 March 1961.

8 Glenvale Players. For a more detailed account of this production, see Cathy Dunphy, "Blind Actors Aim for No-fault Night," *Toronto Star*, 7 January 1986.

9 Wanda C. Fitzgerald, "Stepping from the Wings," *Canadian Theatre Review* 122 (2005): 64.

10 Ibid., 62.

11 Alex Bulmer, personal interview, 2011.

12 Ibid.

13 Bulmer as quoted in Jon Kaplan, "Alex Bulmer's groundbreaking *Smudge* goes inside the mind's eye. Sight unseen," *Now Magazine*, 16 November 2000.

14 Diane Flacks, "Having Cultivated Her Talent Abroad, Alex Bulmer Plants Her Creative Seed Here," *Toronto Star*, 26 May 2009.

15 Paula Citron, "Rochdale Revisited in Multi–media Stage Trip," *Toronto Star*, 10 September 1992.

16 Ibid.

17 Mad Pride Toronto, YouTube Channel, http://www.youtube.com/user/madpridetoronto.

18 Geoffrey Reaume, *Remembrance of Patients Past: Patient Life at the Toronto Hospital for the Insane, 1870–1940* (Toronto: Oxford University Press Canada, 2000).

19 Citron, "Rochdale."

20 Picasso Pro, "Mandate," http://www.picassopro.org/about.html.

21 Alex Bulmer, personal interview, 2011.

22 Picasso PRO website, http://www.picassopro.org/.

23 Stage left website, http://www.stage-left.org/.

24 Ibid.

25 Michele Decottignies, personal email to author, 2011.

26 Stage Left website, 2011.

27 Michele Decottignies, personal interview, 31 May 2010.

28 Ibid.

29 Stage left website.

30 Stage left website.

31 Decottignies, personal interview.

32 Ibid.

33 For further analysis of the generative links between these ideas with relation to theatre, see Ann M. Fox and Joan Lipkin's "Res(Crip)ting Feminist Theater

Through Disability Theater: Selections from the DisAbility Project," *NWSA Journal* 14, no. 3 (Fall 2002): 77–98.

34   Ruth Bieber, "The Truth About Theatre from the Inside Out," *Canadian Theatre Review* 122 (Spring 2005): 56. Readers interested in further information about InsideOut's history and work should watch for a manuscript that Bieber is in the process of preparing for publication.

35   Ibid., 57.

36   Ibid.

37   Ibid.

38   Jeff Goffin, "Help Unwanted Makes Its Point with Humour," *FFWD Weekly*, March 2003, 33.

39   Quoted in Sherri Zickefoose, "Stages of Development: Integrated Theatre Company Gives Disabled a Voice," *Calgary Herald Entertainment Guide*, 27 March–2 April 2003, 2.

40   Barbara Green, "The Inside Out Integrated Theatre Project: Making Theatre an Agent of Change." *Theatre Alberta News* (Winter 2005): 10.

41   Barbara Green with Ruth Bieber, "Inside/Out Theatre," *Bridges* (Fall 2004): 11.

42   Bieber, "The Truth About Theatre from the Inside Out," 58.

43   Ibid.

44   Ibid.

45   Ibid.

46   *FFWD Weekly* (Calgary), "Your Face Here: Pamela Boyd," 17–23 May 2007. In 2008, Restless Dance Company changed its name to Restless Dance Theatre.

47   Michael Ende, *Momo* (New York: Doubleday Penguin, 1984).

48   Momo Dance website, http://www.momodancetheatre.org/about_us.htm.

49   Pamela Boyd, personal interview, 3 December 2007.

50   Ibid.

51   Ibid.

52   Ibid.

53   *FFWD Weekly*, "Your Face Here: Pamela Boyd."

54   City of Vancouver Archives, City of Vancouver, *Vancouver '92*.

55   Realwheels Archive, James Sanders, Artistic Director's Report (Realwheels Annual General Meeting, 15 November 2004).

56   James Sanders, personal interview, 29 December 2009.

57   Realwheels website, www.realwheels.ca.

58   Real Wheels Archive, Realwheels Ad Hoc Collective, "The Realwheels Theatre Project," (an Application to the BC Arts Council for Project Assistance for Professional Theatre, 15 April 2004), 34.

59   Ibid.

60   Realwheels Archive, Sanders, Artistic Director's Report (Realwheels Annual General Meeting, 15 November 2004).

61   Realwheels website.

62 PuSh festival website, http://pushfestival.ca/.

63 Lisa Traiger, "Language in Silence: Deaf, Jewish mime onstage at Gallaudet,"
    Washington Jewish Week, 11 March 2010, http://www.washingtonjewishweek.
    com/main.asp?SectionID=27&SubSectionID=25&ArticleID=12430&TM=
    1884.501.

64 James Sanders, personal email, 19 May 2008.

65 Balancing Acts 5, Festival Headliners, http://www.stage-left.org/festival_
    headliners.htm.

66 S. Siobhan McCarthy, "Using the Arts as a Tool for Healing, Self-Discovery,
    Empowerment and Catharsis," *Canadian Theatre Review* 122 (Spring 2005): 61.

67 Ibid.

68 Ibid.

69 *Scraping the Surface* won Edmonton's Sterling Award for Outstanding New
    Play (1996) and Vancouver's Jessie Richardson Award for Outstanding Script
    and Performance for a Young Audience (1997). The *Ottawa Sun* rated *Still
    Waiting for that Special Bus* "the Pick of the Festival" and gave it five stars (*Arts
    Smarts*, 29). Victoria Maxwell's *Crazy for Life* has garnered several awards and
    nominations: the 2007 Entertainment Industries Council PRISM Award
    Nominee; Winner of the 2005 Moondance International Film Festival Award
    for Best Stage Play; Winner of Solo Collective's Canadian National Emerging
    Playwright's Award; Winner of the Gordon Armstrong Theatre Award; Finalist
    in the Canadian National Playwriting Competition.

70 Balancing Acts 2009 website, http://www.balancing-acts.org/ba9.htm.

71 Carrie Sandahl, "Black Man, Blind Man: Disability Identity Politics and
    Performance," *Theatre Journal* 56, no. 4 (December 2004): 582.

72 Ibid., 602.

73 Andrew Houston, "Lyle Victor Albert's After Shave," *Canadian Theatre Review*
    122 (Spring 2005): 34.

74 Petra Kuppers, *Disability and Contemporary Performance* (New York:
    Routledge, 2003), 3.

75 On this and other points, see Shain's interesting self-reflective thesis and
    article, both with the same title, "Disability, Theatre and Power: An Analysis
    of a One-Person Play," *Canadian Theatre Review* 122 (Spring 2005): 13–18.

76 Alan Shain quoted in *Arts Smarts: Inspiration and Ideas for Canadian Artists
    with Disabilities* (Vancouver: Society for Disability Arts and Culture, 2002), 44.

77 Ibid., 29.

78 Victoria Maxwell, "Making the Invisible Visible," *Canadian Theatre Review* 122
    (Spring 2005): 27.

79 Victoria Maxwell website, http://www.victoriamaxwell.com.

80 James Sanders, quoted in *Arts Smarts*, 44.

81 See, for example, Max-i-mime's aforementioned collaborations with
    Realwheels or Picasso PRO's organization in 2010 of OPEN SIGN STAGE,

evenings in Toronto and Ottawa which invited "Deaf, Hard of Hearing and Allied Artists" to experiment and collaborate with Josette Bushell-Mingo, Artistic Director of Tyst Teater Sweden.

82 Rachel E. Tracie, "Deaf Theatre in Canada: Sign Posts to an Other Land" (abstract from Master's thesis, University of Alberta, 1998).

83 Distinguishing between mime theatre and Deaf theatre, Tracie also offers brief histories of several other Canadian initiatives: Theatre Visuel Des Sourds; A Show of Hands; The Canadian Deaf Theatre; Deaf-Gypsy Mime Company; and Fingers Happy Productions.

84 Tracie, "Deaf Theatre in Canada: Sign Posts to an Other Land," 6.

85 One example is Joanna Bennett's 2006 ASL Showcase which was presented in association with Toronto's Harbourfront Centre and through the support of Equity Showcase, Picasso PRO, and studio lab theatre foundation. The evening of seven drama and comedy performances aimed precisely to "demonstrate to the public and arts community this pioneering form of performance, designed to inspire the community and create a first-ever sign language theatre in Canada, initiating professional opportunities for Deaf artists in the arts," http://media.harbourfrontcentre.com/mediaDisplay.php?id=349.

CHAPTER THREE

1 The performance was part of the interdisciplinary conference, "Madness Manifest: Creativity, Art and the Margins of Mental Health," sponsored by the Department of Dramatic Arts, Brock University, 14 January 2008.

2 Workman Arts Archive (WAA), Workman Theatre Project, "Company Background," 1998; "Company Background," 1999.

3 My research on the history of Workman Arts is based on a wide-ranging analysis of the company archives and interviews with members over a decade. Readers interested in a more exhaustive account of this history should refer to Kirsten Johnston, "Staging Madness: Dramatic Modes of Representing Mental Illness at the Workman Theatre Project, 1989–2001" (PhD dissertation, University of Toronto, 2002).

4 CAMH was formed in 1998 as a result of the merger of the Queen Street Mental Health Centre, Clarke Institute of Psychiatry, the Addiction Research Foundation, and the Donwood Institute.

5 Friedlander, "The theatre of the mind," in *Toronto Star*, 31 March 1992.

6 Lisa Brown, personal interview, 12 May 1999.

7 Lisa Brown, personal interview, 24 June 2008.

8 WAA, Workman Theatre Project, "WTP: A new voice in mental health," *Queen Street Mental Health Centre Tidbits*, November 1990.

9 Brown, personal interview, 1999.

10 For a more comprehensive discussion of the issues of naming associated with the mental health service user movement, see Iain Ferguson, "Challenging a

'Spoiled Identity': Mental Health Service Users, Recognition and Redistribution," in *Disability, Culture and Identity*, eds. Sheila Riddell and Nick Watson (Harlow, Essex: Pearson Education, 2003), 67–87.

11 Brown, personal interview, 2008.

12 Shannon Quesnelle, personal interview, 24 June 2008.

13 Carrie Sandahl, "The Tyranny of Neutral: Disability and Actor Training," in *Bodies in Commotion: Disability & Performance*, eds. Carrie Sandahl and Philip Auslander (Ann Arbor: University of Michigan Press, 2005), 255–67.

14 Workman Arts Season and Training Brochure, 2007–08.

15 John Palmer, personal interview, 21 March 2001.

16 Anonymous, personal interview, 2001.

17 Scott Simmie and Julia Nunes, *The Last Taboo: A Survival Guide to Mental Health Care in Canada* (Toronto: McClelland, 2001).

18 Arsenault quoted in Jon Kaplan, "Arsenault's Innerspeak Maps a Journey toward Mental Health," *Now Magazine*, 20 June 1991.

19 WAA, Vit Wagner, "Play doesn't get mired in its didactic purpose," *Toronto Star*, 20 June 1991.

20 Brown, personal interview, 1999.

21 As we shall explore further in Chapter Seven, the company's work in this regard aligns them with theorists Petra Kuppers and Sander Gilman, both of whom also explore and undermine visual stereotypes associated with mental illness representation.

22 WAA, Robert Cushman, "Little Joy in this Musical," in *National Post*, 14 October 2000.

23 Richard Ouzounian, "Real Sadness in Joy," *Toronto Star*, 8 October 2000.

24 Robert Cushman, "Edward the 'Crazy Man' brings mental illness home," *National Post*, 2 May 2011. A production aimed at young audiences, *Edward the Crazy Man* tells the story of a friendship between a boy and a homeless man who has been diagnosed with schizophrenia. The play by Emil Sher is an adaptation of Marie Day's book of the same title. Two of the production's performers were nominated for the Toronto Alliance for the Performing Arts' Dora Mavor Moore Awards.

25 James I. Charlton, *Nothing About Us Without Us: Disability Oppression and Empowerment* (Berkeley: University of California Press, 1998).

26 Michel Foucault, *Madness and Civilization: A History of Insanity in the Age of Reason* (New York: Vintage Books, 1988, c1965).

27 Dale Peterson, ed., *A Mad People's History of Madness*, (Pittsburgh: University of Pittsburgh Press, 1982), xiv.

28 Paul Anthony Darke, "Now I Know Why Disability Art is Drowning in the River Lethe," in *Disability, Culture and Identity*, eds. Sheila Riddell and Nick Watson (Harlow, England: Pearson Education, 2003), 132.

CHAPTER FOUR

1   Candice Larscheid, personal interview, 8 June 2011.

2   Theatre Terrific Archives (TTA), Sue Lister, "Artistic Director's Report," *Theatre Terrific Update* (Spring 1994): 2.

3   Hilary U. Cohen, "Conflicting Values in Creating Theatre with the Developmentally Disabled: A Study of Theatre Unlimited," *The Arts in Psychotherapy* 12 (1985): 3–10.

4   TTA, Theatre Terrific, "The Big Birthday Bash," *Theatre Terrific Update* (Spring 1995): 1, 7.

5   The Community Living Society (CLS) was founded in 1978. CLS's website describes its origins and purpose as follows: "Initially the Society was established as an independent planning agency to facilitate the movement of individuals from institutional to community living. The community living services pioneered and developed by the CLS over the years are oriented toward nurturing each individual's growth potential to lead a free and dignified life in an integrated community environment. This is achieved by CLS employees being accountable to the individuals they serve. In this way the individuals are given the support and opportunity to choose their activities," http://www.cls-bc.org/.

6   TTA, Liam Lacey, "Theatre 'Opens Horizons' for Disabled Actors," *Globe and Mail*, 14 March 1990.

7   TTA, Connie Hargrave, "All of Life's a Stage," *Transitions* (May–June 2000): 14; TTA, "Connie's Thoughts," 10 October 1986.

8   Larscheid, personal interview.

9   Ibid. and TTA, Richard Watson, "Terrific Theatre at Theatre Terrific," *Abilities* (Spring 1992): 158–9.

10 TTA, British Columbia, Certificate of Incorporation, Theatre Terrific Society, 19 August 1985.

11 TTA, Theatre Terrific Budget Projections and Comparisons, 1987. In 1986 TTS received $50,641 from this grant and in 1987, $65,120. TTA, Hargrave, "Looking Back on 10 Years of Theatre Terrific," *Theatre Terrific Update* (Winter 1995): 1; TTA, Craig Spence, "Actors Face Curtain," *Vancouver Courier*, 1987.

12 Biographical sketch from TTA, Theatre Terrific, *Dancing on the Head of a Pin with a Mouse in My Pocket* (program, 1986).

13 TTA, Colin Smith, "Disabled Drama Extends Horizons," *The Spokesman*, December 1982; TTA, Catherine Ducharme, "Unique Theatre Group," *The Spokesman*, 11 February 1989.

14 Larscheid, personal interview.

15 TTA, Connie Hargrave, "Looking Back," 3; TTA, Kevin Griffin, "Theatre Terrific Certainly is Just That – Terrific," *Vancouver Weekender*, 14 August 1986; TTA, Mark Leiren-Young, "Uneven Play Has Moments," *Georgia Straight*, September 1986, 12–19.

16   TTA, Hargrave, "Connie's Thoughts."

17   TTA, Sue Lister, "Sue's Thoughts for the Day," 9 October 1986.

18   TTA, Hargrave, "Connie's Thoughts."

19   TTA, Ducharme, "Unique Theatre Group," 11; TTA, Laura Busheikin, "Theatre Group Enables the Disabled," *Ubyssey*, 12 August 1987. Famous People Players, founded by Diane Dupuy in 1974, has a long history of training and employing artists with disabilities in black light puppet theatre. The company has achieved considerable commercial success, opening for Liberace in Las Vegas in its early years and now maintaining its own stand-alone premises for dinner theatre in west Toronto, as well as a farm property in Ancaster. The company employs performers with disabilities as puppeteers and in other facets of its dinner theatre program, and offers training in the process. Despite a surface similarity to some disability theatre practices, however, the company has not been particularly engaged with the disability arts and culture movement and vice versa.

20   TTA, Theatre Terrific, "Theatre Terrific," September 1986, including mission statement and background notes.

21   TTA, Theatre Terrific, Notes on The National Theatre Workshop of the Handicapped and Graeae Theatre Company attached to ibid.

22   TTA, Theatre Terrific, *Annual Report* 1988, 1.

23   TTA, Theatre Terrific, "Update," (Spring 1990).

24   TTA, Theatre Terrific, "Direct Access … On the Move." *Theatre Terrific News* (Spring 1988): 1.

25   TTA, Theatre Terrific, "Direct Access to the Heart," *Theatre Terrific Update* (Spring 1994): 1.

26   TTA, Theatre Terrific, "Update," (Spring 1990): 1.

27   TTA, Watson, "Terrific Theatre at Theatre Terrific," 158.

28   TTA, Lacey, "Theatre 'Opens Horizons' for Disabled Actors."

29   TTA, Boby Lukacs, "How Theatre Changed My Life," *Theatre Terrific Newsletter* (Winter 1992): 9.

30   Such testimonial style letters were routinely published, generally anonymously, in the company updates and newsletters.

31   TTA, Kathy Santini, "Terrific Theatre Group Encourages Disabled," *Nanaimo Daily* Free Press, n.d.; TTA, Larry Nelson, "This Theatre Really is Terrific," *Powell River News*, 20 June 1990; TTA, *Alberni Valley Times* "Theatre Terrific Takes Play Production to District Schools," 3 March 1992; TTA, *Comox District Free Press*, "Theatre Terrific Comes Here," 7 April 1993; TTA, Jamie Baxter, "Theatre Terrific Brings World of Disabled to Schools," *Vancouver Sun*, 19 November 1992.

32   TTA, Lacey, "Theatre 'Opens Horizons' for Disabled Actors."

33   Ibid.

34   TTA, Shannon Rupp, "Theatre Terrific is Terrific," *Coquitlam Magazine*, 28 June–

25 July 1989; TTA, Janet Smith, "Theatre Terrific a Catalyst for Change," *The West Ender*, 14 June 1990; TTA, Alison Appelbe, "Theatre a Terrific Experience for Disabled," *Vancouver Courier*, 28 November 1990; TTA, Margaret Peterson, "Theatre Nurtures Conquering Spirit," *Vancouver Courier*, August 1991; TTA, Tina Cresswell, "Actors with a Special Extra," *Prince George Citizen*, February 1990.

35 TTA, Theatre Terrific, Annual Report 1989: Treasurer's Report, 3

36 TTA, Hugh McLeod, Social Development Officer, Secretary of State of Canada to Lorne Kimber, Theatre Terrific Society, 21 July 1988; TTA, Gerry Weiner, Secretary of State of Canada office to Mrs. Nan Purkis, Theatre Terrific Society, 26 February 1990; TTA, Robert de Cotret, Secretary of State of Canada office to Lois McLean, Theatre Terrific Society, 8 June 1992.

37 TTA, Jamie Norris, "Artistic Director Report," *Theatre Terrific Update*, 1996a, 3.

38 Ibid.

39 Ibid.

40 TTA, Jamie Norris, "Artistic Director Report," *Theatre Terrific Update*, 1996b, 3.

41 TTA, Elaine Avila and Trevor Found, "The School," document accompanying letter to "Fran" [Board of Directors] 15 June 1998.

42 TTA, Elaine Avila and Trevor Found, "Dream School," document accompanying letter to "Fran" [Board of Directors] 15 June 1998.

43 In the TTA, *Step Right Up!* program, only Molhoj is identified as a Theatre Terrific member; Beckett who had been involved since the company's early days, defined himself in the biographical notes as a professional actor, with no mention of disability.

44 In addition to Thomas' critical review, Tim Carlson described the show in the *Vancouver Sun* as "halfway there." TTA, Carlson, "Theatre Terrific's New Effort Makes for Some Uneven Entertainment," *Vancouver Sun*, 11 June 1999.

45 TTA, Colin Thomas, "Disability Troupe Dispenses with 'Niceness,'" *Georgia Straight*, 3–10 June 1999; TTA, Colin Thomas, "Step Right Up!" *Georgia Straight*, 17–24 June 1999, 107.

46 TTA, Avila and Found, "Dream School."

47 TTA, Roger Gaudet, Canada Council to Gayle Manketlow, Theatre Terrific Society, 21 February 2000.

48 TTA, "Artistic Director: Theatre Terrific," 2000.

49 TTA, Liesl Lafferty, "From the Artistic Director," *Theatre Terrific Newsletter* (Spring 2001): 1.

50 Liesl Lafferty, "Stage Ability: A Terrific Theatre Experience," *Canadian Theatre Review* 122 (Spring 2005): 65.

51 TTA, Theatre Terrific, "Theatre Terrific – Beyond Disability," F.K. Morrow Grant application, 2004.

52 Lafferty, "Stage Ability" 66.

53 TTA, David A. Bremner and Rebecca Shields, Empyrean Communications Proposal for Theatre Terrific, 12 November 2002.

54   TTA, Pat Mackenzie, "New Artistic Director Brings Strong Vision to Theatre Terrific," *Theatre Terrific Newsletter* (Spring 2005): 1.

55   TTA, Susanna Uchatius, "Notes from the A.D. Desk," *Theatre Terrific Newsletter* (Spring 2005): 2.

56   Ibid.

57   Ibid.

58   Ibid.

59   TTA, "Theatre Terrific Society Mandate," 2006.

60   TTA, Bryson Young, Review of *Ugly*, written and directed by Susanna Uchatius. *Vancouver Sun*, 14 September 2005.

61   Larscheid, personal interview.

62   TTA, Theatre Terrific. "*Workin'* has great run at Fringe Festival," *Theatre Terrific News* (Winter 2007): 1.

63   TTA, Uchatius as quoted in Peter Birnie, "Transcendent Transformations Front and Centre for Theatre Terrific," *Vancouver Sun*, 5 April 2010.

64   TTA, "*The Glass Box* Theatre Terrific 2008 Professional Production Audition Notice," *Theatre Terrific News* (Fall 2007): 2.

65   Ibid.

66   Jean Vanier, *Becoming Human* (Toronto: Anansi Press), 1998.

67   Susanna Uchatius, personal interview, 17 August 2009.

68   Larscheid, personal interview.

CHAPTER FIVE

1   Theatre Terrific Archives (TTA), Elaine Avila, "Visiting Theatre Unlimited," *Theatre Terrific Update* (Spring 1992): 6 and "Visiting Theatre Unlimited," *Theatre Terrific Update* (Fall 1992): 6.

2   International Guild of Disabled Artists and Performers website, http://igodap.ning.com.

3   Ibid.

4   TTA, Trevor Found, "Theatre Terrific in Australia," 1999.

5   TTA, Elaine Avila and Trevor Found, "From the Artistic Directors," *Theatre Terrific Society*, Spring 1999.

6   Michael Scott, "Candoco unable to impress," Arts and Magazine section, *Vancouver Sun*, 22 May 1999.

7   Owen Smith, "Shifting Apollo's Frame: Challenging the Body Aesthetic in Theater Dance," in *Bodies in Commotion: Disability & Performance*, ed. Carrie Sandahl and Philip Auslander (Ann Arbor: University of Michigan Press, 2005), 80.

8   Margaret Birrell and Joan Meister, "Letter to the editor," *Vancouver Sun*, 29 June 1999.

9   Kevin McKeown, "Letter to the editor," *Vancouver Sun*, 29 May 1999.

10   Adrian Chamberlain, "Therapeutic Art Falls Victim to Critics," *Times Colonist*, 5 June 1999.

11   Taylor Burke, "Letter to the Editor," *Vancouver Sun*, 29 June 1999.

12   s4DAC flyer.

13   Pamela Boyd, personal interview, 3 December 2007.

14   Alex Bulmer and Rose Jacobson, "The Picasso Project: A Report from the Field of Disability Arts," December 2004.

15   Diane Flacks, "Having cultivated her talent abroad, Alex Bulmer plants her creative seed here," *Toronto Star*, 26 May 2009.

16   Ibid.

17   Ibid.

18   Ibid.

19   The first of these festivals was entitled Stages: Unmasking Disability Culture: A Disability Arts Festival and was produced by Calgary scope Society and Transition to Independence in February 2002. In December 2002, Calgary scope Society and Stage Left productions produced A Second Look at Disability Culture: Another Disability Arts Festival.

20   For an archive of Art with Attitude events, see: Ryerson School of Disability Studies, "Performances," http://www.ryerson.ca/ds/activism/performances.html.

21   Ibid.

22   Renowned disability, women, and transgendered people's rights and anti-violence leader and activist, Joan Meister (1950–2004), was a founding member of s4DAC and served as chair of its board of directors. She was also a founding member of DAWN (DisAbled Women's Network) Canada.

23   James Sanders, personal interview, 2009.

24   Lisa Brown, personal interview, 2006.

25   *Shameless*, directed by Bonnie Klein, produced by the National Film Board of Canada, 2006.

26   Balancing Acts website, http://www.balancing-acts.org/about.htm.

27   The Canada Council website explains that the Alberta Creative Development Initiative (ACDI) is a partnership between the Alberta Foundation for the Arts and the Canada Council for the Arts in collaboration with the Calgary Arts Development Authority and the Edmonton Arts Council.

28   Balancing Acts website.

29   Jayne Leslie Boase, "Festivals: Agents of Change? Dynamics and Humanism Within Disability and Arts Collaborations," *The International Journal of the Humanities* 3, no. 10 (2006): 133.

30   Canadian Arts and Heritage Sustainability Program, http://www.pch.gc.ca/progs/pcapc-cahsp/index_e.cfm.

31   It is important to note my own participation in the network owing to my background as an academic interested in recording and analyzing disability

theatre activities in Canada and as the education and research director for the 2003 Madness and Arts World Festival. However, I have been restricted in drawing from the compiled minutes of the meetings, which remain private documents. As a result, instead of recording the specific and "in process" opinions of any particular network participant, my observations focus on broad themes of discussion, different disability culture perspectives, and emerging questions and directions in the network and disability arts in Canada.

32 Performance Creation Canada website, http://www.performancecreation canada.ca/.

33 A note in the glossary section of the IETM website explains the acronym and founding of the network: "Created in July 1981 in Polverigi, Italy at the Polverigi International Theatre Festival. An idea of Philippe Tiry, Roberto Cimetta, Velia Papa, Hugo De Greef, Gordana Vnuk, Patrick Sommier, Steve Austen, Jean-Paul Thibaudat. Called the 'Informal European Theatre Meeting.' In 2005, it was decided that the initials would be kept along with the new strap line, 'international network for contemporary performing arts.' IETM is an international non-profit association under Belgian law; the statute was confirmed in 1989." (International Network for Contemporary Performing Arts website, http://www.ietm.org).

34 The first meeting was held from 16–19 March 2006 at the University of Calgary's Faculty of Social Work. Student Holly Genois kept notes as part of a practicum credit. The second meeting ran from 22–24 February 2007 at the Ryerson RBC Disability Studies Centre. A regional meeting open to all interested disability artists was hosted at UBC on 24 April 2006. A second regional meeting held by Stage Left occurred on 30 November 2006. Workman Arts hosted a regional meeting in Toronto on 21 February 2007.

35 In alphabetical order, the participants were: Lisa Brown, Artistic Director of the Workman Theatre Project (Toronto), who inaugurated the Madness and Arts World Festival, now held internationally; Deborah Cohen, Executive Director and Producer of Abilities Arts Festival, Toronto; Michelle Decottignies and her successor as Artistic Director of Balancing Acts, Nicole Dunbar; Catherine Frazee, a founder of the Society for Disability Arts and Culture (S4DAC) and Kickstart in Vancouver, and a professor of disability studies at Ryerson University who organizes the Arts with Attitude and other annual disability arts events in Toronto; Bonnie Sherr Klein, award-winning documentary film-maker and one of the founders of S4DAC; Geoff McMurchy, a principal organizer of S4DAC and the Artistic Director of Vancouver's Kickstart festivals; David Roche, a disability arts comedian who has performed in numerous international, American, and Canadian disability arts festivals and sat on the board of S4DAC; Edmonton dramaturg and director of Speaking of Schizophrenia (SOS) Players, Sam Varteniuk; as well as the current author and several administrative staff. Other participants included Ghislaine (Jessie)

Fraser who was the office manager at s4DAC at the time of the first meeting and, in Toronto, Disability Scholar and Ryerson researcher Richard Ingram.

36 Stage Left, *Newsletter*, 2009, http://www.stage-left.org/docs/SLFallNewsletter.pdf.

37 Geoff McMurchy quoted in *A Legacy for All of Us: A Plan for the Development of Integrated Arts and Culture in British Columbia*, 8 (prepared by Richard Marcuse in collaboration with members of the integrated arts community), http://www.kickstart-arts.ca/brian/BRIANplan07-08-15.pdf. The document further explains, "The people who attended the initial planning meeting were Janet Ashdown, Consumer Initiative Fund, Vancouver Coastal Health, Highs & Lows Choir; Suzanne Bessette, Garth Homer Society art studio program, Victoria; James Sanders, Artistic Director, Realwheels Society; Barbara Sanders, Administrator, Realwheels Society; Susanna Uchatius, Artistic Director, Theatre Terrific; Irwin Oostindie, Gallery Gachet; Pat Danforth, Victoria Disability Arts Festival; Geoff McMurchy, s4DAC Artistic Director; Terry Wiens, Dance Victoria, Coordinator, Tailspin integrated dance workshops; Moe François, Director, Artists Helping Artists; Lawrence Shapiro, dancer representing Helen Walkley, choreographer; Vickie Cammack, Executive Director, PLAN Institute, s4DAC board member; Al Etmanski, President, PLAN, 2010 Legacies Now consultant; Rina Fraticelli, Executive Producer, National Film Board, Pacific & Yukon Region; Lori Baxter, 2010 Legacies Now/Arts Now; Catherine McDonald, General Manager, Theatre Terrific; Judith Marcuse, Artistic Producer, Judith Marcuse Projects, who facilitated the session; and Avril Orloff, who provided graphic recording for the session. The Advisory Group members are Geoff McMurchy of s4DAC; Catherine McDonald of Theatre Terrific; Lori Baxter, of Legacies Now; and Irwin Oostindie, of Gallery Gachet." Marcuse in collaboration, *A Legacy for All of Us*, 8.

38 Sanders, personal interview.

39 *A Legacy for All of Us*, 10.

40 Ibid., 11.

41 Rose Jacobson and Geoff McMurchy, "Focus on Disability & Deaf Arts," January 2009: 4, http://www.picassopro.org/resources.html.

42 Jihan Abbas et al., "Lights … Camera … Attitude!" Ryerson RBC Institute for Disability Studies Research and Education (2004): 1, 13 May 2007, http://www.ryerson.ca/ds/pdf/artsreport.pdf.

43 Canada Council, "Moving Forward: Canada Council for the Arts Strategic Plan 2008–2011," 1 June 2008, http://www.canadacouncil.ca/NR/rdonlyres/06782D43-21B4-4B26-BD60-1B4D96A00921/0/MovingforwardStrategicPlan200811.pdf.

44 See "Expanding the Arts: Deaf and Disability Arts, Access and Equality Strategy," Canada Council, 2011, http://canadacouncil.ca/NR/exeres/5CC65917-7CA0-4EE9-86BA-36DA1663F318.

45 Paul Anthony Darke, "Now I Know Why Disability Arts is Drowning in the

River Lethe," in *Disability, Culture and Identity*, ed. Sheila Riddell and Nick
Watson (Harlow, England: Pearson Education, 2003), 141.

CHAPTER SIX

1 For example, in its layered interrogations of criminal trials, media repre-
   sentations, and prejudice, the production invites comparisons with:
   Nightwood Theatre's 1984 production of *This is For You, Anna* by Suzanne
   Odette Khuri, Ann-Marie MacDonald, Banuta Rubess, and Maureen White;
   Neworld Theatre's 2004 production *Ali and Ali and the Axes of Evil* by Marcus
   Youssef, Guillermo Verdecchia, and Camyar Chai; and Teesri Duniya's 1996
   production of *Counter Offence* by Rahul Varma.

2 Michele Decottignies later notes that after consultation with a legal professional she revised her understanding of the case: "'necessity' does actually exist
   in Canadian law but it doesn't qualify in Latimer's case – he doesn't satisfy the
   criteria: the accused must be in imminent peril or danger; the accused must
   have had no reasonable legal alternative to the course of action he or she
   undertook; the harm inflicted by the accused must be proportional to the
   harm avoided by the accused" (Michele Decottignies, personal email, 10 June
   2011). For my purposes here, it is chiefly important to know the questions
   which guided the company's work, their accuracy in relation to Canadian law
   is a matter for a different kind of critical analysis.

3 Michele Decottignies, "Mercy Killing or Murder," *Canadian Theatre Review* 122
   (Spring 2005): 74.

4 Emil Sher, *Mourning Dove* (Toronto: Playwrights Canada Press, 2005), 79. This
   piece started as a radio play, first broadcast on CBC Radio in 1996; a further
   developed version premiered at the Great Canadian Theatre Company in
   2005.

5 Decottignies, "Mercy Killing or Murder," 74.

6 Decottignies is listed as director in the published CTR script but has since
   asked to be described as a dramaturg given the collaborative process involved
   and her anti-oppressive practice.

7 The first aspect involved extensive research into the case from a critical disability studies perspective. Researchers examined published material and tran-
   scripts related to the case. In the published version of the script, the authors
   cite in particular the relevance of Ruth Enns' *A voice unheard: The Latimer
   Case and People with Disabilities* (Toronto: Fernwood Press, 1999).

8 Decottignies, "Mercy Killing or Murder," 75.

9 Ibid., 71.

10 Ibid.

11 Ibid.

12 Ibid., 76–9.

13 Ibid., 83.

14 Ibid., 84.

15 Ibid., 86.

16 Ibid., 87.

17 Tagline is from Realwheels Archive (RA), Realwheels, *Skydive* promotional package.

18 Barbara Sanders, "In-flight Entertainment," *Alignment: Magazine of the Canadian Association for Prosthetics and Orthotics*, 2007, 36.

19 Ibid.

20 Kevin Kerr, *Skydive* (Vancouver: Talonbooks, 2010), 11.

21 Those interested in the details of the various prototypes and physical issues involved in this experimental development process should consult Sanders, "In-flight entertainment."

22 Ibid.

23 The production was nominated in five categories: Outstanding Production, Critics' Choice for Innovation, Best Sound, Best Direction, and for Sven Johansson's aerial choreography, Significant Artistic Achievement. They won the last three of these.

24 Kerr, *Skydive*, 19.

25 Wasserman, "See Skydive? Jump to It!" *Province*, 28 January 2007.

26 Kerr, *Skydive*, 10.

27 Ibid., 93.

28 Ibid., 95.

29 Ibid., 27.

30 RA, Dylan DeMarsh, "Real Drama," *Solutions* (Summer 2009).

31 Ibid.

32 RA, Ipsos Reid, "Skydive Impact Research" (company report, 20 March 2009), 3.

33 Catherine Frazee, "Disability Pride within Disability Performance," *Canadian Theatre Review* 122 (Spring 2005): 12. Italics as in original. The footnote in relation to the word normals reads as follows: "I am grateful to Disability Studies scholar John Kelly for the charmingly pejorative turn of phrase."

34 Ibid., 10–11.

35 Tobin Siebers, "Disability Aesthetics," *Journal of Cultural and Religious Theory* 7, no. 2 (Spring/Summer 2006): 64.

36 Catherine Frazee, "Excellence and Difference: Notes for Panel Presentation" (for kickstART! Celebration of Disability Arts and Culture, Roundhouse Community Centre, Vancouver, BC), 18 August 2001.

37 Victoria Maxwell, "Making the Invisible Visible," *Canadian Theatre Review* 122 (Spring 2005): 27.

CHAPTER SEVEN

1 Antonin Artaud, "Van Gogh: The Man Suicided by Society," in *Artaud Anthology* 4th edition, ed. Jack Hirschman (San Francisco: City Lights, 1965), 137.

2 Johnston Post-Performance Notes, 7 October 1997.

3 Wolfgang Iser, *The Act of Reading: A Theory of Aesthetic Response* (Baltimore: Johns Hopkins University Press, 1978), 226.

4 Ibid., 229–30.

5 Petra Kuppers, *Disability and Contemporary Performance* (New York: Routledge, 2003), 130.

6 Workman Arts Archive (WAA) Denise Dumol, comp. Summary of the Questions and Comments during Terry Watada's *Vincent* (unpublished play script, 1997).

7 Sander L. Gilman, *Picturing Health and Illness* (Baltimore: Johns Hopkins University Press, 1995), 31–50.

8 WAA, Watada, *Vincent*, 19.

9 Ibid., 1.

10 Ibid., 27.

11 Sandford Budick and Wolfgang Iser, eds. *Languages of the Unsayable: The Play of Negativity in Literature and Literary Theory* (New York: Columbia University Press, 1989), xiv.

12 Ibid., xvii.

13 Ibid., xiv.

14 Ibid., xiii.

15 WAA, Terry Watada, "Notes from the Playwright" (program for *Vincent*, 1993).

16 Budick and Iser, *Languages of the Unsayable*, xix.

17 Ibid., xii–xiii.

18 Sander L. Gilman, *Disease and Representation* (Ithaca: Cornell University Press, 1988), 13.

19 Anonymous, personal interview, 2001. While the theatrical performances of the WA are public, not all members feel comfortable with publicly disclosing their identities as people who have received mental health services. The stigma associated with mental illness has strong practical impacts on people's lives. For further discussion of this stigma as it exists in contemporary Canadian culture, please see Scott Simmie and Julia Nunes, *The Last Taboo: A Survival Guide to Mental Health Care in Canada* (Toronto: McClelland, 2001). For a broader analysis of the stigma associated with mental illness see Otto Wahl, *Telling Is Risky Business: Mental Health Consumers Confront Stigma* (New Brunswick, NJ: Rutgers University Press, 1999).

20 Anonymous, personal interview.

21 Gilman, *Disease and Representation*, 202–30.

22 Ibid., 202.

23 Ibid., 230.

24 Ibid., 242.

25 Ibid.

26 Ibid., 244.

27 Ibid., 243.

28 Ibid.

29 Gilman, *Picturing Health and Illness,* 31–50.

30 Ibid., 36.

31 Ibid., 41.

32 WAA, Watada, *Vincent,* 15–16.

33 Ibid., 13.

34 Lisa Brown, personal interview, 1999.

35 When the conference attendees at Penetanguishene saw *Vincent's* premiere, most had been coping with de-institutionalization for over one year. On 4 February 1992, amendments to the Canadian Criminal Code contained in Bill C-30 became law. To explain these changes to the concerned public, the Ontario Ministry of Health published, WAA, Ontario Ministry of Health, "Questions and Answers about How Bill C-30 (An Act to Amend the Canadian Criminal Code) Will Affect Forensic Mental Health Services in Ontario," May 1992. It explained that these amendments were intended to change provisions for forensic psychiatric patients, individuals defined as person[s] whose mental disorder has resulted in a significant interaction with the criminal justice system. These patients are usually held in the custody of a psychiatric hospital under the authority of both criminal and mental health law. The sections of the criminal code which the Bill changed were those dealing with the "placement and detention of defendants found not guilty by reason of insanity or unfit to stand trial," 2. These sections of the Criminal Code had been virtually unchanged for a hundred-and-fifty years. The amendments sought to reconcile the code with the Canadian Charter of Rights and Freedoms. Many of the amendments attempted to clarify terminology, for example, by replacing "insanity" with "mental disorder" and "not guilty" with "not criminally responsible." Others increased the possibility of conflicting interpretations, most particularly where the ramifications of the Bill for the mandatory treatment of "mentally disordered" individuals in the Province of Ontario were unclear, 6.

36 WAA, Mental Health Centre Penetanguishene and the Ontario Ministry of Health, "Working with the Mentally Ill in a Post-Institutional Era" (conference brochure, June 1993).

37 Lisa Brown and Terry Watada met with the Sabatino family several times during the development of the script and production. Mrs Sabatino, Dominic's mother, and her younger son attended the production at Metropolitan Police Headquarters in 1997.

38 WAA, James MacGowan and Paul Vieira, "Bat-Wielding Man Shot Dead by Police," *Globe and Mail*, 10 August 1992.

39 WAA, Swainson, "Debate Rages over Forcing Mentally Ill into Therapy," *Toronto Star*, 5 October 1992.

40 WAA, editorial, "Pepper vs. patience," *Toronto Star*, 16 August 1992.

41 Ibid.

42 Lester Donaldson was shot and killed by a Toronto police officer on 9 August 1988. Two officers had been sent to Donaldson's home following a complaint by another tenant that Mr Donaldson was violent. Mr Donaldson, a man diagnosed with mental illness, wielded a knife and was shot by a police officer through the abdomen before an Emergency Task Force arrived to support the officers. The case prompted investigations into racial discrimination and discrimination against the mentally ill. Public criticism of the police's handling of the incident led to a coroner's inquest and a criminal investigation by the Ontario Provincial Police. The civilian Public Complaints Commission also investigated "a complaint filed by Mr. Donaldson's widow concerning police behavior at the scene." See: Editorial, "The Aftermath of a Police Shooting," *Globe and Mail*, 16 August 1992.

43 WAA, Watada, "Notes from the Playwright."

44 In 1996, *Vincent* was produced at the Joseph Workman Auditorium on 10 October and for the Family Mental Health Alliance, Etobicoke (FAME) on 9 November. In August 1997, *Vincent* was performed at the Toronto Metropolitan Police Headquarters. *Vincent* then toured to a variety of Toronto venues from 7–17 October 1997. These venues included the George Brown College gymnasium, Ontario Science Centre, Humber College Auditorium, Credit Valley Hospital's Dr. Sane Auditorium, Caritas Hall for Mens Sana, Queensway Hospital Auditorium for Reconnect Mental Health Services, Aldwyn B. Stokes Auditorium for the Clarke Institute, and Noel Ryan Auditorium for the Distress Centre, Peel. A Manitoba tour followed in December, with a performance at the Royal Oak Inn in Brandon, the Prairie Theatre Exchange in Winnipeg, and the Mental Health Centre in Selkirk. The June 2000 remount directed by Michael Kelly for the Alternatives to the Use of Lethal Force by Police conference was held at the Law Society of Upper Canada, Osgoode Hall. In June 2001, a remount, again directed by Michael Kelly, was commissioned for the Crisis in Society Conference in Belleville, Ontario. In the spring of 2002, another remount toured, first to Hamilton's McMaster University, where it played to an audience of health care professionals, and then to the National Arts Centre in Ottawa. In March 2003 *Vincent* was performed as part of the company's Madness and Arts 2003 World Festival (described in Chapter 5). The show was remounted for the festival's second incarnation produced by Theater Sycorax in Münster, Germany in 2006.

45 Budick and Iser, *Languages of the Unsayable*, xiv.

CHAPTER EIGHT

1 Theatre Terrific Archives (TTA), Jan Derbyshire, Joanna Garfinkel, Kyla Harris, Watson Moy, and Susanna Uchatius, *The Glass Box* (Playwrights Theatre Centre, Vancouver BC, 18–28 February 2009).

2 "Southbury Training School," http://www.cga.ct.gov/2000/rpt/olr/htm/ 2000-r-0103.htm).

3 "Theatre Terrific presents 'The Secret Son,'" (Down Syndrome Research Foundation website, April 22, 2009), http://www.dsrf.org/?section_copy_ id+309&section_id+5044.

4 Susanna Uchatius, personal interview, 2009.

5 In "Arthur Miller's Missing Act," in *Vanity Fair*, September 2007, Suzanna Andrews notes that the only major American newspaper to mention Daniel in its obituary for Miller was the *Los Angeles Times*.

6 Uchatius, personal interview.

7 TTA, Susanna Uchatius, *The Secret Son*, Roundhouse Community Centre, Vancouver, BC, 22–5 April 2009.

8 Ibid.

9 Ibid.

10 Lennard J. Davis ed., *Disability Studies Reader* (New York: Routledge, 1997), 1.

11 Helen Meekosha, "A Disabled Genius in the Family: Personal Musings on the Tale of Two Sisters," *Disability and Society* 15, no. 5 (2000): 814.

12 Catherine Frazee, Joan Gilmour, and Roxanne Mykitiuk, "Now You See Her, Now You Don't: How Law Shapes Disabled Women's Experience of Exposure, Surveillance and Assessment in the Clinical Encounter," in *Critical Disability Theory: Essays in Philosophy, Politics, Policy and Law*, eds. Dianne Pothier and Richard Devlin (Vancouver: University of British Columbia Press, 2005), 235.

13 Canada.com, "Art on Wheels" (16 March 2007), http://www.canada.com/story_ print.html?id=f965e782-2ba2-477e-a695-b3487fb8e953&sponsor=.

14 Uchatius, personal interview.

15 Kyla Harris, television interview for *The Glass Box*, http://www.theatreterrific. ca/glass-box.

16 Magnetic North advertising for *The Glass Box*, n.d.

17 Uchatius, personal interview.

18 Michael A. Rembis, "Beyond the Binary: Rethinking the Social Model of Disabled Sexuality," *Disability and Sexuality* 28, no. 1 (March 2010): 58.

19 TTA, Jan Derbyshire, Joanna Garfinkel, Kyla Harris, Watson Moy, and Susanna Uchatius, *The Glass Box*, Playwrights Theatre Centre, Vancouver, BC, 18–28 February 2009.

20 Rosemarie Garland-Thomson, *Extraordinary Bodies: Figuring Physical Disability in American Culture and Literature* (New York: Columbia University Press, 1997), 8.

21 Leonard Cassuto, "Oliver Sacks and the Medical Case Narrative," in *Disability*

Studies: Enabling the Humanities, eds. Sharon L. Snyder, Brenda Jo Brueggemann, and Rosemarie Garland-Thomson (New York: Modern Language Association of America, 2002), 120.

22   Lennard J. Davis, *Enforcing Normalcy: Disability, Deafness and the Body* (London: Verso, 1995), 3.

23   Tobin Siebers, "Disability Aesthetics," *Journal of Cultural and Religious Theory* 7, no. 2 (Spring/Summer 2006): 64.

24   The play within the play title cites the earliest extant complete musical composition, the Seikilos epitaph, roughly dated from 200 BCE to 100 CE. *The Secret Son* included the composition as a refrain throughout the play: "While you live, shine like the sun, let nothing grieve you beyond measure, life exists only a short while and soon time will come to take its tribute."

25   TTA, Uchatius, *The Secret Son*.

26   Ibid.

27   Victoria Ann Lewis quoted in Kathleen A. Tolan, "We Are Not a Metaphor," *American Theatre* (April 2001): 17.

28   Victoria Ann Lewis, *Beyond Victims and Villains: Contemporary Plays by Disabled Playwrights* (New York: Theatre Communications Group, 2006), xxi.

29   Carrie Sandahl, "Ahhhh Freak Out! Metaphors of Disability and Femaleness in Performance," *Theatre Topics* 9, no. 1, (March 1999): 11–30.

30   For a strong overview of the complex problems and issues associated with casting in disability theatre, see Carrie Sandahl, "Why Disability Identity Matters: From Dramaturgy to Casting in John Belluso's Pyretown," *Text and Performance Quarterly* 28 (2008): 225–41. The Alliance for Inclusion in the Arts (formerly the Non-Traditional Casting Project) website also offers useful resources pertaining to these issues, http://inclusioninthearts.org/.

31   Sandahl, "Why Disability Identity Matters," 226.

CHAPTER NINE

1   2010 Legacies Now website, http://www.2010legaciesnow.com/.

2   Patrick Healey, "Advocacy Group Opposes 'Miracle Worker' Casting Choice," *New York Times* (ArtsBeat Blog, 29 October 2009), http://artsbeat.blogs.ny times.com/2009/10/29/advocacy-group-opposes-miracle-worker-casting-choice/.

3   Patrick Healey, "Vision-Impaired Girl Gets Helen Keller Understudy Role," *New York Times*, http://www.nytimes.com/2009/12/09/theater/09disabled.html.

4   On their website, Kickstart explains the service in more detail: "Each patron is given a personal receiver with a single earpiece and volume control that allows him or her to hear both the show and our live audio description at the same time. The broadcast begins 15 minutes before curtain with detailed descriptions of the set, characters and costumes. Once the show begins, the describer transmits pertinent physical action and visual detail between the lines of

dialogue. Brief program notes are provided at intermission." "VocalEye live Audio Description," Kickstart website, http://www.kickstart-arts.ca/vocal-eye/.

5 Ibid.

6 Ibid.

7 See Bert O. State's influential book, *Great Reckoning in Little Rooms: On the Phenomenology of Theater* (Berkeley: University of California Press, 1987).

8 *Rick: The Rick Hansen Story,* Study Guide, 4, http://www.rickhansen.com/Portals/2/Documents/StudyGuide.pdf .

9 *Rick: The Rick Hansen Story* website, http://www.rickhansen.com/.

10 *Rick: The Rick Hansen Story,* Study Guide, 4.

11 Rose Jacobson and Geoff McMurchy, "Focus on Disability and Deaf Arts," January 2009, http://www.picassopro.org/resources.html.

12 Carrie Sandahl, "Why Disability Identity Matters: From Dramaturgy to Casting in John Belluso's Pyretown," *Text and Performance Quarterly* 28 (2008): 226.

13 *The Blue Dragon* ran from 2–27 February in 2010, while *Spine* ran from 10–20 March 2010; the Olympics ran from 12–28 February in 2010, the Paralympics from 12–21 March 2010.

14 "Spine gets back to basics," Cultural Olympiad website, 15 March 2010, http://www.vancouver2010.com/more-2010-information/cultural-festivals-and-events/news/spine-gets-back-to-basics_303974us.html.

15 Ibid.

16 Liz Nichols, "Conjuring a Virtual Online Wonderland," *Edmonton Journal,* 3 February 2010.

17 "Spine gets back to basics."

18 Peter Birnie, "Avatars to Take the Stage in SPINE," *Vancouver Sun,* 3 March 2010.

19 Ibid.

20 Ibid.

21 Peter Birnie, "Playhouse Opens Season with Riveting Miracle Worker," *Vancouver Sun,* 16 October 2009.

22 Ibid.

23 Peter Birnie, "Man in Motion Honoured in One Wheelie," *Vancouver Sun,* 17 March 2010.

24 Ibid.

25 Peter Birnie, "Despite an Orgy of Effects, Spine Fails to Engage," *Vancouver Sun,* 14 March 2010.

26 In the spring of 2010, Vancouver's annual Jessie Richardson Theatre Awards honoured *The Miracle Worker.* The company won for "Outstanding Production, Large Theatre" and production artist Alessandro Juliani was awarded "Outstanding Sound Design or Original Composition, Large Theatre." Direc-

tor Meg Roe also won the "Ray Michal Award for Outstanding Work or Body of Work by an Emerging Director." Although they did not win, young performers Berner and Drabinsky, who alternated playing Helen Keller in the production, were both nominated for "Outstanding Performance by an Actress in a Lead Role, Large Theatre." Further production nominations included "Outstanding Lighting Design, Large Theatre" for John Webber and "Outstanding Set Design, Large Theatre" for Allan Stichbury. While, at the time of writing, neither *Rick:The Rick Hansen Story* nor *Spine* have won theatre awards, Foon's play for the former has been published by Playwrights Canada Press and the production has toured to Edmonton's Citadel Theatre. Plans for a 2012–13 tour of *Spine* have also been cited on the Realwheels company website.

CONCLUSION

1 David A. Freeman, *Creeps* (1970), in *Beyond Victims and Villains: Contemporary Plays by Disabled Playwrights*, ed. Victoria Ann Lewis (New York: Theatre Communications Group, 2006), 7–42. The play was included in both *Modern Canadian Drama*, ed. Richard Plant, 333–79 (Markham: Penguin Books, 1984) and *Modern Canadian Plays*, ed. Jerry Wasserman, 85–100 (Vancouver: Talon Books, 1985).

2 Victoria Ann Lewis, ed., *Beyond Victims and Villains: Contemporary Plays by Disabled Playwrights* (New York: Theatre Communications Group), 2006.

3 Ibid., 4.

4 David A. Freeman quoted in Ibid., 4.

5 Ibid., xxiv.

6 Ibid., xxv.

7 Michele Decottignies, personal interview, 31 May 2010.

8 Catherine Frazee, "Disability Pride within Disability Performance," *Canadian Theatre Review* 122 (Spring 2005): 12.

9 Bonnie Sherr Klein, *The Art of Disability: Some Ideas about Creativity, Health and Rehabilitation* (Vancouver: University of British Columbia, 2001), 5.

10 Ruth Bieber, "The Truth About Theatre from the Inside Out," *Canadian Theatre Review* 122 (Spring 2005): 58.

Bibliography

2010 Legacies Now website. http://www.2010legaciesnow.com/ (accessed 21 June 2010).

Abbas, Jihan, Kathryn Church, Catherine Frazee, and Melanie Panitch. "Lights … Camera … Attitude! Introducing Disability Arts and Culture." Ryerson RBC Institute for Disability Studies Research and Education (2004): 1–58, 13 May 2007. http://www.ryerson.ca/ds/pdf/artsreport.pdf (accessed 15 July 2010).

Andrews, Suzanna. "Arthur Miller's Missing Act." *Vanity Fair*, September 2007. http://www.vanityfair.com/culture/features/2007/09/miller200709?currentPage=all (accessed 1 July 2009).

The Alliance for Inclusion in the Arts website. http://inclusioninthearts.org/ (accessed 30 July 2011).

"Art on Wheels." *Victoria Times Colonist*, 16 March 2007.

Artaud, Antonin. "Van Gogh: The Man Suicided by Society." In *Artaud Anthology*. 4th ed., edited by Jack Hirschman, 135–63. San Francisco: City Lights, 1965.

Arts Smarts: Inspiration and Ideas for Canadian Artists with Disabilities. Vancouver: Society for Disability Arts and Culture, 2002.

Balancing Acts website. http://www.balancing-acts.org/ (accessed 27 October 2009).

Balancing Acts archive. http://www.balancing-acts.org/archives.htm (accessed 15 July 2010).

Balancing Acts 5 website, Festival Headliners. http://www.stage-left.org/festival_headliners.htm (accessed 15 July 2010).

Balancing Acts 9 website. http://www.balancing-acts.org/ba9.htm (accessed 15 July 2010).

Barnes, Colin, and Geof Mercer. *Disability*. Cambridge: Polity, 2003.

Barnes, Colin, Mike Oliver, and Len Barton, eds. *Disability Studies Today*. London: Polity, 2002.

Bennett, Susan. *Theatre Audiences: A Theory of Production and Reception*. London: Routledge, 1990.

Bieber, Ruth. "The Truth About Theatre from the Inside Out." *Canadian Theatre Review* 122 (Spring 2005): 55–8.

Birnie, Peter. "Avatars to Take the Stage in SPINE." *Vancouver Sun*, 3 March 2010.

– "Playhouse Opens Season with Riveting Miracle Worker." *Vancouver Sun*, 16 October 2009.

– "Man in Motion Honoured in One Wheelie." *Vancouver Sun*, 17 March 2010.

– "Despite an Orgy of Effects, Spine Fails to Engage." *Vancouver Sun*, 14 March 2010.

Birrell, Margaret, and Joan Meister. "Letter to the Editor." *Vancouver Sun*, 29 June 1999.

Boase, Jayne Leslie. "Festivals: Agents of Change? Dynamics and Humanism Within Disability and Arts Collaborations." *The International Journal of the Humanities* 3, no. 10 (2006): 133–6.

Budick, Sanford, and Wolfgang Iser, eds. *Languages of the Unsayable: The Play of Negativity in Literature and Literary Theory*. New York: Columbia University Press, 1989.

Bulmer, Alex. "Alex Bulmer on the Hierarchy of Disability." 10 May 2009. http://www.bookofjudithplay.blogspot.ca/2009_05_01archive.html (accessed June 2009).

– *Smudge*. (2000) In *Lesbian Plays: Coming of Age in Canada*. Toronto: Playwrights Canada Press, 2007.

– and Rose Jacobson. "The Picasso Project: A Report from the Field of Disability Arts." December 2004. http://www.picassopro.org/resources.html (accessed December 18, 2009).

Campbell, Andrea. "The Downlow on the MoMo: This Group Will Have You Dancing in Tongues." *FFWD Weekly*, 24–30 May 2007, 46.

Canada Council. "Moving Forward: Action Plan 2008–2011." 1 June 2008. http://www.canadacouncil.ca/NR/rdonlyres/06782D43-21B4-4B26-BD60-1B4D96 A00921/0/MovingforwardStrategicPlan200811.pdf (accessed 1 November 2011).

Canada Council. "Moving Forward: Canada Council for the Arts Strategic Plan 2008–2011: Values and Directions." 1 November 2007. http://www.canadacouncil.ca/aboutus/strat_plan/qw12844551678 1777288.htm (accessed 25 November 2011).

Canada Council. "Expanding the Arts: Deaf and Disability Arts, Access and Equality Strategy," September 2011. http://canadacouncil.ca/NR/exeres/5CC65917-7CA0-4EE9-86BA-36DA1663F318 (accessed 25 November 2011).

Canadian Heritage. "Canadian Arts and Heritage Sustainability Program."
http://www.pch.gc.ca/pgm/pcapc-cahsp/index-eng.cfm (accessed 13 May 2007).

Cassuto, Leonard. "Oliver Sacks and the Medical Case Narrative." In *Disability
Studies: Enabling the Humanities*, edited by Sharon L. Snyder, Brenda Jo Bruegge-
mann, and Rosemarie Garland-Thomson, 118–30. New York: Modern Language
Association of America, 2002.

Chamberlain, Adrian. "Therapeutic Art Falls Victim to Critics." *Times Colonist*, 5
June 1999.

Charlton, James I. *Nothing About Us Without Us: Disability Oppression and Empowerment*. Berkeley: University of California Press, 1998.

Chivers, Sally. "Barrier by Barrier: The Canadian Disability Movement and the
Fight for Equal Rights." In *Group Politics and Social Movements in Canada*, edited
by Miriam Smith, 307–28. Peterborough: Broadview Press, 2008.

Citron, Paula. "Rochdale Revisited in Multi-media Stage Trip." *Toronto Star*,
10 September 1992.

Cohen, Hilary U. "Conflicting Values in Creating Theatre with the Developmentally
Disabled: A Study of Theatre Unlimited." *The Arts in Psychotherapy* 12 (1985):
3–10.

Community Living Society website. http://www.cls–bc.org/ (accessed 2 April 2010).

Corker, Mairian, and Tom Shakespeare, eds. *Disability/ Postmodernity: Embodying
Disability Theory*. London: Continuum, 2002.

Council of Canadians with Disabilities website. "Social Policy." http://www.ccdon
line.ca/en/socialpolicy/ (accessed 28 June 2011).

Cushman, Robert. "Theatre review: Edward the 'Crazy Man' brings mental illness
home." *National Post*, 2 May 2011.

Darke, Paul Anthony. "Now I Know Why Disability Arts is Drowning in the River
Lethe (with thanks to Pierre Bourdieu)." In *Disability, Culture and Identity*, edited
by Sheila Riddell and Nick Watson, 131–42. Harlow, England: Pearson Education,
2003.

Davis, Lennard J., ed. *Disability Studies Reader*. New York: Routledge, 1997.

– *Enforcing Normalcy: Disability, Deafness and the Body*. London: Verso, 1995.

Day, Marie. *Edward the "Crazy Man."* Toronto: Annick Press, 2002.

Decottignies, Michele. "Mercy Killing or Murder: The Tracy Latimer Story."
Canadian Theatre Review 122 (Spring 2005): 67–88.

– and Andrew Houston, eds. "Theatre and the Question of Disability." *Canadian
Theatre Review* 122 (Spring 2005): 1–97.

Degner, Theresia. "Disability Discrimination Law: A Global Comparative
Approach." In *Disability Rights in Europe: From Theory to Practice*, edited by
Caroline Gooding and Anna Lawson, 87–106. Oxford: Hart Publishing, 2006.

Dinsmore, Ted. "Play's Cast is Blind But You'd Never Guess." *Toronto Star*, 16 March
1961.

Dunphy, Cathy. "Blind Actors Aim for No-fault Night." *Toronto Star*, 7 January 1986.

Editorial, "The Aftermath of a Police Shooting." *Globe and Mail*, 30 August 1988.

Ende, Michael. *Momo*. New York: Doubleday Penguin, 1984.

Enns, Ruth. *A Voice Unheard: The Latimer Case and People with Disabilities*. Toronto: Fernwood Press, 1999.

Ferguson, Iain. "Challenging a 'Spoiled Identity': Mental Health Service Users, Recognition and Redistribution." In *Disability, Culture and Identity*, edited by Sheila Riddell and Nick Watson, 67–87. Harlow, Essex: Pearson Education, 2003.

FFWD Weekly (Calgary). "Your Face Here: Pamela Boyd." May 2007, 17–23.

Fitzgerald, Wanda C. "The Glenvale Players: Canada's Premier Group of Blind and Vision-Impaired Theatre Artists." Alliance for Equality for Blind Canadians website. http://www.blindcanadians.ca/publications/cbm/19/glenvale-players-canadas-premier-group-blind-and-vision-impaired-theatre-artists (accessed 21 June 2010).

– "Stepping from the Wings." *Canadian Theatre Review* 122 (2005): 62–4.

Flacks, Diane. "Having Cultivated Her Talent Abroad, Alex Bulmer Plants Her Creative Seed Here." *Toronto Star*, 26 May 2009.

Fleischer, Doris Zames, and Frieda Zames. *The Disability Rights Movement: From Charity to Confrontation*. Philadelphia: Temple University Press, 2001.

Foucault, Michel. *Madness and Civilization: A History of Insanity in the Age of Reason*. New York: Vintage Books, 1988, c1965.

Fox, Ann M., and Joan Lipkin. "Res(Crip)ting Feminist Theater Through Disability Theater: Selections from the DisAbility Project." *NWSA Journal* 14, no. 3 (Fall 2002): 77–98.

Frazee, Catherine. "Disability Pride within Disability Performance." *Canadian Theatre Review* 122 (Spring 2005): 10–12.

– "Excellence and Difference: Notes for Panel Presentation" for kickstART! Celebration of Disability Arts and Culture, Roundhouse Community Centre, Vancouver, BC, 18 August 2001.

– "Notes for Keynote Address by Catherine Frazee for kickstART 2: Festival of Disability Arts and Culture." http://www.s4dac.org/festivals/kickstart/2004/catherine_frazee_keynote.pdf (accessed 10 December 2004).

– Joan Gilmour, and Roxanne Mykitiuk. "Now You See Her, Now You Don't: How Law Shapes Disabled Women's Experience of Exposure, Surveillance and Assessment in the Clinical Encounter." In *Critical Disability Theory: Essays in Philosophy, Politics, Policy and Law*, edited by Dianne Pothier and Richard Devlin, 223–47. Vancouver: University of British Columbia Press, 2005.

– Kathryn Church, and Melanie Panitch, eds. *Out from Under: Disability, History & Things to Remember*. Toronto: School of Disability Studies, Faculty of Community Services, Ryerson University, 2008.

Freeman, David A. *Creeps*. (1970) In *Beyond Victims and Villains: Contemporary Plays by Disabled Playwrights*, edited by Victoria Ann Lewis, 7–42. New York: Theatre Communications Group, 2006.

– *Creeps.* (1970) In *Modern Canadian Drama*, edited by Richard Plant, 333–79. Markham: Penguin Books, 1984.

– *Creeps.* (1970) In *Modern Canadian Plays*, edited by Jerry Wasserman, 85–100. Vancouver: Talon Books, 1985.

Friendly Spike Theatre Band. "Current Events." http://www.friendlyspike.ca/Current %20Events.html (accessed 21 June 2010).

Garland-Thomson, Rosemarie. *Extraordinary Bodies: Figuring Physical Disability in American Culture and Literature.* New York: Columbia University Press, 1997.

Gilman, Sander L. *Disease and Representation: Images of Illness from Madness to Aids.* Ithaca: Cornell University Press, 1988.

– *Picturing Health and Illness: Images of Identity and Difference.* Baltimore: Johns Hopkins University Press, 1995.

"Glenvale Players." In *Canadian Theatre Encyclopedia*, Athabasca University Press. www.canadiantheatre.com (accessed 25 November 2011).

Goffin, Jeff. "Help Unwanted Makes Its Point with Humour." *FFWD Weekly*, March 2003, 20–6.

Green, Barbara. "The Inside Out Integrated Theatre Project: Making Theatre an Agent of Change." *Theatre Alberta News* (Winter 2005): 9–10.

– with Ruth Bieber. "Inside/Out Theatre." *Bridges* (Fall 2004): 10–11.

Grossé, Jocelyn. "Theatre. Breaking Down Barriers. DisArts Collective's Freak Out! Celebrates Diversity Through Art." *FFWD Weekly*, 23 November 2006. http://www.ffwd weekly.com/Issues/2006/1123/the2.htm (accessed 25 November 2011).

Harris, Kyla. "Interview: Intrepid Theatre: Stories on and off Stage." Blip.tv website. http://blip.tv/file/1711267?utm_source=aolvideo&utm_medium=aolvideo (accessed 15 July 2010).

Healey, Patrick. "Advocacy Group Opposes 'Miracle Worker' Casting Choice." *New York Times*, ArtsBeat Blog, 29 October 2009. http://artsbeat.blogs.nytimes.com/ 2009/10/29/advocacy-group-opposes-miracle-worker-casting-choice/ (accessed 25 November 2011).

– "Vision-Impaired Girl Gets Helen Keller Understudy Role." *New York Times.* http://www.nytimes.com/2009/12/09/theater/09disabled.html (accessed December 2009).

Houston, Andrew. "Lyle Victor Albert's After Shave." *Canadian Theatre Review* 122 (Spring 2005): 26–8.

Hurley, Erin. *Theatre & Feeling.* London: Palgrave Macmillan, 2010.

International Guild of Disabled Artists and Performers website. http://igodap. ning.com (accessed 29 June 2010).

International Network for Contemporary Performing Arts website. http://www.ietm. org/ (accessed 15 July 2010).

Iser, Wolfgang. *The Act of Reading: A Theory of Aesthetic Response.* Baltimore: Johns Hopkins University Press, 1978.

Jacobson, Rose, and Alex Bulmer. "The Picasso Project: A Report from the Field of

Disability-Arts." December 2004. http://www.picassopro.org/2PicassoReport.pdf (accessed 25 November 2011).

– and Geoff McMurchy. "Focus on Disability & Deaf Arts in Canada." January 2009. http://www.picassopro.org/resources.html (accessed 18 December 2009).

Johnston, Kirsten M. Post-Performance Notes. 7 October 1997.

– "Staging Madness: Dramatic Modes of Representing Mental Illness at the Workman Theatre Project, 1989–2001." PhD diss., University of Toronto, 2002.

Kaplan, Jon. "Alex Bulmer's groundbreaking *Smudge* goes inside the mind's eye. Sight unseen." *Now Magazine*, 16 November 2000.

Kerr, Kevin. *Skydive*. Vancouver: Talonbooks, 2010.

Kickstart. Promotional Flyer. 2001.

Kickstart. "VocalEye live Audio Description." http://www.kickstart-arts.ca/vocal-eye/ (accessed 31 December 2011).

Khuri, Suzanne Odette, Ann-Marie MacDonald, Banuta Rubess, Tori Smith, Barb Taylor, and Maureen White. "This is For You, Anna: A Spectacle of Revenge." *Canadian Theatre Review* 43 (Summer 1985): 127–66.

Klein, Bonnie Sherr. *The Art of Disability: Some Ideas about Creativity, Health and Rehabilitation*. Vancouver: University of British Columbia Press, 2001.

Kudlick, Catherine. "Disability History: Why We Need Another 'Other.'" *The American Historical Review* 108, no. 3 (June 2003): 763–93.

Kuppers, Petra. *Disability and Contemporary Performance*. New York: Routledge, 2003.

– "Toward the Unknown Body: Stillness, Silence, and Space in Mental Health Settings." *Theatre Topics* 10, no. 2 (2000): 129–43.

Lafferty, Liesl. "Stage Ability: A Terrific Theatre Experience." *Canadian Theatre Review* 122 (Spring 2005): 65–6.

Lewis, Victoria Ann, ed. *Beyond Victims and Villains: Contemporary Plays by Disabled Playwrights*. New York: Theatre Communications Group, 2006.

Linton, Simi. "Disability and Conventions of Theatre." http://www.similinton.com/about_topics_2.htm (accessed 28 June 2011).

Longmore, Paul K. "The Second Phase: From Disability Rights to Disability Culture." http://www.independentliving.org/docs3/longm95.html (accessed 25 November 2011). Originally published in *Disability Rag & Resource*, September/October 1995.

Mad Pride Toronto YouTube Channel, *The Edmond Yu Project* Parts 1–3. www.youtube.com/user/madpridetoronto (accessed 7 July 2010).

Marcuse, Richard, in collaboration with members of the integrated arts community. *A Legacy for All of Us: A Plan for the Development of Integrated Arts and Culture in British Columbia*. http://www.kickstart-arts.ca/brian/BRIANplan07-08-15.pdf (accessed 25 November 2011).

Maxwell, Victoria website. http://www.victoriamaxwell.com (accessed 15 July 2010).

– "Making the Invisible Visible." *Canadian Theatre Review* 122 (Spring 2005): 26–8.

McCarthy, S. Siobhan. "Using the Arts as a Tool for Healing, Self-Discovery, Empowerment and Catharsis." *Canadian Theatre Review* 122 (Spring 2005): 59–61.

McKeown, Kevin. "Letter to the Editor." *Vancouver Sun*, 29 May 1999.

Meekosha, Helen. "A Disabled Genius in the Family: Personal Musings on the Tale of Two Sisters." *Disability and Society* 15, no. 5 (2000): 811–15.

MoMo Dance Theatre website. http://www.momodancetheatre.org/about_us.htm (accessed 15 July 2010).

Neufeldt, Aldred H. "Growth and Evolution of Disability Advocacy in Canada." In *Making Equality: History of Advocacy and Persons with Disability in Canada*, edited by Deborah Stienstra and Aileen Wight-Felske, 11–32. Toronto: Captus Press, 2003.

Nichols, Liz. "Conjuring a Virtual Online Wonderland." *Edmonton Journal*, 3 February 2010.

Patston, Philip. "Who's behind IGODAP? And why?" http://www.igodap.org/founder.htm (accessed 10 December 2004).

Performance Creation Canada website. http://www.performancecreationcanada.ca/ (accessed 15 July 2010).

Peters, Yvonne. "From Charity to Equality: Canadians with Disabilities Take Their Rightful Place in Canada's Constitution." In *Making Equality: History of Advocacy and Persons with Disability in Canada*, edited by Deborah Stienstra and Aileen Wight-Felske, 119–36. Toronto: Captus Press, 2003.

Peterson, Dale, ed. *A Mad People's History of Madness*. Pittsburgh: University of Pittsburgh Press, 1982.

Picard, Andre. "Vancouver Airport Wins New Hansen Prize." *Globe and Mail*, 12 June 2004.

Picasso Pro website. http://www.picassopro.org/ (accessed 21 June 2010).

Picasso Pro. "Mandate," http://www.picassopro.org/about.html (accessed 21 June 2010).

Porter, Roy. *A Social History of Madness: Stories of the Insane*. London: Phoenix/Orion Books, 1996.

Prince, Michael J. "Canadian Federalism and Disability Policy Making." *Canadian Journal of Political Science* 34, no. 4 (December 2001): 791–817.

PuSh International Performing Arts Festival website. http://pushfestival.ca/ (accessed 7 July 2010).

Rae, Robert. "Disability, invisibility and theatre: which nation are we staging?" *International Journal of Scottish Theatre* 2, no.1 (2001). http://erc.qmu.ac.uk/OJS/index.php/IJoST/article/view/78/html (accessed 28 June 2011).

Realwheels. "Skydive: An Action-Adventure-Comedy for the Stage." Promotional package. nd.

– Realwheels Website. www.realwheels.ca (accessed 7 July 2010).

Reaume, Geoffrey. *Remembrance of Patients Past: Patient Life at the Toronto Hospital for the Insane, 1870–1940*. Toronto: Oxford University Press Canada, 2000.

Rembis, Michael A. "Beyond the Binary: Rethinking the Social Model of Disabled Sexuality." *Disability and Sexuality* 28, no. 1 (March 2010): 51–60.

Restless Dance. http://www.restlessdance.org/ (accessed 18 December 2009).

Rick: The Rick Hansen Story. Study Guide. http://www.rickhansen.com/Portals/2/Documents/StudyGuide.pdf (accessed 5 July 2010).

Rick: The Rick Hansen Story. Website. http://www.rickhansen.com/ (accessed 5 July 2010).

Riddell, Sheila, and Nick Watson, eds. *Disability, Culture and Identity*. Harlow, England: Pearson Education, 2003.

Rubenfeld, Michael and Sarah G. Stanley. *The Book of Judith*. Centre for Addiction and Mental Health grounds, Toronto, Ontario. 19–31 May 2009.

Ryerson School of Disability Studies website, "Performances." http://www.ryerson.ca/ds/activism/performances.html (accessed 15 July 2010).

Sandahl, Carrie. "Ahhhh Freak Out! Metaphors of Disability and Femaleness in Performance." *Theatre Topics* 9, no. 1, (March 1999): 11–30.

– "Black Man, Blind Man: Disability Identity Politics and Performance." *Theatre Journal* 56, no. 4 (December 2004): 579–602.

– "The Tyranny of Neutral: Disability and Actor Training." In *Bodies in Commotion: Disability & Performance*, edited by Carrie Sandahl and Philip Auslander, 255–67. Ann Arbor: University of Michigan Press, 2005.

– "Why Disability Identity Matters: From Dramaturgy to Casting in John Belluso's Pyretown." *Text and Performance Quarterly* 28 (2008): 225–41.

– and Philip Auslander. "Disability Studies in Commotion with Performance Studies." Introduction in *Bodies in Commotion: Disability & Performance*, edited by Carrie Sandahl and Philip Auslander, 1–12. Ann Arbor, MI: University of Michigan Press, 2005.

Scott, Michael. "CanDoCo Unable to Impress." Arts and Magazine section, *Vancouver Sun*, 22 May 1999.

– "Is Disabled Dance Only Victim Art?" *Vancouver Sun*, 19 May 1999.

Shain, Alan. "Disability, Theatre and Power: An Analysis of a One-Person Play." MA thesis, Carleton University, 2006.

– "Disability, Theatre and Power: An Analysis of a One-Person Play." *Canadian Theatre Review* 122 (Spring 2005): 13–18.

Shakespeare, Tom, and Nicholas Watson. "The Social Model of Disability: An Outdated Ideology? Exploring Theories and Expanding Methodologies." In *Research in Social Science and Disability* 2, 9–28. Stamford, CT: JAI Press, 2001.

Shameless. Directed by Bonnie Sherr Klein. Produced by the National Film Board of Canada. 2006. Film.

Sher, Emil. *Mourning Dove*. Toronto: Playwrights Canada Press, 2005.

Siebers, Tobin. "Disability Aesthetics." *Journal of Cultural and Religious Theory* 7, no. 2 (Spring/Summer 2006): 63–73.

– *Disability Theory*. Ann Arbor: University of Michigan Press, 2008.

– *Disability Aesthetics*. Ann Arbor: University of Michigan Press, 2010.

Simmie, Scott, and Julia Nunes. *The Last Taboo: A Survival Guide to Mental Health Care in Canada*. Toronto: McClelland, 2001.

Skotch, Richard K. "American Disability Policy in the Twentieth Century." In *The New Disability History*, edited by Paul K. Longmore and Lauri Umansky, 375–92. New York: New York University Press, 2001.

Smith, Owen. "Shifting Apollo's Frame: Challenging the Body Aesthetic in Theater Dance," In *Bodies in Commotion: Disability & Performance*, edited by Carrie Sandahl and Philip Auslander, 73–85. Ann Arbor: University of Michigan Press, 2005.

– "Judith Snow Inside Her Third Cycle of 30 Years." Blog entry, 1 February 2011. http://thirdcycle.blogspot.com/2011/02/february-1-2011.html (accessed June 27, 2011).

Snyder, Sharon L., Brenda Jo Brueggemann, and Rosemarie Garland-Thomson, "Introduction: Integrating Disability into Teaching and Scholarship." In *Disability Studies: Enabling the Humanities*, edited by Sharon L. Snyder, Brenda Jo Brueggemann, and Rosemarie Garland-Thomson, 1–12. New York: Modern Language Association of America, 2002.

"Southbury Training School." http://www.cga.ct.gov/2000/rpt/olr/htm/2000-r-0103.htm (accessed 15 August 2009).

"Spine gets back to basics." Cultural Olympiad website, 15 March 2010. http://www.vancouver2010.com/more-2010-information/cultural-festivals-and-events/news/spine-gets-back-to-basics_303974us.html (accessed 21 June 2010).

Stage Left. "Balancing Acts." http://www.balancing-acts.org/about.htm (accessed 27 October 2011).

– *Newsletter* (Fall 2009). http://www.stage-left.org/docs/SLFallNewsletter.pdf (accessed 16 December 2009).

Stage Left Productions website. http://www.stage-left.org/ (accessed 27 December 2011).

State, Bert O. *Great Reckoning in Little Rooms: On the Phenomenology of Theater*. Berkeley: University of California Press, 1987.

Suleiman, Susan, and Inge Crosman, eds. *The Reader in the Text: Essays on Audience Interpretation*. Princeton, NJ: Princeton University Press, 1980.

Taylor, Burke. "Letter to the Editor." *Vancouver Sun*, 29 June 1999.

The Enchantment. Directed by Gille Blais. Produced by Colette Blanchard and the National Film Board of Canada. 1994. Film.

"Theatre Terrific presents 'The Secret Son.'" Down Syndrome Research Foundation website, 22 April 2009. http://www.dsrf.org/?section_copy_id+309&section_id+5044 (Accessed 15 August 2009).

Tolan, Kathleen A. 2001. "We Are Not a Metaphor." *American Theatre* (April 2001): 17–21, 57–9.

Tracie, Rachel E. "Deaf Theatre in Canada: Signposts to Another Land," Master's thesis, University of Alberta, 1998.

Traiger, Lisa. "Language in silence: Deaf, Jewish mime onstage at Gallaudet." *Washington Jewish Week*, 11 March 2010. http://www.washingtonjewishweek.com /main.asp?SectionID=27&SubSectionID=25&ArticleID=12430&TM=1884.501 (accessed 15 July 2010).

Vanier, Jean. *Becoming Human*. Toronto: Anansi Press, 1998.

Varma, Rahul. *Counter Offence*. Toronto: Playwrights Canada Press, 1997.

Vernon, Ayesha. "The Dialectics of Multiple Identities and the Disabled People's Movement." *Disability and Society* 14, no. 3 (1999): 385–98.

Victoria Maxwell Media Kit. http://www.victoriamaxwell.com/media/Email%20 Web%20Can%20info%20kit.pdf (accessed 7 July 2010).

Wahl, Otto. *Media Madness: Public Images of Mental Illness*. New Brunswick, NJ: Rutgers University Press. 1995.

– *Telling Is Risky Business: Mental Health Consumers Confront Stigma*. New Brunswick, NJ: Rutgers University Press, 1999.

Wasserman, Jerry. "See *Skydive*? Jump to It!" *Province*, 28 January 2007.

Watada, Terry. "Tale of a Mask." In *Canadian Mosaic: 6 Plays*, edited by Aviva Ravel, 43–83. Toronto: Simon and Pierre, 1995.

Youssef, Marcus, Guillermo Verdecchia, and Camyar Chai. *The Adventures of Ali & Ali and the aXes of Evil: A Divertimento for Warlords*. Vancouver: Talon Books, 2005.

Zickefoose, Sherri. "Stages of Development: Integrated Theatre Company Gives Disabled a Voice." *Calgary Herald Entertainment Guide*, 27 March–2 April 2003, 1–2.

ARCHIVAL SOURCES

The archives below refer to the collections of documents maintained by the listed companies. With the exception of the City of Vancouver archives, these are not organized archives with conventional archival filing systems. As a result, I refer to each document individually.

City of Vancouver Archives

City of Vancouver. *Vancouver '92: An Overview of City Programs for People with Disabilities*. Document Number PD 2226, n.d.

Realwheels Archives (Vancouver, BC)

DeMarsh, Dylan. "Real Drama." *Solutions* (Summer 2009).

Ipsos Reid. "Skydive Impact Research: Topline Results." Company report, 20 March 2009.

Moore, Mavor. Quoted in "Realwheels Society – Past, Present and Future." Direct Access Application Documents, n.d.

Realwheels. Skydive promotional package, n.d.

Realwheels Ad Hoc Collective. "The Realwheels Theatre Project." Application to the BC Arts Council for Project Assistance for Professional Theatre, 15 April 2004.

Sanders, Barbara. "In-Flight Entertainment." *Alignment: Magazine of the Canadian Association for Prosthetics and Orthotics* (2007), 36–8.

Sanders, James. Artistic Director's Report from the Realwheels Annual General Meeting, 15 November 2004.

Theatre Terrific Archives (Vancouver, BC)

Alberni Valley Times. "Theatre Terrific Takes Play Production to District Schools." 3 March 1992.

Appelbe, Alison. "Theatre a Terrific Experience for Disabled." *Vancouver Courier,* 28 November 1990.

Avila, Elaine, and Trevor Found. "Dream School." Document accompanying letter to "Fran" [Board of Directors], 15 June 1998b.

– "From the Artistic Directors." Theatre Terrific Society, Spring 1999.

– "The School." Document accompanying letter to "Fran" [Board of Directors], 15 June 1998.

– "Visiting Theatre Unlimited," *Theatre Terrific Update* (Spring 1992).

– "Visiting Theatre Unlimited," *Theatre Terrific Update* (Fall 1992).

Baxter, Jamie. "Theatre Terrific Brings World of Disabled to Schools." *Vancouver Sun,* 19 November 1992.

Bernhard, Kate. "One on One: Teaching Kids About Life," *Theatre Terrific Update* (Spring/Summer 1989): 3.

Birnie, Peter. "Transcendent Transformations Front and Centre for Theatre Terrific." *Vancouver Sun,* 5 April 2010.

Bremner, David A., and Rebecca Shields. Empyrean Communications. Proposal for Theatre Terrific, 12 November 2002.

British Columbia, Province of. Certificate of Incorporation, Theatre Terrific Society, 19 August 1985.

Busheikin, Laura. "Theatre Group Enables the Disabled." *Ubyssey,* 12 August 1987.

Canada.com. "Art on Wheels." 16 March 2007. http://www.canada.com/story_print.html?id=f965e782-2ba2-477e-a695-b3487fb8e953&sponsor= (accessed 1 July 2009).

Carlson, Tim. "Theatre Terrific's New Effort Makes for Some Uneven Entertainment." *Vancouver Sun,* 11 June 1999.

Comox District Free Press. "Theatre Terrific Comes Here." 7 April 1993.

Cotret, Robert de, Secretary of State of Canada. Official communication to Lois McLean. Theatre Terrific Society, 8 June 1992.

Cresswell, Tina. "Actors with a Special Extra." *Prince George Citizen,* February 1990.

Down Syndrome Research Foundation. "Theatre Terrific Presents 'The Secret Son.'"
    22 April 2009. http://www.dsrf.org/?section_copy_id+309&section_id+5044
    (accessed 15 August 2009).

Ducharme, Catherine. "Unique Theatre Group." *The Spokesman*, 11 February 1989.

Editorial, *Globe and Mail*. "The Aftermath of a Police Shooting." 30 August 1988.

Fitzgerald, Nicole. "Ups and Downs for Theatre Terrific's New Artistic Director."
    Terminal City, July 2001, 13–19.

Found, Trevor. "Theatre Terrific in Australia." Theatre Terrific Society, Spring 1999.

Gaudet, Roger, on behalf of Canada Council. Letter to Gayle Manktelow. *Theatre
    Terrific Society*, 21 February 2000.

The Glass Box. Devised by Jan Derbyshire, Joanna Garfinkel, Kyla Harris, Watson
    Moy, and Susanna Uchatius. Playwrights Theatre Centre, Vancouver, BC, 18–28
    February 2009.

Griffin, Kevin. "Theatre Terrific Certainly is Just That – Terrific." *Vancouver
    Weekender*, 14 August 1986.

Harris, Kyla. Television interview for *The Glass Box*. http://www.theatreterrific.ca/
    glass-box (accessed 1 August 2009).

Hargrave, Connie. "All of Life's a Stage." *Transitions* (May–June 2000): 14.

– "Connie's Thoughts." 10 October 1986.

– "Looking Back on 10 Years of Theatre Terrific." *Theatre Terrific Update* (Winter
    1995): 1–3.

Lacey, Liam. "Theatre 'Opens Horizons' for Disabled Actors." *Globe and Mail*,
    14 March 1990.

Lafferty, Liesl. "From the Artistic Director." *Theatre Terrific Newsletter* (Spring
    2001): 1.

Leiren-Young, Mark. "Uneven Play Has Moments." *Georgia Straight*, September
    1986, 12–19.

Lister, Sue. "Artistic Director's Report." *Theatre Terrific Update* (Spring 1994): 2.

– "Highlights from the Artistic Director." *Theatre Terrific Update* (Winter 1995): 4.

– "Sue's Thoughts for the Day." 9 October 1986.

Lukacs, Boby. "How Theatre Changed My Life." *Theatre Terrific Newsletter* (Winter
    1992): 9.

Mackenzie, Pat. "New Artistic Director Brings Strong Vision to Theatre Terrific."
    Theatre Terrific Newsletter (Spring 2005): 1.

Magnetic North Advertising for *The Glass Box*, n.d.

McLeod, Hugh, Social Development Officer, Secretary of State of Canada. Official
    communication to Lorne Kimber. Theatre Terrific Society, 21 July 1988.

Nelson, Larry. "This Theatre Really is Terrific." *Powell River News*, 20 June 1990.

Norris, Jamie. "Artistic Director Report." *Theatre Terrific Update* (Winter 1996a): 3.

– "Artistic Director Report." *Theatre Terrific Update* (Fall 1996b): 3.

Peterson, Margaret. "Theatre Nurtures Conquering Spirit." *Vancouver Courier*,
    August 1991.

Richmond News. "Terrific Classes Build Self-Esteem in Participants." 27 October 1993.

Rossi, Cheryl. "Inclusive Theatre Terrific Uncovers Arthur Miller's Secret; Diverse Ensemble Cast Explores 'Universal Stories.'" *Vancouver Courier*, 22 April 2009.

Rupp, Shannon. "Theatre Terrific is Terrific." *Coquitlam Magazine*, 28 June–25 July 1989.

Santini, Kathy. "Terrific Theatre Group Encourages Disabled." *Nanaimo Daily Free Press*, n.d.

Smith, Colin. "Disabled Drama Extends Horizons." *The Spokesman*, December 1982.

Smith, Janet. "Theatre Terrific a Catalyst for Change." *The West Ender*, 14 June 1990.

Spence, Craig. "Actors Face Curtain." *Vancouver Courier*, 1987.

Theatre Terrific. Annual Report, 1988.

– Annual Report: Treasurer's Report, 1989.

– "Artistic Director: Theatre Terrific." 2000.

– "The Big Birthday Bash." *Theatre Terrific Update* (Spring 1995): 1, 7.

– Budget Projections and Comparisons, 1987.

– "Dancing on the Head of a Pin with a Mouse in My Pocket," program. 1986.

– "Direct Access … On the Move." *Theatre Terrific News* (Spring 1988): 1.

– "Direct Access to the Heart." *Theatre Terrific Update* (Spring 1994): 1.

– "*The Glass Box*: Invitation to a Work-In-Progress Presentation." 16 May 2008. http://www.theatreterrific.ca/the_glass_box_workinprogress_presentation (accessed 15 August 2009).

– "*The Glass Box* Theatre Terrific 2008 Professional Production Audition Notice." *Theatre Terrific News* (Fall 2007): 2.

– "Notes on The National Theatre Workshop of the Handicapped and Graeae Theatre Company." Attached to "Theatre Terrific," September 1986.

– *Step Right Up!* Program, n.d.

– "Theatre Terrific." September 1986.

– "Theatre Terrific – Beyond Disability." F.K. Morrow Grant application, 2004.

– *Theatre Terrific Newsletter* (Fall 1992): 6.

– *Theatre Terrific Newsletter* (Spring 1992): 6.

– "Theatre Terrific Society Mandate." 2006.

– "Update." *Theatre Terrific Update* (Spring 1990).

– "*Workin'* has great run at Fringe Festival." *Theatre Terrific News* (Winter 2007): 1.

Thomas, Colin. "Disability Troupe Dispenses with 'Niceness.'" *Georgia Straight*, June 1999, 3–10.

– "Step Right Up!" *Georgia Straight*, 17–24 June 1999, 107.

Uchatius, Susanna. "Notes from the A.D. Desk." *Theatre Terrific Newsletter* (Spring 2005): 2.

– *The Secret Son*. Roundhouse Community Centre, Vancouver, BC, 22–25 April 2009.

– "Theatre Terrific Troupe," *Theatre Terrific Newsletter* (Fall 2005): 1.

Watson, Richard A. "Terrific Theatre at Theatre Terrific." *Abilities* (Spring 1992): 158–9.

Weiner, Gerry, Secretary of State of Canada. Official communication to Mrs Nan Purkis, Theatre Terrific Society, 26 February 1990.

Young, Bryson. Review of *Ugly,* written and directed by Susanna Uchatius. *Vancouver Sun,* 14 September 2005.

Workman Arts Archival Sources (Toronto)

Ardal, Maja (Book), and Joey Miller (Music). *Joy. A Musical. About Depression.* Unpublished play, 2000.

Arsenault, Louise. *Innerspeak.* Unpublished play, 1991.

Barrie, Shirley. *Tripping Through Time.* Unpublished play, 1993.

Bender, Melissa. Quoted on the Workman Arts website. http://www.workmanarts. com/Theatre/index.cfm (accessed 9 June 2009).

Cushman, Robert. "Little Joy in this Musical." *National Post,* 14 October 2000.

Dumol, Denise, comp. "Summary of the Questions and Comments during Vincent Performances." 1997.

Editorial, *Toronto Star.* "Pepper vs. Patience." 16 August 1992.

Friedlander, Mira. "The Theatre of the Mind." *The Toronto Star,* 31 March 1992.

Gregory, John. *Worlds Away?* Unpublished play, 1992.

Kaplan, Jon. "Arsenault's Innerspeak Maps a Journey Toward Mental Health." *Now Magazine,* 20 June 1991.

Lurie, Steve. "Mentally Ill at Risk Unless Police Educated." *Globe and Mail,* 15 August 1992, letter.

MacGowan, James, and Paul Vieira. "Bat-Wielding Man Shot Dead by Police." *Globe and Mail,* 10 August 1992.

Mental Health Centre Penetanguishene and the Ontario Ministry of Health. "Working with the Mentally Ill in a Post-Institutional Era." Conference Brochure, June 1993.

Ontario Ministry of Health, Mental Health Facility Branch. "Questions and Answers about How Bill C-30 (An Act to Amend the Canadian Criminal Code) Will Affect Forensic Mental Health Services in Ontario." May 1992.

Ouzounian, Richard. "Real Sadness in Joy." *Toronto Star,* 8 October 2000.

Swainson, Gail. "Debate Rages over Forcing Mentally Ill into Therapy." *Toronto Star,* 5 October 1992.

Editorial, *Toronto Star.* "Pepper vs. Patience." 16 August 1992.

Wagner, Vit. "Play Doesn't Get Mired in its Didactic Purpose." *Toronto Star,* 20 June 1991.

Watada, Terry. *Vincent.* Directed by Ines Buchli, Penetanguishene, June 1993.

– "Notes from the Playwright." Program for *Vincent,* 1993.

– *Vincent.* Unpublished play script, 1997.

Workman Arts. http://www.workmanarts.com/About/index.cfm (accessed 9 June 2009).

Workman Theatre Project. "Notes for Penetanguishene 1992–1997," n.d.

– Company Background, 1998.

– Company Background, 1999.

– Registration Sheet, 2007.

– Season and Training Brochure, 2007–08.

– "WTP: A New Voice in Mental Health." *Queen Street Mental Health Centre Tidbits*, November 1990.

Index

Shannon, Robert, 169
Sher, Emil, 109
Sherr Klein, Bonnie, 5, 77, 90, 94, 173
Siebers, Tobin, xiii, 11, 16; and disability
    aesthetics, 121, 150–1
Simmie, Scott, 56
Simon Fraser University, 26, 80; and
    the Fei and Milton Wong Experi-
    mental Theatre, 165, 168
Sison, Carmela, 167
Skydive, 15, 37–39, 93, 163, 173; play
    analysis of, 114–9; and disability the-
    atre aesthetics, 119–24
slowrunning, 81
Smudge, 24, 90, 173
SNIFF (Sensory Narrative in Full
    Form) Inc., 23, 26
Snow, Judith, 4, 24, 91
social model, 9–11
Society for Disability Arts and Culture
    (S4DAC). See Kickstart
Socks, see Time to Put My Socks On
Solo Disability Performance, 41–5
SOS Players, 19, 51
Soul Journey, 61
Spine, 16, 37–38, 93, 156; play analysis of,
    165–8, 170
Spiraling Within, 79, 173
Srivastava, Tia, 110–11
Stackhouse, Ruth Ruth, 25
Stage Left, 15, 21, 29–33, 36, 39–40, 42,
    64, 96–7, 163; and Mercy Killing or
    Murder?, 107–14, 119–24, 173; and fes-
    tivals, 91–2, 94, 96; see also Balancing
    Acts
Stanley, Sarah, 55
States, Bert O., 161
Step Right Up!, 75–7
Still Waiting for that Special Bus, 41–2
Stjernholm, Kjell, 87, 89
Stratiy, Angela Petrone, 46

Sullivan, Sam, 89, 155, 157, 159
Syllabub, 71–2

Tale of a Mask, 58, 138
TAPIT/new works (US), 61
Tarragon Theatre, 24, 171
That's So Gay!, 42
The Blue Dragon, 165
The Chant, 48–9
The Church of 80% Sincerity, 41
The Edmond Yu Project, 25, 126, 173
The Glass Box, 16, 82, 173; play analysis
    of, 143–4, 147–50, 173
The Matilda Show, 147, 173
The Miracle Worker, 16; play analysis of,
    156–161, 170
The Secret Son, 82; play analysis of,
    143–7, 150–53
The Store, 38
Theatre Bagger, 38
Theatre of the Oppressed, 29-30
Theater Sycorax (Germany), 13, 61–2, 94
Theatre Terrific, 15–16, 21, 37, 42, 87–8,
    92, 163; origins and early develop-
    ment, 65–74; and Direct Access, 70–4;
    critical response, 72, 76, 81; funding,
    68, 72–4, 77, 79–80, 84, 101; mandate,
    69–70, 75, 78, 80–1, 85; training, 67–
    71, 80–1, 84; repertory group, 75–8,
    80; play histories, 71–3, 75–7, 79, 81–3;
    and The Glass Box, 143–4, 147–50; and
    The Secret Son, 143–7, 150–53
Theatre Unlimited, 65, 87
Third Eye Looming, 54–5, 58, 62
Tied Together, 26
Time to Put My Socks On, 42
Tolan, Kathleen, 152
Toronto Summerworks, 28
Toronto Theatre Alliance (TTA), Cross
    Cultural Alliance. See Picasso Pro
Torwl, Meg, 30, 42, 83